THE ROYAL FAMILY AT WAR

Also by Theo Aronson

THE GOLDEN BEES
The Story of the Bonapartes

ROYAL VENDETTA
The Crown of Spain (1829–1965)

THE COBURGS OF BELGIUM

THE FALL OF THE THIRD NAPOLEON

THE KAISERS

QUEEN VICTORIA AND THE BONAPARTES

GRANDMAMA OF EUROPE
The Crowned Descendants of Queen Victoria

A FAMILY OF KINGS
The Descendants of Christian IX of Denmark

ROYAL AMBASSADORS
British Royalties in Southern Africa 1860–1947

VICTORIA AND DISRAELI
The Making of a Romantic Partnership

KINGS OVER THE WATER
The Saga of the Stuart Pretenders

MR RHODES AND THE PRINCESS: a play

PRINCESS ALICE
Countess of Athlone

ROYAL FAMILY
Years of Transition

CROWNS IN CONFLICT
The Triumph and the Tragedy of
European Monarchy 1910–1918

THE KING IN LOVE
Edward VII's Mistresses

NAPOLEON AND JOSEPHINE
A Love Story

HEART OF A QUEEN
Queen Victoria's Romantic Attachments

THE ROYAL FAMILY
AT WAR

Theo Aronson

JOHN MURRAY

To the memory of
R.I.B. (Jock) WEBSTER

© Theo Aronson 1993

First published in 1993
by John Murray (Publishers) Ltd.,
50 Albemarle Street, London W1X 4BD

A catalogue record for this book is available from the British Library

ISBN 0–7195–5015–7

Typeset in 12½/13½ Linotron Bembo by Wearset, Boldon,
Tyne and Wear
Printed and bound in Great Britain at the University Press, Cambridge.

Contents

Illustrations

ACKNOWLEDGEMENTS

Plates 1, 3, 9, 10, 26, 27, 31, Windsor Castle Royal Archives © 1992, Her Majesty the Queen; 2, 6, 7, 8, 11, 12, 13, 16, 17, 19, 20, 21, 22, 24, 25, 28, from *Royal Family in Wartime*, Anon.; 4, 29, from *Queen Mary* by Louis Wulff, published by Sampson Low, Marston and Co.; 5, Michael Bloch; 14, Author's Collection; 15, 23, 30, Imperial War Museum; 18, from *Our Princesses*, by Lisa Sheridan, published by John Murray.

Author's Note

I<small>T WAS AS</small> a schoolboy, growing up in South Africa, that I first saw King George VI and Queen Elizabeth. The year was 1947, and the King and Queen, with their two daughters, were paying a three-month-long state visit to the country. A particular feature of this tour was the series of short stops made at remote railway stations and sidings as the royal train travelled through South Africa's vast hinterland. On these occasions the royal family would alight to talk to the little knot of people gathered there.

It was on such a railway siding, set in a desolate, sun-baked, scrub-covered landscape, that I had my first view of the family. Even as a schoolboy, I was impressed by the aplomb with which King George VI and Queen Elizabeth carried out what must have been, for them, the most thankless of duties. In my mind's eye, I can still see them as they moved slowly down the single line of spectators: the King handsome, sun-tanned and courteous; the Queen dressed, even for this handful of unimportant people, with great panache.

The apparent interest and enthusiasm with which the royal couple asked their routine questions and listened to the predictable answers were masterly. With anyone who looked at all shy or shabby they would make a special effort. 'I am so glad to meet you,' the Queen would say. 'How kind of you to come and see us.' It was, despite the smallness of its scale, an exercise in professionalism.

This encounter first awakened my interest in this attractive and conscientious couple. In the years since then, my interest has deepened. In my capacity as a writer of royal historical biography, I have been able to study them more fully. I have often needed to research and deal with aspects of George VI's reign. Queen Elizabeth, now the Queen Mother, has granted me several audiences – for this and other books – during which Her Majesty has spoken to me about those days, and I have had many conversations with other leading royal figures of the period – Princess Margaret; Princess Alice, Countess of Athlone; Princess Alice, Duchess of Gloucester; and Lord Harewood – as well as with members of the various royal households. The more I have learned about the reign of George VI, the more my admiration for the King and Queen – and for the entire royal family during those turbulent years – has increased.

In spite of the social, political and military upheavals of the period, George VI's reign was surprisingly successful. Starting off with very little taste, talent or training for his immense task, the King was none the less able to bequeath to his daughter, Queen Elizabeth II, a throne of great stability and popularity. There can be no doubt that much of this popularity was due to the conduct of the royal family during the reign's greatest upheaval: the Second World War. 'This War', as Winston Churchill once wrote to the King, 'has drawn the Throne and the people more closely together than was ever before recorded.' And in bringing the throne and people closer together, the Second World War saw a consolidation of the monarch's position. The crown became a symbol not only of the nation at war but also of the extraordinary fusion of all sections of the population. No less than for its country, was this the British monarchy's finest hour.

It is with this aspect of the monarchy that this book is concerned. Far from being a detailed study of George VI's political, diplomatic and military activities during the Second World War, it is an account of the lives, as much private as public, of the entire royal family during these years. Its main theme is the contribution made not only by the King and Queen, but also by many major and minor royal figures of the time; and how, to a greater or lesser extent, this contribution ensured that the crown emerged from the war with its prestige greatly enhanced.

In dealing with this subject, I have had to set myself certain limits. To prevent the cast of characters from becoming too unwieldly, I have concentrated on the immediate family of King George VI, including his brothers and their wives, and his sister's family. I have also dealt with the Earl of Athlone, who was both the King's uncle and, as Governor-General of Canada, his representative. But I have not included Lord Louis Mountbatten on the grounds that he was merely one of the King's many second cousins and because, unlike Lord Athlone, he was not an official wartime representative of the monarchy.

My chief thanks are to Queen Elizabeth the Queen Mother who, in the course of my research, has several times received me to relate her memories of the reign of King George VI. For me, these audiences have been occasions of exceptional interest and pleasure. I am also indebted to Her Majesty for allowing me to reproduce some of her previously unpublished letters.

Other members of the royal family who have several times received me to give information are Princess Margaret, Countess of Snowden; Princess Alice, Duchess of Gloucester; and the late Princess Alice, Countess of Athlone, with whom I was especially friendly. I am also grateful for my conversations with Princess Alice's daughter and son-in-law, Lady May and Sir Henry Abel Smith, and with King George VI's nephew, the Earl of Harewood.

Members, past and present, of the various royal households to whom I am indebted for help and information are, in alphabetical order: Sir Alastair Aird, Comptroller to Queen Elizabeth the Queen Mother; Sir Simon Bland,

Private Secretary to the Duke of Gloucester; Miss Mary Goldie, Secretary to Princess Alice, Countess of Athlone; the Dowager Viscountess Hambleden, Lady of the Bedchamber to Queen Elizabeth; Mrs Kathleen Harvey, Lady-in-waiting to Princess Alice, Duchess of Gloucester; the late Miss Joan Lascelles, Lady-in-waiting to Princess Alice, Countess of Athlone; Lord Napier and Ettrick, Private Secretary to Princess Margaret; the late Sir Shuldham Redfern, Secretary to the Earl of Athlone; Mr William Tallon, Page of the Back Stairs to Queen Elizabeth the Queen Mother; Group Captain Peter Townsend, Equerry to King George VI; and Mr Neville Usher, Aide-de-camp to the Earl of Athlone.

I am grateful to Queen Elizabeth II by whose gracious permission previously unpublished extracts from the diaries and letters of Queen Mary, as well as previously published material from the Royal Archives, of which Her Majesty holds the copyright, are reproduced here. For arranging this, and for other help and information, I must thank the Queen's Librarian, Mr Oliver Everett. As always, Miss Frances Dimond, Curator of the Royal Photographic Collection, has been most helpful and efficient. Mr Hugo Vickers very kindly arranged for me to quote hitherto unpublished extracts from the private papers of Lord Hardinge of Penshurst, at one time Private Secretary to King George VI. I must thank the Hon. David Astor, Sir Edward Ford and Mr Michael Bott, Keeper of the Archives and Manuscripts, for use of previously unpublished royal correspondence in the Astor Papers at the University of Reading; and Mr Michael Coney for material in the Public Record Office, Kew. Mr Roy C. Nesbit has kindly allowed me to put forward his theory about the plane crash in which the Duke of Kent was killed, and Mrs Yvone Sterenborg has allowed me access to her extensive royal cuttings collection. I am grateful to HarperCollins and Mr Alan Tadiello for the use of material from the diaries of Harold Nicolson at Balliol College, Oxford; and to Mr Paul Kemp and Mr Stephen

Nash of the Imperial War Museum, London.

Others who have helped me to a greater or lesser extent are the late Mr Toby Barker, Ms Anne Barlow, Mr Michael Bloch, Ms Sarah Bradford, Mr Mervyn Clingan, Mr David Griffiths, Mr R.H. Hubbard, Mr Andrew Lownie, Mr John Van Der Kiste, the late Mr R.I.B. Webster and Mrs Emily Wood. I am grateful to the staffs of the British Library, the Newspaper Library at Colindale, the Bristol Reference Library, the Bath Reference Library and especially to Mrs S. Bane and her always efficient staff at the Frome Library. I am indebted to the authors and publishers of all the books listed in my Bibliography but three books that have proved especially useful are the biographies of King George VI by Sarah Bradford, John Wheeler-Bennett and Patrick Howarth.

As always, my greatest debt is to Brian Roberts for his enthusiasm, encouragement and expertise.

Part One

THE KING AMONG HIS PEOPLE

1

The Unknown King

ON THE NIGHT of 23 August 1939, King George VI broke off his holiday at Balmoral to return to London. Having driven to Perth, he boarded a special coach attached to the night express and arrived at Euston Station at eight the following morning. At Buckingham Palace he was handed a letter from the Prime Minister, Neville Chamberlain. It confirmed what he had already been told. The announcement, two days before, of the signing of a non-aggression pact between Nazi Germany and Soviet Russia had brought the prospect of war much closer. This newly signed pact would allow Hitler to move against Poland without fear of any Russian intervention. The British government's reaction, Chamberlain assured the King, had been to issue a declaration to the effect that the pact would in no way weaken the Anglo-French resolve to stand by Poland. Parliament was to meet in special session that day for the passing of an Emergency Defence Bill.

Also waiting for the King was a more personal letter. It was from his mother, Queen Mary, at Sandringham. In her stiff but sincere fashion, the old Queen wrote to commiserate with her son. Having, as the consort of King George V, faced a similar prospect in 1914, Queen Mary understood what George VI, as man and monarch, must be going through. More than most would Queen Mary have appreciated how little her son must be relishing the idea of having yet another exacting duty thrust upon him. For by now it was almost certain that this shy, insecure, self-doubting man was about to be called upon to fulfil one of the most assertive of roles: that of the supreme symbol of the nation at war.

By that summer of 1939, George VI had been King for just over two and a half years. Born on 14 December 1895, he was 43 years old. The claim, by one historian, that King George VI's title on ascending the throne should have been 'the Unknown',[1] was hardly less valid in August 1939. Until his unexpected accession on the abdication of his brother Edward VIII in December 1936, he had lived – as the Duke of York – in the shadow of his formidable father, King George V, and of his popular brother, the Prince of Wales, afterwards Edward VIII. The former had been widely respected; the latter idolized.

The little that the general public knew about the new King was hardly reassuring. George VI lacked any strong public presence. Slight and fine-boned, he looked frail. It was rumoured that he was physically weak, that he suffered from 'falling fits' (epilepsy), that he would never stand the strain of his new position. The fact that, in the year of his accession, the sovereign's customary Christmas broadcast was cancelled and the proposed Indian Durbar postponed merely strengthened suspicions about his lack of physical stamina. An intensely shy man, the King never enjoyed public appearances. He tended to look tense, hesitant, ill at ease; he lacked any sense of royal showmanship. One had only to watch the incessant working of his jaw muscles to appreciate that he was under severe strain. Never one for the spontaneous gesture, the King was almost incapable of making small talk. But the most debilitating handicap of all, for a man in public life, was his speech impediment. Although, by the time of his accession, George VI had overcome the worst of his stammer, his public delivery remained slow, hesitant, monotonous.

In short, as Stanley Baldwin, the Prime Minister of the day, admitted, there was 'a lot of prejudice against him. He's had no chance to capture public imagination as his brother did. I'm afraid he won't find it easy going for the first year or two.'[2]

Although many of the rumours about the King's short-comings were groundless, some of the public's reservations about his suitability for his task were valid. Indeed, the King shared them. He appreciated, more than anyone, to what extent he lacked the presence, personality and experience for his role. To him, the Abdication crisis and the prospect of ascending the throne had had the quality of a nightmare. One royal relation described him as being 'mute and broken' at the idea of becoming King;[3] another claimed that he was 'absolutely appalled'.[4] He likened himself to 'the proverbial sheep being led to the slaughter'.[5] On finally realizing that nothing could save him from his fate, he broke down, he admitted, 'and sobbed like a child'.[6] During the first few months of his reign he felt overwhelmed by the magnitude of his task: by the relentless publicity; by the volume of work in the boxes ('I've never even seen a State Paper,' he wailed to his cousin, Lord Louis Mountbatten);[7] by the necessity for public speaking; and by the strain of public appearances.

But gradually, as the first numbing shock wore off, George VI began to impress those about him by his less showy qualities: his common sense, his dedication, his integrity and his moral courage. The new King might not have been particularly quick, clever or original but he had a reassuring dependability. Unlike his flashier elder brother, he was very conscientious; he was determined, as he put it, 'to make amends' for the abdicated King's selfish and disruptive behaviour.[8] George VI was anxious to bring back to the throne not only the respectability of King George V's reign but also a sense of monarchical continuity and stability.

Those who had half expected the King to be, not only simple but also simple-minded (Edouard Daladier, the French Prime Minister, dismissed him as 'a moron'),[9] were surprised to find that he was somewhat complex. When relaxed, and out of the public eye, he could be talkative, interesting, amusing. He had a wit that was sometimes dry, sometimes salty. Lord Tweedsmuir, the Governor-General of Canada, described him as a 'wonderful mixture . . . of shrewdness, kindliness and humour',[10] while a surprised President Roosevelt, who came to know George VI in the course of his state visit to North America in 1939, claimed that the King 'knew a great deal about foreign affairs in general but also about social legislation'.[11]

But the qualities that were beginning to impress court and government circles were precisely those which were most difficult to project in public. In spite of his increasingly regal demeanour, his nationwide public appearances and the un-doubted success of his state visits to France, Canada and the United States, he remained, to the general public, an unchar-ismatic, reserved, remote figure, utterly lacking in the ability to enthuse the crowds in the way that his brother had been able to do.

It was not until after his return from the North American tour in the summer of 1939, during which he and the Queen had been given a tumultuous welcome by less inhibited crowds, that he began to feel more confident. Quite clearly, people in North America had liked him for himself, not merely as the wearer of the crown. He returned, too, with a new conception of his role. If his first task, after the Abdication, had been to stabilize the monarchy, he now wanted to make it more human, more accessible, more modern. 'There must be no more high-hat business,' he explained to one of his entourage during the tour, 'the sort of thing that my father and those of his day regarded as the correct attitude – the feeling that certain things couldn't be done.'[12] What he now wanted to be was 'a people's King'.[13]

This was easier said than done. How exactly, in the Britain of the 1930s – still stratified, class-conscious, unequal in terms of wealth and opportunity – was he going to achieve this? Clement Attlee, Leader of the Labour Opposition, had already spoken out against the monarchy living in a style 'based upon conceptions of Kingship now out of date'. 'Great and numerous residences, an army of attendants, a titled entourage and the habitual observance of elaborate ceremonial', argued Attlee, remained a barrier between the crown and the people.[14] Even if George VI was not ready to change the monarchy to the extent visualized by Attlee, he was certainly anxious to remove some of the barriers. But how, given the ingrained formalities of his position and his own natural reserve, could he possibly hope to bring crown and people closer together?

During the course of George VI's short reign and of her own long widowhood, Queen Elizabeth was to establish herself firmly as one of the most popular women not only in Britain but throughout the world. So it is difficult to appreciate that, on George VI's accession, she, too, was a relatively unknown figure.

Thirty-six years old at the time, she had no more wanted to be Queen than her husband wanted to be King. Not only did she realize how great a strain the burden of sovereignty would place on her husband but she also had some reservations about her own aptitude for the task. After all, it had been with considerable reluctance that she had agreed to marry the Duke of York: she had dreaded the restrictions of life as a member of the royal family. She, too, was rather shy and, contrary to general belief, remained so throughout her life. 'I'm a very shy person,' she once admitted. 'I thought that I would become less shy with the passing years but it hasn't happened.'[15] Fortunately, this was a superficial trait only; it did not denote any lack of self-confidence. With characteristic determination Queen Elizabeth fought her shyness and, if she never conquered it, she certainly mastered it.

To the general public the prospect of her becoming a successful Queen seemed unlikely. She had been known, during her thirteen-year marriage, as 'the little Duchess': a small, smiling, fussily dressed figure, completely lacking the commanding presence of her mother-in-law, Queen Mary. She had been born, on 4 August 1900, a commoner – as Lady Elizabeth Bowes-Lyon, the youngest daughter of the 14th Earl of Strathmore – and not since Tudor times had a commoner become Queen. Might not a princess, born and bred, have made a more suitable consort? This was certainly the view of some of the older generation of the royal family. The new King's redoubtable aunt, Princess Alice, Countess of Athlone, maintained that only those of royal birth and training could hope to sustain the role with any success. 'You've got to start early,' she would insist, 'it's not really something that you can pick up.'[16] The fashionable set who had once surrounded Edward VIII considered Queen Elizabeth to be woefully unsmart, and he himself is reported as having referred to her as 'that common little woman'.[17] Lacking chic, lacking stature, lacking *gravitas*, lacking royal birth, could the new Queen possibly make a success of her role?

Unlike George VI, the Queen lost very little time in proving that she could. Of immediate appeal to the public was the fact that she was a mother of a young family; this gave the monarchy a reassuringly respectable air. Equally appealing were her looks. Although she was not a great beauty, Queen Elizabeth was one of those women who can give an illusion of beauty. Her particularly Celtic looks – her marshmallow complexion, her bright blue eyes, her jet-black hair – were striking, especially when enlivened by her radiant smile. Her clothes, now designed by the up-and-coming couturier, Norman Hartnell, became both more elegant and more romantic. By the use of pastel shades and sumptuous styles, he complimented her conscious presentation of herself as a graceful, feminine, pretty-as-a-picture Queen.

With the Queen's newly acquired aura of romance went a newly acquired aura of majesty. She might be small but by her erect carriage, increasingly assured manner and unhurried gestures, she achieved great dignity. This dignity might have seemed, on ceremonial occasions during the early years of the reign, to be somewhat studied (Eleanor Roosevelt considered her 'a little too self-consciously regal')[18] and some found her manner 'condescending',[19] but one can appreciate what the Queen was trying to achieve. About her talent for public appearances, however, there were no reservations whatsoever. The Queen quickly revealed a certain showmanship; as much as the King disliked appearing before the crowds, so did she come to enjoy it. She perfected a way of tilting her head, of waving her right hand, of smiling her warm smile, of seeming to seek out, for one flattering second, every single face. 'She really does seem to convey to each individual in the crowd that he or she has had a personal greeting,' wrote the admiring Harold Nicolson.[20]

Eleanor Roosevelt pronounced her 'perfect as a Queen, gracious, informed, saying the right thing and kind',[21] and professed herself astounded that the Queen 'should remain so perfectly in character all the time. My admiration for her grew every minute she spent with us.'[22]

It was the Queen who, on the North American tour of 1939, was responsible for inaugurating that casual and spontaneous mingling with the crowds that was to be such a feature of their wartime visits. Having just laid the foundation stone of a building in Ottawa and having been told that some of the masons were Scots, she insisted on breaking away from the official party in order to go and speak to them. Again, at the unveiling of a war memorial, she decided to go down among the thousands of veterans. Never, claimed the Governor-General, Lord Tweedsmuir, would he forget the agonized look on the faces of the detectives as Their Majesties moved unescorted and unprotected through the crowd. The Queen, he went on to say, 'has a perfect genius for the right kind of publicity'.[23]

However, such royal informality had not yet been experienced by British crowds. To the majority of them the Queen, for all the dazzle of her smile and the wave of her gloved hand, remained a distant figure: an other-worldly creature to be cheered in a passing car or carriage. She seemed hardly more real than the fairy-tale Queen who sat, in a spangled crinoline among the hydrangeas, in one of Cecil Beaton's official portraits.

About her true personality, the general public knew almost nothing. For beneath the melting charm and the irrepressible *joie de vivre* was a certain steeliness. The Queen's views were firmly held and her convictions deeply felt. Once her husband had become King, she directed her considerable talents and energies into ensuring that his reign would be a success. The King's frequent public allusions to his wife's help in carrying out his duties were far from conventional tributes. They were in heartfelt appreciation of her constant support, encouragement and inspiration. Their characters were complementary. Where he was hesitant, she was assured; where he was a worrier, she was serene; where he was introspective, she was outgoing; where he was short-tempered, she was long-suffering. Whatever he lacked, she provided.

And never were the Queen's qualities of tranquillity, optimism and resilience to prove more valuable, not only to her husband, but also to the monarchy and the country, than during the years of war that lay ahead.

In the days that followed the King's sudden return from Balmoral to London in late August 1939, he did what he could to avert the imminent catastrophe. Diffident he might be, but he was enough of a monarch to appreciate that his status conferred certain advantages. While giving the government his unqualified support in their declared intention of honouring their pledge to Poland, he was anxious to use his position as a royal head of state to make personal approaches to other heads of state. Through his Principal Private Secretary, Sir Alexander Hardinge, he suggested to the Foreign Office that he send a friendly message direct to the Emperor of Japan. Might not such a gesture of friendship, in the light of the recent Soviet-German pact, help detach anti-Russian Japan from the Axis Powers? When 'dealing with Orientals,' argued the King, 'direct communications between Heads of State may be helpful'.[24] Politely, the Foreign Office declined his offer.

Denied an approach to the Japanese Emperor, the King suggested one to the German Führer. But the Prime Minister was having none of it. The British monarchy could hardly risk a rebuff from Hitler. The moment, explained Chamberlain tactfully, was not opportune.

With each day that passed, it became less opportune. The other frantic appeals for peace and offers of negotiation which were criss-crossing Europe seemed to be making very little impression on Hitler. The Führer continued to keep the world in suspense; sometimes seeming to be on the verge of striking at Poland, at others to be hanging back. Indeed, by 28 August – the fifth day after the King's return to London – it looked as though the unshakeability of the Anglo-French-Polish alliance was causing Hitler to have second thoughts about the advisability of a Polish invasion. Sir Miles Lampson, the British Ambassador in Egypt, calling at Buckingham Palace on 29 August, found the King in 'admirable form'.

'H.M. thought that there would now be peace and that this time Hitler's bluff had been called,' reported Lampson. The King seemed almost more concerned about the fact that the machinations of the 'villain Hitler' had disrupted the grouse-shooting at Balmoral. His Majesty had never known better sport: '1,600 brace in six days', he boasted.[25]

It was, not unnaturally, to his family that George VI looked for comfort during these uncertain days. With the Queen and his two young daughters still at Balmoral and with Queen Mary at Sandringham, the King had to rely on his two brothers: Prince Henry (Harry), Duke of Gloucester, and Prince George, Duke of Kent. The differences in temperament between the brothers – the unassertive King, the bluff Duke of Gloucester and the debonair Duke of Kent –

tended to matter rather less in times of stress and, *en garçon* (all three wives were away), the brothers found themselves being drawn closer together.

'Harry and George have dined with me nearly every night,' reported the King to Queen Mary on 28 August. 'I have seen more of them in the last week than I have during the year.'[26] On the day before, the three brothers had attended morning service in Westminster Abbey, 'as quietly and simply as any other worshippers'.[27] That evening they were joined by Prince George's wife, the *soignée* Princess Marina, who had come hurrying home from a family holiday in Yugoslavia.

But the King's chief family support arrived, in the person of the Queen, at Euston Station on the morning of 29 August. Having left their two daughters at Balmoral, the Queen was able to devote her full attention to the King. Even the first glimpse of her as, with back straight, head tilted and a serene smile on her lips, she was driven to the Palace, was reassuring. For the King, the Queen's presence was invaluable. In the week that was left before the outbreak of war, husband and wife were rarely separated.

The Queen's return happened to coincide with the day that Adolf Hitler finally decided to attack Poland. During the following three days, while Hitler was cynically offering Poland impossible terms for negotiation, the King carried out his constitutional duties: he presided over the Privy Council, he granted audiences to ministers, he visited the War Office, the Admiralty, the Air Ministry and the Central War Room. On 1 September – the day that Germany invaded Poland – he signed an order for complete mobilization. He was wildly cheered when, that same afternoon, he visited the Prime Minister in Downing Street; the King was said to have been 'deeply touched' by this spontaneous demonstration of loyalty.[28]

By 11 a.m. on 3 September, Hitler having failed to reply to the Anglo-French ultimatum, the country was at war. At six that evening the King, whose only partially mastered stammer made public speaking an ordeal, broadcast to the Empire. In simple terms, he outlined the reasons why Britain had been obliged to go to war and, in equally simple terms, called upon 'my people at home and my people across the seas' to stand firm and united in the 'dark days ahead'.[29]

A few days later he started a diary which he was to keep throughout the war years. In it, in his straightforward, unhistrionic fashion, he entered his thoughts about the outbreak of war and his memories of the declaration of the First World War in August 1914, when he had been a midshipman on HMS *Collingwood* in the North Sea. 'Today we are at war again', he mused, 'and I am no longer a midshipman in the Royal Navy.' The country, he wrote more conventionally, 'is calm, firm and united behind its leaders'.[30]

But how did he really feel as he faced not only the prospect of having to assume the demanding role of a King-at-War, but also the hardships and horrors that a war was bound to bring?

'We were stunned,' admitted the Queen in later years. 'Sorrowful, of course, but mainly stunned.'[31]

The King's two daughters, the 13-year-old Princess Elizabeth and the 9-year-old Princess Margaret, were still at Balmoral. With the return of the King and then the Queen to London during the last days of August 1939, the princesses had been moved from Balmoral Castle to Birkhall, a smaller house on the estate. 'Who *is* this Hitler, spoiling everything?'[32] Princess Margaret had demanded on an earlier occasion. Now, with the sudden departure of her parents, the move to Birkhall and the future appearing so uncertain, he seemed to be spoiling things again. But as the King and Queen were determined that their daughters' lives should be disrupted as little as possible, their governess, Marion Crawford (known, inevitably, as 'Crawfie') was instructed to 'stick to the usual programme as far as you can'.[33] This meant the established pattern of lessons, homework and recreation. Crawfie's increasingly heavy workload ('I had to prepare, the night before, lessons for two children, both of different ages, both extremely bright')[34] was lightened by the recruitment of a French teacher. Princess Elizabeth continued her lessons in constitutional history – by now by post – which Sir Henry Marten, Vice-Provost of Eton, had been giving her ever since she turned 13.

Not unnaturally, these lessons in constitutional history made the Princess even more aware of her position as Heir Presumptive. (She was not yet Heir Apparent as the 39-year-old Queen could still have given birth to a son, who would have become the future sovereign.) They also tended to emphasize the differences between the two princesses. As Princess Elizabeth, deeply conscious of her status and re-sponsibilities, became ever more tidy and methodical, so did Princess Margaret become less so. Both blue-eyed, brown-haired, attractive girls, the elder was quieter, steadier, more serious-minded. The younger was livelier, prettier, more mercurial.

Although a good part of the princesses' day was devoted to lessons, it was not all work. Even on remote Deeside, the war brought diversions. The princesses would hand round tea and cake to the women who gathered at Birkhall to sew as part of the war effort, and would greet, somewhat self-consciously, the evacuee children from the Glasgow slums who were being accommodated on the Balmoral estate. Most of these city-bred children hated life in the country. 'They were terrified by the strange sounds,' re-membered the Queen, 'by things like the wind in the trees at night.'[35]

What the princesses found menacing was the voice of the traitorous William Joyce, known as Lord Haw-Haw. His affected tones, broadcasting from Germany, had only to be heard on the radio for the princesses to bombard the set with books or cushions. Much more acceptable were the filmed antics of Charlie Chaplin and the Keystone Cops. And most acceptable of all were the telephone calls, at six each evening, from the King and Queen.

When parents and daughters were to be reunited, no one was certain. With Christmas approaching – by which time they had been apart for over three months – the princesses were taken shopping in Aberdeen where, at Woolworths, they bought most of their presents. On 18 December, the Queen telephoned to say that they would all be spending Christmas together at Sandringham. Although the Norfolk coastline was one of the most vulnerable to enemy invasion, the curious inactivity of the so-called 'phoney war' – that static six-month-long period between Hitler's conquest of Poland and his attack on Norway – allowed the King to spend Christmas, as usual, at his beloved Sandringham.

The reunion was a joyful one. The royal family – the King, the Queen and the two princesses – were very close. 'There was something unique about the King's home life,' claimed Princess Alice, who had experienced the home lives of many generations of the royal family. 'The four of them made a small, absolutely united circle. They shared the same jokes and they shared each other's troubles.'[36] Amongst themselves, they behaved with the utmost naturalness; there was none of that stultifying formality that had blighted the boyhoods of George VI and his brothers. Unsophisticated in their own tastes, the King and Queen encouraged simplicity in their daughters. Providing one did one's duty, life should be the greatest possible fun. As a result, the princesses grew up in an atmosphere of family jokes, parlour games, sing-songs and charades. This closeness, this insularity almost, was to be intensified during the long years of war.

The joys of the family Christmas at Sandringham were tempered, for the King, by the prospect of his Christmas broadcast. Not until that was over, he was always to sigh, could he enjoy Christmas. As usual, he spoke live. This Christmas broadcast, the first of the war, was a particularly significant one. Coming in the middle of the phoney war, when the reason for taking up arms – the defeat of Hitler –

seemed in danger of being submerged in a flood of peace moves and defeatist talk, it was designed to serve as a rallying cry. It was also meant as a message of comfort. In his mail, the King had come across a poem entitled 'The Desert', published privately in 1908; being deeply moved by its sentiments, he decided to end his broadcast with a few lines from it.

'I feel', he said in his slow, measured fashion, 'that we may all find a message of encouragement in the lines which, in my closing words, I should like to say to you:

I said to the man who stood at the Gate of the Year, "Give me a light that I may tread safely into the unknown." And he replied, "Go out into the darkness, and put your hand in the Hand of God. That shall be better than light, and safer than a known way."

'May that Almighty Hand guide and uphold us all.'[37]

Absent from the family circle at Sandringham that Christmas was Queen Mary. On 4 September, the day after war was declared, she had left Sandringham for Badminton House, the Gloucestershire home of her niece, Mary, daughter of her late brother Adolphus, Marquess of Cambridge, and now wife of the 10th Duke of Beaufort.

She went under protest. For the 72-year-old Queen, the thought of leaving, not so much Sandringham, but her London home, Marlborough House, was distressing. For one thing, Marlborough House, into which she had moved from Buckingham Palace on the death of her husband, King George V, had become almost an extension of her own personality. Its dignified, sumptuously decorated rooms, crammed with the treasures that she had spent a lifetime collecting, made a perfect setting for this indomitable old Queen. Indeed, with her highly stylized appearance, Queen Mary looked not unlike some painstakingly executed work of art. But stronger, even, than her attachment to Marlborough House was the Queen's sense of royal obligation. It would not be 'at all the thing', she declared, for a member of the royal family to be seen 'deserting' the capital in wartime.[38] Patiently, the King explained that her presence in London would cause unnecessary trouble and anxiety. Only on being convinced of this did Queen Mary agree to leave.

Her departure from Sandringham for the West Country was more in the nature of a royal progress than a flight. The Queen's Daimler headed a cavalcade of cars including almost her entire Marlborough House staff of sixty-three, plus dependants, and over seventy pieces of personal luggage. 'Quite a fleet', she noted tersely. Her eight-and-a-half-hour journey ('a lovely drive')[39] was broken at Althorp, where she was given lunch by Lord and Lady Spencer. There was another, unscheduled, stop. Queen Mary suddenly announced that she needed to go to the lavatory. They were forced to pull up at 'a lonely inn', reported Lady Cynthia Colville, her lady-in-waiting, 'where the inn-keeper was most helpful'. By way of thanks, Queen Mary afterwards sent him a small silver knife; he, in turn, sent her a silver chain. 'A most suitable souvenir,' remarked one of Lady Cynthia's sons.[40]

Queen Mary arrived at Badminton House that evening. Her niece, the Duchess of Beaufort, is said to have watched the arrival and, worse still, the unloading of this royal caravan with 'astonishment'.[41]

'Pandemonium', she reported to a friend, 'was the least it could be called! The [Queen's] servants revolted, and scorned our humble home. They refused to use the excellent rooms assigned to them. Fearful rows and battles royal were fought . . . The Queen, quite unconscious of the stir, has settled in well.'[42]

For the duration of the war, this most formal, punctilious and metropolitan of queens was to be subjected to all the unfamiliarities and uncertainties of life in the country.

★

One of King George VI's chief anxieties during the phoney war was a personal one: the behaviour of his elder brother, Edward VIII, now Duke of Windsor.

Nothing more vividly illustrated George VI's sense of insecurity, during the early years of his reign, than his dealings with his brother. Ever since Edward VIII had abdicated the throne to marry the twice-divorced Wallis Warfield Simpson and had gone to live in exile in France, the new King had remained apprehensive about his brother's intentions. Acutely conscious of the fact that he lacked his brother's charm, spontaneity and crowd-pleasing qualities, he was afraid that the ex-King might force his way back into the public spotlight. 'All my ancestors succeeded to the throne after their predecessors had died,' he once grumbled. 'Mine is not only alive, but very much so.'[43] Sir Ronald Lindsay, the British Ambassador in Washington, visiting George VI at Balmoral, claimed that 'really the King does not yet feel safe on his throne, and up to a point he is like the medieval monarch who has a hated rival claimant living in exile . . .'[44] The Ambassador need not have gone as far back as that for his analogy; there was a more recent parallel. The Duke of Windsor, with his winsome, Stuart-like appeal, was, like Bonnie Prince Charlie, a 'King over the Water'. This was why George VI would not hear of the Duke of Windsor's return from exile.

But his brother's threat to his position (which he may well have exaggerated) was not the only reason for George VI's unyielding attitude. He, and even more so the Queen, could not forgive the Duke for what they considered to be his shameful dereliction of royal duty. They resented the fact that his selfishness had forced them to ascend the throne. 'Who', answered the Queen sharply, on being told that the lines under the Duke's eyes had disappeared since the Abdication, 'has the lines under his eyes now?'[45] They steadfastly refused to have anything to do with his wife, whom they regarded as a showy, scheming *arriviste*, or to accord her the title of Royal Highness. To them, she remained 'Mrs S'. Besotted by Wallis, the Duke resented this family cold-shouldering of his wife more bitterly than anything else; it rankled for the rest of his life.

Nor did the King feel that, in political matters, the Duke could be relied upon to behave with the necessary royal circumspection. On several occasions since the Abdication – by a highly publicized visit to Nazi Germany in 1937, by a broadcast appeal for peace in the United States in 1939, by a direct appeal to Hitler to prevent war, and by a series of other indiscretions – the Duke of Windsor had not only focused attention on himself but had also broken the code by which no king, not even an ex-king, should involve himself in controversial political issues. The Duke, as the King once grumbled to a Cabinet minister, 'had never had any discipline in his life'.[46] The statement by Charles Bedaux – the shady businessman in whose French château the Windsors had been married and who was partly responsible for the Duke's tour of Nazi Germany – that the Duke of Windsor planned to study working conditions in various countries with a view to returning to Britain as the champion of the working classes was hardly guaranteed to calm the King's apprehensions.

The outbreak of the war intensified all these problems. The Duke of Windsor, anxious to be of some service to his country, suggested that he return to Britain to discuss the matter with the King. To this George VI reluctantly agreed, and he ordered that a plane be sent to the South of France to pick up the Duke and Duchess. But it was not going to be as easy as that. Only if his wife were received as a member of the royal family, insisted the Duke, would he accept his brother's offer of a plane. As George VI, backed by the Queen and Queen Mary, was prepared to do no such thing, the plan fell through. The Windsors came by sea instead. They were neither met nor accommodated by any member of the royal family. The Duke, without the Duchess, was granted one short meeting with the King. His brother's mood, reported George VI to another of his brothers, the

Duke of Kent, was 'his usual swaggering one, laying down the law about everything'.[47] He seemed, noticed the astonished King, to be utterly unconcerned about the effects of the Abdication; 'He has forgotten all about it.'[48]

The Duke, oblivious to the awkwardness which his presence – and still more, that of the Duchess – might cause, was anxious to be given a job in Britain. The King was having none of it. He feared both his brother's popularity and the Duchess's unpopularity. The Duke hardly endeared himself to the military authorities by wanting to know if his brother, the Duke of Gloucester, who was serving as Chief Liaison Officer with the British Field Force in France, was being paid. To the Duke of Windsor's disappointment – for he was nothing if not mercenary – he was told that the Duke of Gloucester was giving his services free. In the end, the Duke of Windsor was sent back to France as liaison officer with the British Military Mission to General Gamelin. His contacts with the British troops, ran the King's instructions, were to be kept to the minimum.

Even so, the Duke of Windsor managed on a series of tours of inspection, to draw far too much attention to himself: the famous boyish charm seemed to be working all its old magic. The Duke of Gloucester lost no time in reporting back on his brother's hogging of the limelight. 'Needless to say,' he wrote to the King, 'everybody was very polite to him but one could see nobody was at ease or very pleased.'[49] Nor were matters helped by the youngest brother, the Duke of Kent, asking the King if it were true that the Dukes of Windsor and Gloucester had inspected the troops together but that 'the former seemed to get all the attention'.[50]

The Duke of Windsor's own view, however, was that he was getting far too little attention. His job was too ill-defined, too unrewarding; his talents, he felt, could be better employed. From Paris, the Duchess, whose opinions the Duke not only respected but constantly quoted, complained that her husband's job was 'too inactive, besides a lot of pressure from the Palace which makes it impossible to do well'. Even the war, she continued, 'can't stop the family hatred of us'.[51]

In January 1940, without advising the King, the Duke suddenly flew to London. Having complained to various politicians and diplomats about what he considered to be his shabby treatment, he had a meeting with his old champion of the Abdication days, Lord Beaverbrook. Between them, the two men agreed that the Duke would be far better employed by returning to Britain to start a 'Peace Movement'. This would be a countrywide campaign to drum up support for a negotiated peace with Germany. This treasonable project was discarded only when the Duke was told that any such prolonged stay in the country would make him liable for British income tax. When set against this 'appalling' prospect,[52] the Duke's enthusiasm for saving Britain by negotiating with Germany very quickly evaporated. He hurried back to France.

But by then a suspicion that the Duke of Windsor was, at best, a security risk and, at worst, a traitor, had taken root. There were certainly grounds for such suspicions. Before the war, the Duke had been an open admirer of the Fascist dictatorships of Hitler and Mussolini. Considering Communism to be a far greater threat than Fascism (and, in fairness, he was not alone in this) he had been an outspoken advocate for some sort of understanding between Britain and Germany. Since his abdication, the Duke had hobnobbed with various Fascist sympathizers and his celebrated visit to Germany in 1937 had had its climax in a meeting with Hitler at Berchtesgaden.

None of this would have mattered had the Duke's attitude not confirmed the Nazis in their belief that, as a champion of their cause, he could be of considerable value to them. Before and during his reign, he had been assiduously cultivated by successive German ambassadors (Wallis Simpson, who was rumoured to have had an affair with Joachim von Ribbentrop, the pre-war German Ambassador, was undoubtedly courted by him), and even now the Nazis thought that they might be able to make use of the ex-King to further their own ends. His 'work', they imagined, 'was by no means finished'. He could still 'come back as a social-equalizing King'.[53] Indeed, soon after the Duke's return to France in January 1940, Count Zech, the German Minister to the Netherlands, assured Berlin that he was in a position to 'establish certain lines leading to the Duke of Windsor'.[54]

George VI, concerned enough about his brother's threat to his position, was soon to have a more serious concern still: the Nazis' plans for setting the Duke of Windsor on his throne.

2

A Definite Job

'I wish I had a definite job like you,' wrote George VI plaintively to Lord Louis Mountbatten at one stage during the phoney war. 'Mine is such an awful mixture...'[1] It certainly was. On the one hand, he was the Supreme Commander of his country's fighting forces, the all-transcending national symbol; on the other, his position as a constitutional monarch precluded him from playing any active part in the waging of the war. Militarily, he was negligible. Indeed, in the eyes of some, there seemed to be no meaningful role for a monarch in wartime; the royal family were regarded as 'peacetime luxuries'.

'I think it's all a bit silly – kings and queens in wartime,' one working-class woman is reported to have said during this period. 'I don't think they're wanted. All them things are all right in peacetime – we like to have ceremonies and royal robes – but now it's up to us all, not kings and queens.'[2]

George VI's ill-defined position was made no easier by the general military stalemate: by the six-month 'War of Nerves' in which an apprehensive Europe simply waited for Hitler to make his next move. Within his constitutional limitations, the King did what he could to fulfil his role. He was involved in various political and diplomatic moves, he made tours of inspection, and, late in 1939, he visited the British and French armies in France. It would be impossible, reported one of the King's equerries fulsomely to the Queen, 'to imagine a greater success ... and I trust His Majesty's natural modesty will not prevent him from realizing his achievement'.[3] But the King remained dissatisfied, frustrated, unfulfilled. Sir Alexander Cadogan, Permanent Under-Secretary at the Foreign Office, visiting the King one day during this period, found him 'rather depressed and a little *défaitiste*'.[4] His depression mirrored the national mood. 'I am very worried over the general situation,' he confided to his diary in March 1940, 'as everything we do or try to do appears to be wrong, and gets us nowhere.'[5]

All this changed, with dramatic suddenness, on 9 April 1940, when Hitler invaded Denmark and Norway. During the following nine tumultuous weeks, with the German blitzkrieg culminating in the fall of France in mid-June, George VI was involved in a series of national and personal upheavals.

The first was the resignation of the Prime Minister, Neville Chamberlain. Faced by the combined opposition of Labour, the Liberals and some Conservatives – all anxious for more dynamic leadership, untainted by the pre-war policy of appeasement – Chamberlain was obliged to offer the King his resignation.

George VI was very sorry to see him go. Throughout Chamberlain's tireless efforts to maintain peace, climaxing in the shameful sacrifice of Czechoslovakia at Munich in 1938, the King and Queen had given him their full support. The 'pro-Chamberlain appeasement point of view', complained the King's Private Secretary, Alexander Hardinge, 'prevailed at court ... from the highest to the lowest'.[6] Although, with hindsight, the royal couple's championship of Chamberlain appears misguided, it was perfectly understandable at the time. They were appalled by the prospect of war; particularly a war that was expected to involve the bombing of civilian populations. 'It all seemed to be coming so soon after the last dreadful war,' said the Queen many years later, 'everyone had suffered so much, and so recently.'[7] One can appreciate why they allowed themselves to be convinced, by Chamberlain and the Foreign Secretary, Lord Halifax, that appeasement was the only alternative to war.

It was a view shared by the majority of their subjects. 'They all complain about Chamberlain nowadays,' remembered the Queen, 'but at the time he had a great deal of support.'[8] With this, the despairing Hardinge agreed. 'London Society', he complained, 'is 99% pro-appeasement.'[9] And not only London Society: on the night of Chamberlain's return from Munich, the Prime Minister, appearing between the King and Queen on the Palace balcony, had been rapturously cheered by a great multitude of people. If this royal seal of approval had been too overtly political a gesture on the part of a constitutional monarch, very few regarded it as such at the time. The royal couple also knew – as many of their subjects did not – how ill-prepared the country was for war. 'At least', argued the Queen, 'Chamberlain gave us another year in which to get ready.'[10]

So it was with genuine regret and some resentment that George VI accepted Chamberlain's resignation on 10 May 1940. Both the King and Queen wrote to thank him for the great support he had given them during 'these last desperate and unhappy years';[11] the Prime Minister's farewell broadcast, reported the Queen, had reduced their eldest daughter to tears.

Although the King would have preferred the urbane Lord Halifax as Chamberlain's successor, he was obliged to send for the man to whom he was 'bitterly opposed'[12] – Winston Churchill. George VI shared the widespread view of Churchill as an unreliable political adventurer. And so did the Queen. In the summer of 1939, during a press campaign to have Churchill readmitted to the Cabinet, Chamberlain had been seated between the Queen and the Duchess of Kent at a dinner at Buckingham Palace; 'neither left me in any doubt', recorded Chamberlain, 'as to their opposition to the idea of Churchill's inclusion'.[13] Nor had the King forgotten Churchill's championship of Edward VIII during the Abdication crisis. Nevertheless these two men – George VI who would have been happier with Chamberlain, and Churchill who would, presumably, have been happier with Edward VIII – were brought together in a partnership that was to develop into a famous wartime institution. Together, George VI and Winston Churchill would come to symbolize the spirit of Britain at war.

As one by one the countries bordering the North Sea fell before the German onslaught, so did the King find himself becoming involved in the fortunes of his fellow monarchs. It was an involvement which, as the war progressed, and more and more monarchs sought sanctuary in Britain, would enhance his stature and increase his self-confidence. His uncle-by-marriage, the stork-like King Haakon VII of Norway, having fled the invading Germans in a British warship, was given refuge in Buckingham Palace. With him was his only son, Crown Prince Olav. They were followed, a fortnight later, by Queen Wilhelmina of the Netherlands. Twice, the redoubtable old Queen had telephoned George VI directly, begging for British military aid. Only on being assured that this was impossible did she reluctantly agree to seek sanctuary in Britain. She arrived – to be met at Liverpool Street Station by the King – with nothing other than the clothes she stood up in and a tin hat supplied by the commander of the destroyer in which she had escaped. Installed in Buckingham Palace, Queen Wilhelmina was treated with every kindness by the King and Queen. Her youngest grandchild, Princess Irene – daughter of Princess Juliana and Prince Bernhard – who was to have been christened in state in Amsterdam on 31 May, was christened instead in the chapel at Buckingham Palace; her godparents were Queen Elizabeth and 'the Dutch armed forces'.[14]

More controversial was the behaviour of King Leopold III of the Belgians. Having, as the active Commander-in-Chief of the Armed Forces (as well as the head of government), resisted the German invasion with the utmost gallantry, he realized that he would not be able to hold out much longer.

But instead of fleeing his country to set up a government-in-exile as his fellow monarchs, King Haakon and Queen Wilhelmina, had done, he decided that his place was with his army and his people. In an official letter to George VI, written several days before his surrender, King Leopold informed him of his decision. 'I am convinced that I am acting in the best interests of my country,'[15] he added in an accompanying, more personal note.

George VI's reply was to express grave concern at King Leopold's decision. Although the British King understood that, as Commander-in-Chief of the Army, Leopold III might feel obliged to remain with his troops, he felt that, as a monarch, he should leave the country to establish his government elsewhere.

On 28 May 1940, having given his French and British allies advance warning, King Leopold surrendered. His surrender was cynically misrepresented by the Allied authorities as an act of gross betrayal. Needing an excuse for the rout and subsequent evacuation of their own forces, they turned King Leopold into a scapegoat. His treacherous and totally unexpected surrender, they claimed, had left them dangerously exposed to the enemy. The 'Traitor King' had stabbed them in the back.

George VI's suspicions – that these accusations were false – were very soon confirmed. He deeply resented this denigration of a fellow sovereign. While agreeing that King Leopold would have been wiser to have left Belgium, he refused to join in the general outcry against him. He insisted that the King of the Belgians continue to receive 'all the honours, privileges and respect due to him'.[16]

The relentless German advance was halted just long enough to allow for the 'miracle of Dunkirk' – the successful embarkation of British and French troops at the end of May and the beginning of June. This was followed, a fortnight later, by the fall of France. By then Italy, with cynical opportunism, had entered the war on the side of Germany. The ending of the Franco-British alliance, which had never been a particularly harmonious one, left the King feeling strangely elated. 'Personally,' he admitted to Queen Mary on 27 June, 'I feel happier now that we have no allies to be polite to and to pamper.' He was thankful, he wrote in his diary some months later, that France had fallen so soon after Dunkirk; it had obliged the country 'to reorganize the Army at home, and gave us time to prepare the Air Force'.[17]

For Britain now stood alone against a ruthless, powerful and victorious enemy and King George VI was about to take up that 'definite job' for which he had been longing.

With Britain facing the threat of invasion and the certainty of bombing raids, the safety of the royal family had to be seriously considered. In an order to the Wehrmacht, Hitler had made clear his intention of preventing the escape of any sovereign from an invaded country. From the start, the King refused to consider leaving his kingdom. 'It just never occurred to us,' said the Queen afterwards. 'We never gave it a thought.'[18] There was a suggestion, soon after the fall of France, that the two princesses might be sent to Canada; quite a large number of upper-class children, including some of the princesses' relations, were being evacuated to Canada and the United States. But the Queen's oft-quoted answer to this suggestion was equally unequivocal: 'The children could not go without me, I could not possibly leave the King, and the King would never go.'[19] Instead, Princess Elizabeth and Princess Margaret were moved, first to the Royal Lodge in Windsor Great Park and then to the safety of Windsor Castle itself. Officially, it was given out that they were living in 'a house in the country'.[20]

Although the King and Queen usually spent weekends at Windsor, they spent every working day at Buckingham Palace. They would travel to and from London in an armour-plated car and always had their gasmasks and steel helmets with them. At the Palace, a distinct air of amateurishness marked the precautions taken for their safety. The royal air-raid shelter had been the housemaids' basement sitting-room. Reinforced by balks of timber, divided by beaver-board partitions, fitted out with baskets of sand and hand-pumps, it was neither particularly safe nor convenient. Not until the worst of the raids were over was a proper shelter built.

Security was equally haphazard. King Haakon, then a guest at Buckingham Palace, once asked the King what measures had been taken against a possible German parachute attack on the Palace. He would illustrate the procedure, answered the King confidently. He pressed the alarm signal to summon the Coates Mission, a specially chosen body of officers and men from the Brigade of Guards and the Household Cavalry, whose duty it was to protect the royal family day and night. There was no response. An embarrassed equerry went hurrying off to find out what had gone wrong. Apparently the police sergeant on duty had assured the officer of the guard that 'no attack was impending'. Only after all had been explained, and police co-operation obtained, did a party of guardsmen come dashing into the garden. Much to the astonishment of King Haakon and the great amusement of the King and Queen, they 'proceeded to thrash the undergrowth in the manner of beaters at a shoot rather than of men engaged in the pursuit of a dangerous enemy'.[21]

Appreciating, perhaps, that he could not place his entire trust in the Coates Mission, the King had shooting ranges laid down in the gardens of Buckingham Palace and Windsor Castle. Here, he and his equerries practised with rifles, pistols and tommy-guns. It was his intention, the King once told a guest, in the event of a German occupation of the country, to offer his immediate services, in any capacity, to the leader of a British resistance movement. The Queen was equally resolute. She was taking instruction in firing a revolver. 'I shall not go down like the others,'[22] she assured the admiring Harold Nicolson.

This was all very well but the government was taking more practical measures. As the monarch must on no account be allowed to fall into enemy hands, plans were drawn up in the event of the royal family having to get out of London. Two armoured cars were converted to passenger use for a rapid spiriting away of the family. Even before the outbreak of war, Madresfield, the Worcestershire home of the Earl and Countess of Beauchamp, had been rented as a possible place of royal refuge. ('The West Country will come into its own,' noted that incorrigible snob, Sir Henry ('Chips') Channon.)[23] Madresfield was merely the first of a number of houses selected (Pitchford Hall in Shropshire and Newby Hall in North Yorkshire were others) because of their relative accessibility to Liverpool. 'There was a line of them,' claimed Princess Margaret, who was not told about this until long after the war; 'we were to be shunted from one to the other until we reached Liverpool.'[24] Members of the Coates Mission, dressed in civilian clothing to allay suspicions, paid secret visits to these various houses in order to judge their suitability.

From Liverpool, if necessary, the royal family would be evacuated to Canada. Even the King would surely, in the end, have to agree to this. Having strongly disapproved of King Leopold's refusal to leave his country and set up a government-in-exile, George VI would hardly lay himself open to the same charge. He would never allow himself to become a hostage or a puppet king.

The King's steadfastness in the face of the Nazi threat was well illustrated during that last, nerve-racking lull between the fall of France and the Battle of Britain. On 2 August (the day after Hitler issued his directive for the 'final' onslaught on Britain), the King received a secret letter from King Gustav V of Sweden. In it, the old monarch offered to act as a mediator between the British King and the German Führer 'in order to examine the possibilities of peace'. Having, with constitutional correctness, passed the letter on to his government, the King, in his diary, made his own uncompromising views very clear. 'How can he talk of peace with Germany now after they have overrun and demoralized the people of so many countries in Europe? Until Germany is prepared to live peacefully with her neighbours in Europe, she will always be a menace. We have got to get rid of her aggressive spirit, her engines of war and the people who have been taught to use them.'[25]

George VI's sense of purpose, burgeoning as the situation worsened, was gradually becoming apparent to those beyond court circles. Harold Nicolson, meeting the King and Queen at a lunch party that July, professed himself astonished at how much the King had changed. 'I always thought him a rather foolish loutish boy,' he wrote to his wife, Vita. 'He is now like his brother [the Duke of Windsor]. He is so gay and she so calm. They did me all the good in the world . . . those two [are] resolute and sensible. *We shall win.* I know that. I have no doubts at all.'[26]

Three weeks before the fall of France, the King's brother, the Duke of Gloucester, returned to England from active service in France. Born on 31 March 1900, Prince Henry was then 40 years of age. The least complex of George V's four surviving sons, he was a bluff and convivial figure, very different from the King. 'Gourmand and more carefree about what he ate and drank . . .', noted one member of the royal household, Prince Henry was 'a jovial type, reacting instantly to the most faintly funny remark with a gusty, high-pitched giggle. He always made you feel good, if not particularly clever.'[27] With his prominent blue eyes, ruddy complexion and thickening waistline, he looked a true Hanoverian.

That the Duke's military service in France had been at all active was due more to his own efforts than to the demands of his job. Faced with the perennial problem of what to do with a soldier-prince in wartime, the military authorities had played safe by appointing him Chief Liaison Officer with the British Field Force in France. By giving him this ill-defined posting, they hoped, while keeping him well out of harm's way, to create the impression that he was playing a militarily significant role.

This conflict – between the restrictions of his princely
status and his own ambitions – had characterized the Duke
of Gloucester's entire military career. For, after sport (hunting, shooting, riding and polo) his consuming passion was
soldiering. He had consented to marriage, at the relatively
late age of 35, only on being assured that such a step would
not spoil his chances of one day commanding his regiment –
the 10th Royal Hussars. Yet his military career had been a
sadly frustrated one. Although a competent enough officer,
he had been prevented, as a King's son, from taking part in
any active service that was likely to prove politically controversial. As most military action tended to be politically
controversial, the Duke of Gloucester had always been
prevented from joining his regiment abroad. To his increasing despair, he had had to content himself with carrying out
the customary princely duties; duties for which he had very
little taste or talent.

The accession of his brother, George VI, in 1936, had
finally put paid to his dream of commanding his regiment.
Created Regent Designate (and so he would remain until his
niece, Princess Elizabeth, turned 18 on 21 April 1944), the
Duke of Gloucester had been obliged to give up his career
and to accept the purely ceremonial promotion to Major-
General.

His marriage, embarked upon somewhat matter-of-factly
in November 1935, had proved surprisingly successful. His
bride had been Lady Alice Montagu-Douglas-Scott, the
34-year-old daughter of the 7th Duke of Buccleuch. Small,
shy, pretty, the Duchess of Gloucester shared many of her
husband's interests. No more than he did she have the taste
for intellectual or sophisticated society. She was happiest on
horseback, in her garden, with her dogs or her paintbox. Yet
behind the Duchess's quiet façade lay great reserves of
strength. In common with all the wives of George V's sons,
the Duchess of Gloucester was a woman of dedication and
resilience.

If the Duke of Gloucester had seemed to have married for

marrying's sake, he had, after five years, developed a close and loving relationship with his wife. However, by the summer of 1940, they still had no children. Although neither of them was very articulate, their letters to each other exuded a warm compatibility. With the Duke away in France and their London home, York House in St James's Palace, taken over by the Red Cross, the Duchess of Gloucester had established herself in their recently acquired country house, Barnwell Manor in Northamptonshire. Being country-loving people, the couple were devoted to this large, rambling mansion.

In France, the Duke of Gloucester threw himself into his vaguely defined duties with characteristic gusto: visiting bases, inspecting troops, attending conferences, escorting visitors. To his brother, the King, he sent back a series of reports which, despite their somewhat schoolboyish tone, were very informative. To his wife at Barnwell Manor he issued a stream of instructions regarding fences, drains, roads, hedges and crops.

These orders could not have been entirely welcome to the Duchess. With most of the male servants and employees conscripted into the forces, she was obliged to run the extensive Barnwell estate with the help of a few old men and women. 'My goodness how we worked,' she remembered in later years. 'Most of the garden had to be turned over to vegetables but it was the weeds that thrived.' 'We seemed', she added with typically wry humour, 'to be growing Weeds for the War Effort.'[28] To these tasks were added additional public duties; chief amongst them the Duchess's appointment as Air Chief Commandant of the Women's Auxiliary Air Force – the famous WAAF.

Even at remote Barnwell the Duchess was thought to be in danger of being kidnapped by German parachutists. 'Never, at any time, however,' she says drily, 'were we given instructions as to what to do in this event.' The only security supplied was in the shape of a single detective – 'a Welshman soon nicknamed "the faithful corgi"'[29] –

although what protection he could have afforded if faced by a party of enemy parachutists it is difficult to imagine.

In their determination to keep the Duke of Gloucester out of harm's way, the military authorities were not being wholly successful. Always accident-prone, he was involved in several car accidents and, in his eagerness to concern himself with whatever was going on, he was constantly being caught up in dangerous situations. 'Motoring about is not nice as many villages are being bombed,' runs one letter from the Duke to his wife. 'We got caught in the middle of a town on Thursday and just had time to quit the car and lie down in a narrow alleyway, when the earth reverberated. We were not hurt but slightly bruised by falling tiles.'[30] The Duke's characteristic understatement masked the fact that he had been wounded sufficiently badly to require medical attention. 'I have got royal blood on me!' exclaimed the soldier responsible for dressing the Duke's wounds.[31]

But even the resilient Duke of Gloucester suffered from occasional bouts of depression. He was more sensitive than his manner suggested. He always dreaded the parting from his wife at the end of his occasional leaves ('My beloved Alice,' he wrote on one occasion, 'I did hate leaving you yesterday so very much that I could hardly keep a straight face . . .'),[32] and reporting back to Headquarters was like 'being back at school, only worse!!'[33] Even soldiering, as experienced on the French front, soon lost its attractions. 'I think I hate this country and war more than ever,' he admitted to the Duchess in February 1940. 'It is such an awful waste of everything.'[34]

He did not have to endure it much longer. With the relentless advance of the German forces towards the Channel, the Duke of Gloucester was ordered home. His presence, as he explained wryly to his mother, Queen Mary, had been an embarrassment to GHQ, 'because wherever I went, or had been, I was bombed'. The King, on welcoming his brother to Buckingham Palace, was able to assure their mother that the returned soldier was 'very calm and has no ill effects to his nerves'.

Queen Mary was very relieved. She had only just heard that Lord Frederick Cambridge, her nephew and the brother of her hostess at Badminton, had been killed in action. The unmarried, 32-year-old, who has been described as a 'charming and lively personality, with a little of the air of an eighteenth-century prince',[35] had made his home at Badminton. Queen Mary, who had been very fond of him, felt his death keenly. 'Heard the news of dear Freddy's death is confirmed,' she wrote in her diary. 'Too sad . . . Had to break the news of Freddy's death to Mary [her niece], she was awfully brave.'[36]

'How dreadful everything is,' sympathized the Duchess of Gloucester with her mother-in-law, 'I do hope and pray the tide may turn soon in our favour.'[37]

Far from turning, the tide was rising more rapidly than ever.

At this critical moment, when Britain stood braced for an expected German invasion, the King was obliged to give his attention once again to the problems caused by the Duke of Windsor.

With the fall of France, the Duke and Duchess of Windsor had fled to Spain. Arriving at the Ritz Hotel in Madrid, the Duke was handed a telegram from Churchill, in which the Prime Minister urged him to move on to Lisbon, from where a flying boat would take him and his wife back to England. Not, the Duke again stipulated, unless his wife was accorded full royal honours; they were not prepared to find themselves 'regarded by the British public as in a different status to other members of my family'.[38]

That the Duke of Windsor should be haggling about status at a time like this seemed incredible to the King but it strengthened his growing conviction that his brother should not, after all, be allowed to come back. Between them, the King and Churchill decided that the Duke of Windsor should be offered an appointment as Governor of the Bahamas. Churchill, on telling his friend Lord Beaverbrook about the plan, asked if he thought the Duke would accept the appointment. 'He'll find it a great relief,' answered Beaverbrook. 'Not half as much as his brother will,' commented Churchill.[39]

Yet even this relatively unimportant posting (the Duchess of Windsor had to consult an atlas) was considered by certain members of the royal family to be too good, if not for the Duke of Windsor, then certainly for 'Mrs S'. The King feared that 'she' would be 'an obstacle',[40] and the Queen is said to have protested that a woman with three husbands living would not 'be acceptable to the people of the Islands and might set a precedent for a general lowering of standards'.[41] With this Princess Alice agreed. She could imagine the distress of the 'nice old-fashioned people of the Bahamas' and the joy of 'the vulgar drinking Americans who will flock there', she wrote to the Queen.[42] If the Duke could not be King because of the woman he had married, then how, the Princess asked pertinently, could he now be the King's representative? The astonished Queen Mary could only imagine that Churchill had got it all wrong: the Duke, she believed, had merely asked Churchill to find him a house in the Bahamas and Churchill, misunderstanding, had made him Governor. 'A great mistake', pronounced the old Queen.[43]

All these petty misgivings paled, however, beside the necessity of getting the Duke of Windsor away as soon as possible. The social embarrassments likely to be caused by the couple in the Bahamas were as nothing when set against the political dangers of their continued stay in Europe. The first (subsequently amended) draft of the message which Churchill sent to the Dominion prime ministers announcing the Duke's appointment as Governor of the Bahamas stated that 'the activities of the Duke of Windsor on the Continent in recent months have been causing His Majesty and myself grave uneasiness as his inclinations are well known to be pro-Nazi and he may become a centre of intrigue. We regard it as a real danger that he should move freely on the Continent.'[44]

How pro-Nazi and how dangerous the Duke of Windsor was during this period is now almost impossible to gauge. So many of the documents dealing with his activities during this period seem to have been unaccountably lost or remain firmly closed to public inspection. His pre-war convictions – that Britain should remain neutral and allow Germany and Italy to destroy Communism – appear not to have changed. His admiration for Fascism seems to have suffered very little diminution; even after the outbreak of war he would happily show guests photographs of himself with Hitler at Berchtesgaden. First in Madrid and then in Lisbon, he seems to have spoken very freely and indiscreetly, leaving his listeners with the impression that he thought Britain would lose the war, that he disapproved of Churchill's government, that he was anxious to 'make propaganda for peace'.[45]

Deplorably, but significantly, he approached the Germans with a request to keep an eye on his houses in Paris and at Cap d'Antibes for the duration of the war. They were only too ready to oblige. Both houses were scrupulously protected and when, later in the war, the Germans occupied the South of France, they are said to have paid the rent on the Duke's property. He arranged for some of his furniture to be stored in Italy and even obtained the Nazis' permission for the Duchess's maid to go to Paris to collect some of her mistress's things.

Not unnaturally, all this gave the Nazis the impression that they might be able to make use of the Duke of Windsor: perhaps as a propagandist, perhaps as a peace negotiator, perhaps, even, as a puppet king. When still Prince of Wales, the Duke had spoken to Prince Louis Ferdinand, grandson of Kaiser Wilhelm II, in approving terms of dictatorships; such a strong man might one day be needed in Britain, he had said. That he had regarded himself as the chief contender for the role was only too apparent. Hitler, whose all-consuming goal was the destruction of Soviet Russia, was still hoping to conclude peace with Britain – if not immediately, then after severe German bombing had brought the country to its knees. He seems to have imagined that a sustained bombardment would lead to the fall of Churchill's government, the flight of King George VI and a negotiated peace with a British equivalent of France's Marshal Pétain. And who, mused the Führer, would be more willing to play this part than the frustrated, embittered, Nazi-sympathizing Duke of Windsor?

During the weeks that the Duke and Duchess spent in the Iberian peninsula, Nazi agents and sympathizers, urged on by Joachim von Ribbentrop, the German Foreign Minister, began paying them court. The reports which they sent back (which may well have been exaggerated) certainly gave the impression that the Duke was more than ready to co-operate. One agent, in repeating his conversations with the Duke, claimed that the ex-King spoke out strongly against the British government, that he described his brother, George VI, as totally stupid, and the Queen as a clever intriguer, and that he was considering issuing a public statement about his opposition to present British policy. When it was suggested that the Duke might one day regain the British throne, 'the Duchess, in particular, became very thoughtful'.[46]

As well she might. The Duchess of Windsor, who had never really appreciated, as any Englishwoman would have done, just how preposterous the idea of her becoming Queen would have been, might still have been harbouring hopes of wearing a crown. With her social assurance, her matchless elegance and – when she chose to exercise it – her winning charm, she no doubt imagined herself well-equipped for the role. Her estimation of her abilities was shared, it seems, by Adolf Hitler. 'She would have made a good Queen,' he remarked to the interpreter who accompanied the Duke and Duchess to Berchtesgaden.[47]

The British authorities, knowing how abjectly in love the Duke was with his wife, always regarded her with the utmost suspicion. Hardinge, the King's Private Secretary, commenting on the Duchess's 'anti-British activity', claimed that 'we never forget the power that she can exert on him to avenge herself on this country'.[48]

Hardinge was right to remember it. The Duchess of Windsor was extremely bitter about what she regarded as her ill-treatment at the hands of the British. When, in May 1940, the American playwright and journalist, Mrs Henry (Clare Boothe) Luce, spoke of her horror at the prospect of the bombing of Britain, the Duchess's reply was sharp. 'After what they did to me, I can't say I feel sorry for them – a whole nation against a lone woman!'[49]

By late July 1940, with the Windsors comfortably accommodated in the home of a suspected Nazi sympathizer near Lisbon, the Germans were ready to put into operation a plan, code-named 'Willi', by which the Duke – softened by a bribe and frightened by the threat of a bomb on the ship due to take him to the Bahamas – would be coerced into returning to Spain. The Duke and Duchess would be 'kidnapped' while on a shooting expedition near the Portuguese-Spanish border. The degree to which the Duke was willing to co-operate with his 'kidnappers' is uncertain. But for one reason or another, he seemed very anxious to delay his departure for the Bahamas.

Not until the Duke's lawyer, Walter Monckton, by now in charge of the British Censorship Bureau, suddenly flew out to Lisbon was the matter resolved. The British authorities, aware of what was happening, were determined to get the Duke away as quickly as possible. In the face of Monckton's forceful arguments, the Duke stopped vaccillating. He agreed to sail as planned.

Whatever the Duke's involvement in the Nazis' plans, there can be little doubt that he believed that, in the all too likely event of Britain losing the war, he would have an important role to play.

How much did George VI know about all this and how seriously did he take it? In public he tended to make light of the 'quisling activities' of his brother.[50] But Hardinge gave them more weight and one must assume that his concern mirrored that of his master. 'Germans expect assistance from the Duke and Duchess of Windsor,' read Hardinge's précis of one intelligence report. 'Latter desiring at any price to become Queen. Germans have been negotiating with her since June 27th ... German purpose to form Opposition Government under Duke of Windsor, having first changed public opinion by propaganda. Germans think King George will abdicate during attack on London.'[51]

The Windsors finally set sail for the Bahamas on 1 August 1940. According to a cable sent by the German Minister in Lisbon to Ribbentrop, the Duke had agreed to go only because a refusal to do so would 'disclose his intentions prematurely'. With the proposed German assault on Britain not yet having started, the time was not quite ripe for the Duke's emergence as the Man of the Hour. When that hour did strike – when either a defeated Britain or a triumphant Germany called upon him to negotiate a peace – he would 'make himself available'.[52] Only one prearranged code-word would be needed to bring him hurrying back to Europe.

How much of this was wishful thinking on the part of the Nazi authorities one does not know. Although the Duke of Windsor might have been prepared to play some sort of peacemaking role, one cannot seriously believe that he would have allowed himself to become King of England by grace of Adolf Hitler. He was, for all his faults, too much of a patriot to be a traitor.

3

'God Bless Your Majesties!'

IF ONE IMAGE, more than any other, has come to symbolize the wartime role played by King George VI and Queen Elizabeth, it is of them visiting the bombed cities of their kingdom. There they stand among the rubble, the King in naval uniform, the Queen in pastel-coloured clothes, talking to groups of elderly men, aproned women and raggedly dressed children. Slowly they move among the crowds, questioning, listening, encouraging; their interest is so patently genuine, their sympathy so heartfelt.

'I was very greatly impressed by the simplicity of both of them,' wrote Lord Woolton, the Minister for Food, after accompanying the royal couple on some of their tours through the devastated streets. 'They were so easy to talk to and to take round, and fell so readily into conversation with the people whom they were seeing, without any affectation or side. They were, in fact, very nice people doing a very human job.'[1] Before the war, royal visits had been meticulously orchestrated occasions, with the King and Queen being monopolized by aristocratic lords-lieutenant or obsequious mayors and town clerks; now they could mingle, quite freely, with the sort of people they would never normally have met. By this informal moving about among those who had lost, sometimes relations, sometimes everything they owned, the King and Queen were able to forge a bond between crown and people that would have been all but impossible in peacetime.

The most horrifying feature of the Battle of Britain was the bombing. For several months, from late August 1940, the cities of Britain were subjected to massive bombing raids. Not only London but also cities like Coventry, Southampton, Plymouth, Bristol and Birmingham suffered death and devastation on a tremendous scale. In under two weeks of bombing in September 1940, over 10,000 civilians were killed or injured, four-fifths of them in London. And invariably, on the day after these raids, there would be the King, often accompanied by the Queen, picking his way through the splintered glass and still smoking wood, doing what he could to bring comfort and encouragement. For a man of his temperament, shy and inarticulate with strangers, it was never easy but he forced himself on. 'I think they liked my coming to see them . . .', he confided to his diary after a visit to Coventry.[2] One of his 'main jobs in life', he wrote after yet another harrowing tramp through the shattered streets of some provincial city, 'is to help others, when I can be useful to them'.[3] The opinion of one of the survivors was much less tentative. 'We suddenly felt that if the King was there everything was all right and the rest of England was behind us,' he said.[4]

Inevitably, the King's unexpected appearances gave rise to a crop of stories. 'Come round the back!' shouted one householder in answer to a knock on his jammed front door; obediently, his royal visitor tramped round to the back door.[5] On another occasion a soldier, dashing out of a railway station, handed his ticket to the uniformed King on the misapprehension that he was the ticket collector. Those accompanying him on his tours of inspection were often astonished by his understanding of the issues and by his memory for faces. Once, on inspecting a line of sailors, the King stopped in front of one of them and said, 'I know your face. Weren't you on the same ship as I was at the Battle of Jutland?' The man had indeed served with him over twenty-five years before but, far from being gratified at having remembered him, King George was annoyed with himself.

'I couldn't remember his *name*,' he afterwards complained to one of his entourage.[6]

His bravery was tinged with fatalism. On being asked if he was worried about being assassinated while on one of his tours, his answer was that there was no point in worrying. If someone wanted to kill him, he said, there was nothing to stop them from doing so.

The London Blitz of September 1940 was particularly severe in the East End, where the districts near the docks suffered most. Again and again, when the raids were over, the King and Queen would appear suddenly in the ruined streets. Within minutes of leaving their car, the small police escort would be swept aside, leaving the couple to walk, often unaccompanied, through the rapidly swelling crowd. 'Masses of men and women,' wrote one observer, 'still dazed by the bombs, thronged about them, swallowed them up, separated them from their staff, and took them to their hearts. Nothing like the warmth of these receptions in hours of disaster has been seen before . . .'[7]

Yet strangely enough, noted another observer, the royal couple were never jostled. 'However tight and heaving the throng, a small circle of space formed round the King and Queen, and they bore this vacuum along with them as they went . . . the royal couple were hedged, as the true saying goes.'[8]

These royal visits to the badly bombed working-class areas carried a certain risk. There were mutterings about the poor East End having been bombed while the rich West End had remained unscathed. Discontent at the fact that the working classes had to make do with inadequate air-raid shelters and the railway arches under Hungerford Bridge, while 'society' people had access to the deep shelters under expensive clubs and hotels, was understandably widespread. The Communist Member of Parliament, Phil Piratin, even went so far as to lead a crowd of demonstrators to the Savoy to demand entrance to the hotel shelter. Only the unexpected sound of the All Clear prevented a potentially awkward confrontation. Inevitably, the King and Queen were affected by this situation.

With the King and Queen still being regarded, by some, as symbols of a privileged aristocracy, their visits to the East End could easily have appeared condescending; might there not be resentment of the fact that while Cockney lives and houses were being shattered, the King and Queen were living in the comfort and safety of their palace? 'It's all very well for them', complained one East End housewife, 'traipsing around saying how their hearts bleed for us and they share our suffering, and then going home to a roaring fire in one of their six houses.'[9] Harold Nicolson, noting the discontent in the East End, claimed that the royal couple had been booed in the course of one of their visits.

But such manifestations of ill-feeling were rare. And the speed and completeness with which the King and Queen overcame these occasional pockets of what were claimed to be 'Communist'-inspired resentment were not the least of their achievements. The great majority of the public appreciated the fact that the royal couple, who could very easily have stayed at home, had taken the trouble to visit the devastated areas. Any royal apprehensions about the warmth of their reception were soon dispelled by the looks of near-adoration in the eyes of the crowds who gathered to see them. 'Good luck!', 'God bless you!', 'Thank Your Majesties for coming to see us!' they would shout.[10] Sometimes, the Queen, overcome by emotion, would have to blink back the tears.

In the course of one of these visits the couple were told about a woman who had already been bombed out of two homes and was now being housed in a third. They immediately asked to see her. A policeman knocked on the door and the woman, with a baby on her hip, came out.

'We heard of your misfortune,' said the Queen. 'May we come in and talk to you? The King and I would so much like to bring you such comfort as we can, and hear your story.'

'Oh, do come in,' said the astounded housewife.

'We understand this is your third home,' said the King.

'That's right,' she answered. 'He burned us out of one and he flooded us out of another, but he'll never get us out of here!'[11]

The royal couple were deeply moved by such encounters. 'I feel quite exhausted after seeing and hearing so much sadness, sorrow, heroism and magnificent spirit,' wrote the Queen to Queen Mary in October 1940, 'the destruction is so awful and the people so wonderful . . .'[12]

Writing to Lady Astor after the bombing of Plymouth in March 1941, the Queen assured her that 'I have been thinking of you all without ceasing. I have been praying that the people may be helped to find courage, and ability to face such a terrible ordeal, and I am certain that they have all this spirit already.

'Words are not invented to say even mildly what one feels, but having just left you [the King and Queen had visited Plymouth a few days before] after such a happy and inspiring day, one feels it all so bitterly, and so personally. My heart does truly ache for those good mothers and children and all the splendid workers.

'That is one of the hard things about being King and Queen of a country that one loves so much. Every time this sort of murderous attack is made, one feels it, as if our own children were being hurt. All we can do, is to do our very best, and leave the rest in God's hand . . .'[13]

Yet so inspiring was what the King and Queen called 'the spirit of the people' that, at times, they would feel strangely elated. 'Often we would come back from seeing the most terrible devastation feeling quite cheerful,' claimed the Queen in later years. 'There was something so uplifting about people's behaviour. So many times people would say to me "Ah well, no use complaining". They were always ready to tackle whatever had to be done. Everybody worked wonderfully together. Really, we would come home feeling quite cheered up.'[14]

The growing identification of the King and Queen with

the suffering of their subjects was considerably strengthened by the bombing of Buckingham Palace on 13 September 1940. A daring enemy bomber-pilot flew straight up the Mall and, watched by the astonished King as he sat in his little sitting-room, dropped six bombs on the Palace. 'The whole thing happened in a matter of seconds,' wrote the King afterwards. 'We all wondered why we weren't dead.'

It had indeed been, as one old police constable remarked to the Queen as she inspected the damage, 'a magnificent piece of bombing, Ma'am, if you'll pardon my saying so'.[15]

It was so magnificent that the badly shaken King suspected that it had been executed by someone with a detailed knowledge of the Palace: perhaps by one of his many German relations, as part of a Nazi plot to kill him and place his brother, the Duke of Windsor, on the throne.

Be that as it may, the bombing of Buckingham Palace had tremendous propaganda value. Photographs of the royal couple picking their way through the debris appeared throughout the world. 'Almost before the wreckage had cooled off,' noted one member of the household, 'here they were, the two of them. Calmly making their way about like people crossing a river on stepping stones.'[16]

In his diary the King recorded that he and the Queen had forged a new bond with the people 'as Buckingham Palace has been bombed as well as their homes, and nothing is immune'.[17] The Queen's more robust remark has become another of those wartime classics. 'I'm glad we've been bombed,' she said. 'It makes me feel I can look the East End in the face.'[18]

For the bombing of the Palace not only produced a wave of sympathy for the royal couple, it also silenced the occasional carping. Even though the King and Queen had hardly been bombed out of house and home, the fact that their lives had been in danger roused feelings of intense anger and fervent loyalty. If the Germans had realized 'the depths of feeling which the bombing of Buckingham Palace has aroused throughout the Empire and America', wrote

Lord Louis Mountbatten to the King, they would have been well advised 'to keep the assassins off'.[19]

'What a wicked thing to do!' raged one young woman. 'If they hurt the King or Queen or the Princesses we'd be so mad we'd blast every German out of existence.'[20]

Altogether, Buckingham Palace was bombed nine times during the war. 'Seldom have I spent such a night,' wrote one of the King's equerries on first taking up his duties. 'Towards midnight, the sirens wailed and immediately there came the crash of bombs and the answering blast of anti-aircraft fire. There in my bedroom somewhere – I was not sure where – in that enormous house, I felt lost and terrified, certain that I should soon be buried under tons of Victorian masonry . . .'[21]

'It fills me with cold rage,' wrote one middle-aged house-wife in her diary on hearing that the Palace had again been bombed. She went on to note that the King and Queen, while visiting some heavily bombed areas of London one day, had had to take shelter in a police station when the air-raid warning sounded. They had taken tea with the ARP workers. 'Many people remarked that Hitler couldn't have gone out visiting like that – he would have needed an armed bodyguard.'[22]

It was due to his many contacts with people like those ARP workers – with policemen, firefighters, demolition squads and Civil Defence services engaged in dangerous war work – that George VI decided to create two decorations for civilians equivalent to the Victoria Cross for servicemen in action. These decorations were to be the George Cross and the George Medal. They would be awarded for acts of civilian bravery and devotion to duty. As medals were one of his passions, the King was responsible not only for their instigation but also for their design.

'Many and glorious are the deeds of gallantry done during these perilous but famous days,' he broadcast on 23 September 1940. 'In order that they should be worthily and promptly recognized, I have decided to create a new mark of honour for men and women in all walks of civilian life. I propose to give my name to this new distinction . . .'[23]

By this imaginative gesture, George VI identified himself ever more closely with the suffering and bravery of his subjects. It became another step on the road towards his ambition of establishing himself as 'A People's King.'

'For him we had admiration, for her adoration,' said one survivor of the Blitz about the King and Queen.[24] If these war years helped establish George VI as a people's king, they undoubtedly established Queen Elizabeth as the nation's darling. It was a position she maintained for the rest of her long life.

'Wherever you go in the world,' the Queen once remarked, 'there's always a wonderful Scotswoman doing a wonderful job of work.'[25] She could hardly have better summed up her own wartime contribution. Never were the Queen's outstanding qualities more in evidence than during these turbulent years.

A professional to her fingertips, she had given serious thought to her presentation of herself as a wartime queen. Although she had become Commander-in-Chief of several women's regiments, she was never seen in uniform. 'There were too many of them; one would have been changing all day long,' she said in later years.[26] But one suspects that she had other reasons. For one thing they would not have suited her; for another, she must have felt that morale would be strengthened and the mystique and glamour of monarchy better served by her looking as attractive and normal as possible. 'I just wore my old things,'[27] she afterwards protested but, according to her couturier, Norman Hartnell, there was rather more to it than that. Between them, they decided that she would, as always, avoid dark colours and stick to her usual pastel pinks, blues and lilacs, although now in rather 'dustier' shades. 'She wished to convey the most comforting, encouraging and sympathetic note possible . . .', he claimed.[28]

So it was in her off-the-face hats, suede gloves, hydrangea colours, pearls and high-heeled shoes that the Queen moved amongst the shabbily dressed crowds. Of course she wore her best clothes when visiting the East End, she once exclaimed: 'If the poor people had come to see me *they* would have put on their best clothes.'[29]

Her instincts, as always, were correct. 'Oh, ain't she lovely,' called out the admiring Cockney women, 'ain't she just *bloody* lovely!'[30]

During the first weeks of the war, when gas attacks were considered a distinct possibility, the Queen always carried her gas-mask in the regulation-issue khaki case suspended on white webbing from her shoulder. But not for long. It was one day noticed that her gas-mask was being carried in a satchel covered in violet velvet to match the colour of her coat.

The Queen's dislike of being seen in uniform was brought home vividly to a member of the Civil Service, then working in Glasgow. He had been sent, from a unit of servicewomen in some remote station, a rare, possibly pre-war, photograph of the Queen in uniform. The photograph had been enlarged, and the official was asked if he could possibly arrange for the Queen to autograph it, so that it could be hung up in the canteen. The official's request was met with a very cool refusal from the Palace. The Queen, he was told, was surprised to receive such a request from a department of the Civil Service, which was apparently prepared to distribute the photograph 'at will'. Abashed, the official wrote back to explain the circumstances. The servicewomen had obtained the photograph 'in good faith and had hoped to honour their premises by giving it a favoured place'. Back came, not the original picture, but a large Cecil Beaton portrait of the Queen 'in a wide foaming white gown', diamond necklace and tiara, duly and 'graciously' signed.[31]

With not even Beaton's black and white photographs doing justice to the Queen's best features – her superb colouring and her graceful movements – spectators were usually surprised by her good looks. 'The hospital hummed and buzzed the next day,' wrote Lady Astor to one of the Queen's ladies-in-waiting after a royal visit to Plymouth, 'and Her Majesty would have been pleased if she could have heard all the things the soldiers said. What struck them most was how much more beautiful she is than her photographs – in fact, one of the officers said that he almost felt like writing to the papers about it.'[32]

Lady Astor went on to say that one young Canadian soldier had locked himself in a lavatory because he had not wanted the Queen to see his disfigured face. On being told this, the Queen sent him a signed photograph and a sympathetic message.

Gestures such as this – part heartfelt sympathy, part public relations – were very typical of the Queen. Appreciating how much people had lost in the bombing raids, she arranged for furniture which had been stored away for decades in Windsor Castle to be sent to the East End. She helped finance and organize the so-called 'Queen's Messengers': a body of especially enlisted women entrusted with the task of bringing food, emergency supplies and, equally important, advice and encouragement to the badly bombed towns and cities. She saw to it that she was photographed at one of her famous Buckingham Palace 'sewing bees' – those gatherings of women engaged in knitting and sewing for the troops – although her contribution, other than as an example, seems to have been slight. The Queen always seemed to be busy on the same piece of knitting, noted one sharp-eyed member of the Palace staff.

When Lord Woolton told the Queen that people regarded her as the embodiment of 'practical sympathy', she was delighted. 'Do you really think that people think of me like that, because it is so much what I want them to think – and it's true. It's what I try to be,' she replied.[33] Her projection of herself, in other words, was proving successful. This same professionalism characterized her dealings with the press. Throughout her life, she was the one member of the royal family whom the newsmen never criticized. Press photographers idolized her. She knew when to look at the camera, when to wave her famous wave and when to smile her famous smile. In the wartime newsreels that were shown all over the world, her star quality was immediately apparent.

Lord Woolton tells a revealing anecdote about the Queen's awareness of what made a good press picture. While she was touring a communal feeding centre, a grubby child in its mother's arms leaned forward to grab the Queen's famous triple string of pearls. As the moment had just been missed by a photographer, Lord Woolton murmured something to the effect that the Queen had broken a pressman's heart. 'Without showing the slightest sign that she had heard me,' he continued, 'she moved back into position for the baby again to play with her pearls, and so that the pressman could take his photograph.'[34]

On another occasion the Queen delighted both press and onlookers by proving herself to be the only person capable of coaxing a terrified little dog out of a hole in the rubble.

To all these qualities, the Queen brought something more: a strong personal magnetism. Those who accompanied her on her tours of hospitals or munitions factories or bomb damage felt her magnetism to have an almost physical dimension. The crowds could sense it immediately. On one occasion an official spoke to her about it. 'We all feel a warmth radiating from you,' he said. 'I can't describe it, something intangible. Do you feel that you are giving something out?'

Her answer was disarmingly frank. 'I must admit that at times I feel something flow out of me. It is difficult to describe what I mean. It makes me feel very tired for a moment. Then I seem to get something back from the people – sympathy, goodwill – I don't know exactly – and I feel strengthened again, in fact, recharged. It's an exchange, I expect: I don't know . . .'[35]

Whatever it was, it helped win for the monarchy enormous popularity as, day after day, the Queen carried out her exhausting and often harrowing duties.

'What days we are living in,' wrote the Duke of Kent to a friend in the summer of 1940, 'and what changes.'[36] The chief change for the 37-year-old Duke was that he, the least military-minded of the late King George V's four surviving sons, had been obliged to get into uniform. In spite of the fact that his naval career had ended, ignominiously, over ten years before (ill-health had been given as the reason for his early retirement from a service he loathed), the Duke of Kent had rejoined the Navy on the outbreak of war. As a Prince of the Blood, it was imperative that he be seen to be making some sort of contribution to the national struggle.

Yet the very fact of his being a prince prevented him from making any really worthwhile contribution. The Admiralty desk job, to which he was posted on rejoining the Navy, he found boring in the extreme..His subsequent jobs, first with the Ministry of Labour and then as Chief Welfare Officer of the Royal Air Force, were hardly more stimulating. A great deal of his time was spent touring civil defence installations, inspecting factories, looking at bomb-sites and visiting RAF bases. He considered it all very tedious. According to Cecil Beaton, 'the Duke of Kent refused to take the war more seriously than a tiresome interruption to his life'.[37]

The Duke, who had been born on 20 December 1902, was a man of somewhat specialized tastes and interests. The best-looking of the brothers – tall and slim with dark blue eyes and a flashing smile – he was also the odd man out. Where even the Duke of Windsor shared the hunting, fishing and shooting tastes of his breed, the Duke of Kent's interests were more cultured. Ready enough to drive fast cars and fly planes, he was just as happy visiting art galleries, listening to records or playing Cole Porter on the piano. He loved the cinema, the theatre and the ballet; Gertrude

Lawrence once discovered him backstage, trying on one of her wigs.

But the Duke of Kent was more than just a sophisticated playboy. His nature had its darker side. Like all the sons of George V, he had a quick temper: he was mercurial, moody, easily irritated and notoriously impatient. Chips Channon, who knew him well, claims that the Duke had drunk deeply from life. Society was full of stories about his womanizing; in later years a well-known figure in London society, Michael Canfield, was claimed to be his son. But there were just as many rumours about his less conventional sexual tastes. The Duke of Kent was apparently bisexual. Noël Coward is said to have been one of his many male lovers, and Randolph Churchill told Sir Robert Bruce Lockhart that the Duke had been obliged to pay a large sum for the recovery of certain love letters to a young man in Paris. He was once arrested, together with a well-known homosexual, in a notorious nightclub, and only after his identity was discovered was he released from the police cells.

Equally scandalous had been the Duke's drug-taking. There was talk of hashish-smoking sessions with a decadent young South American, and in 1929 one of his women friends – an American by the name of Kiki Preston – introduced him to more serious drug-taking. He became so badly addicted that the Duke of Windsor, at that stage Prince of Wales, and to whom he was very close, was obliged to take him in hand. Kiki Preston was forced to leave England and the two brothers retired to the country where the younger one was kept under strict surveillance. By the following year, his addiction appears to have been conquered. Even King George V, who seldom had a good word to say for his eldest son, was moved to write and congratulate him on all he had done for his younger brother.

It has been claimed, on the flimsiest evidence, that the Duke of Kent shared his elder brother's admiration for the Fascist regimes of Hitler and Mussolini; that he, too, saw Germany and Italy as dynamic modern states from whose policies Britain had a great deal to learn. It is unlikely. Although the Duke of Kent might have been irked by the stuffiness of court and government circles, he was not particularly interested in politics. Prince Louis Ferdinand, a grandson of Kaiser Wilhelm II, visiting from Nazi Germany, seems to have been more impressed by the Duke's elegance than his politics. He liked the Duke of Kent, the Prince confided to a friend, because he was 'artistic and effeminate and used strong perfume'.[38]

So it had been with considerable relief that King George V and Queen Mary heard the news, in August 1934, of their youngest son's engagement. His choice of bride was what one might have expected. Not for him some pretty little English débutante, but the 27-year-old Princess Marina of Greece and Denmark. Very much part of the complicated network of interrelated European royal families, Princess Marina brought a breath of Continental air into the by then thoroughly British royal family. She brought also a chic unknown since the heyday of Queen Alexandra. 'I agree with Winston', wrote Churchill's secretary, John Colville, 'in thinking the Duchess of Kent the most beautiful woman whom I have ever seen. She is excellently dressed, her hair is as well done as it can be, and her natural beauty is only increased by the taste with which she paints and clothes herself.'[39]

During the years before the war, and with the Duke's hedonistic bachelorhood behind him, the Kents established themselves – in their Belgrave Square home and a mansion called Coppins in Buckinghamshire – as a highly fashionable couple, playing host to the likes of Noël Coward, Somerset Maugham and Douglas Fairbanks Junior. 'He was one with the most charm left at the job,' claimed the Duchess of Windsor, 'and they made a couple more up with the advances of this world.'[40] Princess Marina, who gave birth to a son in 1935 and a daughter just over a year later, tended to leave the running and decorating of their houses to her husband. When the visiting Lady Airlie once complimented

the Duchess on 'the beautifully arranged rooms and perfectly chosen meal', she laughed. 'My husband chose the dinner
and the wine – and the flowers and everything else,' admitted Princess Marina. 'He enjoys doing it, and so I always
leave the household affairs to him. I let him make all the
decisions over furniture and decorations. He has a wonderful
sense of colour and design.'[41]

A theory persists to this day that, at the time of Edward
VIII's abdication, there had been a plan to put the Kents,
rather than the Yorks, on the throne. Not only was the
Duke of Kent the father of a male heir but with his
impressive bearing and social aplomb, and with a wife who
had been born a princess, he would also fulfil the ceremonial
demands of the position to perfection.

It is an implausible story. Neither the British constitution
nor royal tradition allowed for any such cavalier treatment
of the order of succession. The Abdication had been trauma-
tic enough; this would have been no time for tampering with
the dynastic rights, not only of the Duke of York and his
two daughters, but of the Duke of Gloucester. Nor is there
any documentary evidence, in the papers of the then Prime
Minister, Stanley Baldwin, to back up the rumour.

The outbreak of the war meant the postponement of an
appointment for which the Duke of Kent would have been
eminently qualified: that of Governor-General of Australia.
Together the Duke and Duchess would have made an
excellent vice-regal couple. Typically, the Duke's chief
concern seems to have been the decorating of Government
House in Canberra. By the use of 'oatmeal-coloured silk
tweed curtains, pale blue satin-covered sofas and chairs, and
white Grecian rugs,' enthused one society columnist, the
Duke of Kent had planned to 'revolutionize' the appearance
of their Australian home.[42] Be that as it may, the postponement of the Duke's appointment robbed him of the opportunity of exercising his various talents on a wider scale.

Not unexpectedly, the Duke of Kent's most valuable
wartime contributions were his official visits to foreign

countries. In June 1940 Churchill sent him to Portugal as head of the British delegation attending the 800th anniversary celebrations of Portuguese independence. His mission was designed to underline Britain's long-standing friendship with Portugal ('our oldest ally' was a much-bandied phrase) and to assure Dr Antonio Salazar, the Portuguese dictator, that Britain was far from being the spent force depicted in Nazi propaganda.

Lisbon, at that time, was a cauldron of intrigue. It was full, not only of rich refugees but also of political agents of every sort. To prevent a rumoured Nazi *coup d'état*, Salazar could not appear to be associating too closely with the British. Nor was the Portuguese dictator's position made any easier by the fact that the Duke of Windsor, who at that stage had still not set sail for the Bahamas, was due to arrive in Lisbon from Madrid at the very time that the Duke of Kent would be there. Those who subscribe to the theory that the Duke of Kent shared his brother's enthusiasm for the Nazi regime maintain that the two princes planned to make use of a Lisbon meeting for political discussions. What, precisely, they planned to discuss and what practical effects such discussions could possibly have had is never made clear. To claim some sort of enduring political collusion between the brothers is to underestimate the repugnance felt by the royal family – including the Duke of Kent – for the Duke of Windsor's marriage. Once such devoted companions, the Dukes of Windsor and Kent had been estranged since the Abdication. A proposed meeting between them in 1937 had been cancelled because of the Duchess of Kent's adamant refusal to be seen in the company of the Duke of Windsor's wife. The Duchess of Windsor always complained about the Kents' continued cold-shouldering of them.

So, far from providing the opportunity for a little political plotting, a Lisbon meeting between the brothers would be very awkward for all concerned. Fortunately, in answer to Salazar's request, the Duke of Windsor agreed to remain in Madrid until his brother's Portuguese visit was over. The

Duke of Kent, spared this family embarrassment, acquitted himself with his customary charm and diplomacy.

These qualities were as much in evidence the following year when he paid official visits to Canada and the United States. With both the King and Churchill anxious to sustain the special relationship between Britain and the United States, the Duke of Kent's three-day stay with the Roosevelts was considered particularly important. In the course of a packed schedule – part official, part social – he clearly impressed his hosts. His appreciation for what Eleanor Roosevelt described as 'the constant flow of aid from this country' was very apparent. It again manifested itself in his enthusiastic letter of thanks. 'The gratitude of the British people for what you have done for us is immeasurable and their admiration is unbounded,' he wrote, 'but I feel I must add my own word of admiration for all you are doing . . .'[43]

When the Kents' third child, a son, was born just under a year later – on 4 July 1942, American Independence Day – the couple asked the President to act as one of the godparents. In accepting, Roosevelt expressed himself 'thrilled and very proud', and the boy was given, as the last of his four names, that of Franklin. 'Tell the King', cabled the President, 'that I will hold him to strict accountability until I am able to take over the responsibility of a godfather myself.'[44]

In its small way, the gesture helped strengthen the bond of personal friendship between the British monarchy and the American presidency and, by extension, between Britain and the United States.

If the Duke of Kent was scoring his successes abroad, his wife was scoring hers at home. In many ways, the war was the making of Princess Marina. Until its outbreak she, like so many members of the royal family, had been a somewhat remote figure to the general public. Although the most cosmopolitan of the royal women, and very conscious of the royal birth that set her apart from her sisters-in-law, the

Queen and the Duchess of Gloucester, she had lived a somewhat domestic life. The Princess was happiest in the company of her children and of her many Continental relations. One family friend mentions 'her loyalty and gentle sweetness'.[45] Indeed, the Kents' glittering circle had tended to be made up of her husband's friends, rather than hers. 'I know the change did me good,' she once wrote to her hostess after being entertained at a country house, 'though I *was* shy at the idea. I suppose I do "vegetate" and one gets used to it . . .'[46]

But her appointment as Commandant of the Women's Royal Naval Service, the Wrens, early in 1940, changed all that. Almost overnight, the Duchess of Kent became both more accessible and more assured. Although, like the Queen, Princess Marina disliked wearing uniform, it was because of the elegance with which she wore hers and its specially designed hat ('No woman wants to wear a hat that makes her look unattractive, war or no war,' she maintained)[47] that she improved the image of the Wrens. And if she did occasionally infringe dress regulations by wearing high-heeled shoes, silk stockings and even earrings with her uniform, no one really minded. Her striking appearance, allied to the efficiency with which she carried out her duties, did wonders for morale. 'She brought a human touch to even a routine inspection,' claimed one associate. 'Walking down a line of girls, she would stop and talk to each one personally, not just a conventional sentence or two, but with genuine interest.'[48]

She had a disarming way of admitting her shortcomings. She could never, she confessed, get used to calling a kitchen a 'galley' or a bedroom a 'cabin'. Her salute, a sort of wilting hand gesture far removed from the crisp regulation version, was described as 'not in the least military'.[49] To any zealous soldier or sailor trying to interest her in some complicated piece of weaponry or machinery, she would simply admit, with a wistful smile, that she did not understand it and was never likely to.

Such was her growing popularity that it needed only one broadcast appeal (coupled with photographs of her in that dashing hat) for volunteers, for the Admiralty to be flooded with applications. Over three thousand poured in on the first day. 'Whatever you do,' begged one despairing Admiralty official, 'don't on any account let the Duchess broadcast again.'[50]

Her wartime duties were not confined to the Wrens. She was employed in a humbler capacity as well. Anonymously, as 'Nurse Kay' – or as anonymously as she could hope to get away with – she worked at University College Hospital in London as a nursing auxiliary. Here, beside the other voluntary nurses, she made beds, washed patients, changed dressings, tidied lockers, carried trays and emptied bedpans.

As the Kents' two eldest children, Prince Edward and Princess Alexandra, had been 'evacuated' to spend long periods with their grandmother, Queen Mary, at Badminton (a not altogether successful venture: the old Queen found the children unruly and they found her unsympathetic) they were able – when out of uniform – to devote much of their attention to their private interests. 'I played backgammon with Princess Marina, whilst the Duke strummed Debussy,' wrote Chips Channon of an evening spent with the couple at Coppins. 'He is extremely intelligent, well-informed but sometimes very nervous and irritable. She, on the other hand, is perfect . . .'[51] The Duke still found time to pursue one of his passions: the collecting of paintings, furniture, porcelain and silver. Coppins, said Channon, was 'full of rich treasures, and gold boxes, étuis and pretty expensive objects always being exchanged or moved about. The Duke adores his possessions . . .'[52]

Whenever he was on a tour of inspection in the West Country, the Duke would visit his mother, Queen Mary, at Badminton. The old Queen had always found the company of her youngest son very congenial. She could talk to him, she admitted to her brother, the Earl of Athlone, 'openly and with ease'. Her two other sons, the King and the Duke of

Gloucester, she complained, 'are *boutonnés*'.[53] Indeed, of all her sons, the Duke of Kent was the only one who shared Queen Mary's tastes. Mother and son would spend many happy hours exploring the antique shops of Bath. The Duke took an interest not only in his mother's magpie collections but also in her sumptuous jewels and clothes.

'He often used to say I looked nice,' sighed Queen Mary after his death. 'Nobody else ever did.'[54]

Only gradually had Queen Mary accommodated herself to living at Badminton. In the early days, she had found life in the country, with its talk of crops and livestock, very strange. She longed to be back in London, close to her family and in the centre of things. Imbued with an unbending sense of royal duty, she felt that she should be making more of a contribution at this critical time. To the Duke of Kent she complained about 'not doing more publicly'.[55] During the phoney war she was always getting up at dawn to take the train to London for the day. It needed the Blitz to put an end to these pleasurable excursions.

But as Queen Mary was always one for making the best of things, for giving her days some sense of purpose, she eventually adjusted herself to her new way of life. This adaptation to rural living was not without its comic side. For one thing, she never looked like a countrywoman. Not for her a headscarf and Wellington boots. Even when wielding a saw or a spade, Queen Mary would be formally dressed in pastel-coloured ankle-length coat and skirt, gloves, earrings and a toque anchored uncompromisingly on her rigidly dressed wig. (The man from Steiner, the ladies' hairdresser in Grosvenor Street, who dressed and fitted Queen Mary's wigs, claimed that she was 'virtually bald'.[56]) With Queen Mary's knowledge of country estates largely confined to the inspection of country houses, her ignorance of farming was almost total. 'So *that's* what hay looks like,' she exclaimed on having her attention drawn to a particularly good crop.[57] And in her zeal to collect scrap for the war effort, she was quite likely to load up her old green Daimler with any implements left in the fields by the farmers. She once arrived home in triumph, dragging a gratifyingly large iron contraption for her dump. It turned out to be a neighbour's plough.

It was for her clearing up of the Badminton estate, however, that Queen Mary became most celebrated. So irked by untidiness, so determined to achieve something worthwhile, she set about creating what she regarded as a sense of order in her immediate surroundings. With her niece, the Duchess of Beaufort, having tactfully diverted her attention away from the garden, Queen Mary directed her energies into organizing the clearing of ground, the thinning of plantations and the stripping of ivy from trees, walls and buildings. Ivy was her particular aversion. Each morning she would emerge from her own suite of rooms – drawing-room, dining-room, bedroom, bathroom and sitting-room – to embark on her day's 'wooding'. Accompanied by her 'wooding squad', made up of an assortment of far less dedicated equerries, ladies-in-waiting, secretaries, soldiers and guests, the Queen threw herself wholeheartedly into her self-appointed task.

No one was allowed to shirk his or her 'wooding' duties. Even the King, who once spent a night at Badminton during his mother's stay there, could not escape. Early the following morning he was to be found, axe in hand, hacking away with the rest of them. By the time Queen Mary left Badminton after six years, not a trace of ivy was to be seen. One of her most treasured possessions was a map of the estate, presented to her by the Duke of Beaufort's agent, on which, marked in blue, were the areas she had helped clear.

The work was not without its hazards. Osbert Sitwell, who often visited Queen Mary, described one 'wooding' expedition. 'The despatch-rider of that morning was a new recruit . . . temporarily replacing a more permanent predecessor who had already been injured: two chauffeurs had been knocked out, and another man, now helping, still wore a black patch over one eye which, I was told, a splinter had entered. We were made to begin attacking an enormous centuries-old thicket of hawthorn, bramble and wild rose . . .'[58]

Eventually, Osbert Sitwell would accept Queen Mary's invitations only on the understanding that 'my doctor absolutely forbade me to clear or cut timber'.[59]

There were times when even her long-suffering nephew-by-marriage, the Duke of Beaufort – always known as 'Master' – lost patience with her passion for thinning out and chopping down. She was determined that a large cedar growing outside the drawing-room windows should be felled: it excluded the light, she complained. This was true but it happened to be the tree in which Lord Fitzroy Somerset, afterwards Lord Raglan of Crimean War fame, had played as a boy. On no account would the Duke of Beaufort allow it to be sacrificed. For once, Queen Mary was obliged to yield to an even more resolute will.

After the fall of France, with Britain facing invasion, it was suggested that Queen Mary go to Canada where her brother, Lord Athlone, was Governor-General or, failing that, that she join the King and his family at Windsor Castle. She refused to do either. By now she had fully accustomed herself to living at Badminton. 'I am more independent here than I should be at Windsor, which is an armed camp,' she told a friend.[60] Not even the threat of air-raids (enemy bombers were always passing on their way to Bath and Bristol) could budge her. She would simply 'descend', as she put it, to the shelter where, surrounded by yawning, dressing-gowned members of the household, she would sit, back erect and immaculately dressed, doing the crossword puzzle. In time, she refused even to make use of the shelter.

Queen Mary was apprehensive, however, about being captured by the Nazis. In the event of a German invasion, arrangements had been made for a plane to fly her from Badminton to a secret destination. Against this eventuality, she had three suitcases permanently packed; one she kept herself, the other two were in the care of her two dressers. A fourth suitcase, for her jewels, was to be packed at the last moment.

She was very strict about observing all wartime regulations concerning food, heating and clothing. Petrol rationing deprived the old Queen of one of her chief pleasures: visiting places of historic or artistic interest in the neighbourhood. Her ancient Daimler was used chiefly, these days, for conveying her 'wooding squad' to outlying parts of the estate. Humphries, the chauffeur who had been with her for many years and was by now considered to be 'long past it', had a tendency to ignore the roads and simply go bumping across the countryside. 'The large, old-fashioned Daimler rocked and swayed in the most frightening fashion, to the consternation of all its occupants except Queen Mary,' complained one passenger. Although the Queen might utter an occasional 'Oh dear! I wish he wouldn't do it!'[61] she would never have dreamed of reproaching Humphries.

More broad-minded than the general public ever imagined, Queen Mary one day caused her companions great amusement. They had set out in the Daimler to visit a Lord and Lady Ailesbury who lived nearby. As they neared the Palladian country house, Queen Mary suddenly exclaimed, 'Of course, I remember Lady Ailesbury now! Nearly forty years ago! She was a Miss Madden, and flirted outrageously with my cousin the Grand Duke of Mecklenburg-Strelitz – the Grand Duchess was quite jealous!'

When they arrived at the house, and Lady Ailesbury ('an enormous pyramid of red granite decked out in black velvet and strung with pearls') was dropping a deep curtsey to Queen Mary, the Queen, very seriously but with an air of 'undisguised mischief', remarked, 'I believe you were a *great* friend of my cousin, the Grand Duke of Mecklenburg-Strelitz?'

'Yes,' exclaimed the anguished Lady Ailesbury, '*and of the Grand Duchess.*'[62]

Queen Mary's stay in the country brought her into

contact not only with the unfamiliarities of farm life but also with the sort of person whom she would never normally have met. And, equally significant, many people were meeting a member of the royal family – a representative of the monarchy – for the first time. The four despatch-riders who had been assigned to her for the duration of the war, and whom she had immediately incorporated into her 'wooding squad', became devoted to her. During breaks from ivy-stripping, she would hand round cigarettes and they would all, the Queen included, sit happily smoking and chatting.

Yet more people were met during the course of her countless self-imposed public duties. Everywhere – while organizing the collection of scrap, visiting factories and hospitals, inspecting bomb-sites, serving in canteens, helping at fêtes, calling on villagers, attending ENSA concerts, even joining in singsongs – Queen Mary would talk to people. Just occasionally, her normally unmistakable presence would remain unrecognized. Once, when she was in a canteen serving tea to a row of astonished soldiers and sailors, an elderly NCO shouted 'Hi, Missus, give us a cuppa tea quick, please.'[63] Queen Mary was highly amused. She had never been called 'Missus' before, she remarked.

To any servicemen whom she happened to pass on the road, she would give lifts. On being told by her overawed passengers that their friends at camp would never believe that they had driven in the same car as Queen Mary, she ordered the striking of a number of small metal medallions bearing her royal cipher and crown. One of these was presented to anyone to whom she had given a lift.

The Queen was often highly diverted by her conversations with her passengers. 'What do you do in civilian life?' she asked one young WAAF corporal.

'I am a tap-dancer, Your Majesty,' replied the girl, 'but I'm afraid that after four years in the WAAF I have *lost my art*.'[64]

Nor did Queen Mary ever resent the good-natured informality of some of the servicemen from the Commonwealth or, as she would have called it, the Empire. To Lord Athlone, Queen Mary once described an experience during a visit to Bath. 'Some Australian soldiers and airmen happened to be there and asked me to be photographed "with the boys",' she wrote. 'I said yes and they crowded round me and I suddenly felt an arm pushed through mine and an arm placed round my waist in order to make more room, I suppose. It really was very comical and *unexpected* at my age.'[65]

One important factor in the continuing popularization of the monarchy was the attitude of Winston Churchill. Throughout the war years, the Prime Minister paid lavish tribute to the contribution of King George VI and Queen Elizabeth. It could have been very different. The first few years of Churchill's wartime premiership saw him at his most impressive. During the Battle of Britain, when the country faced the threat of invasion, suffered the horrors of the Blitz and fought off the German air attack, Churchill's bulldog-like qualities seemed to epitomize the spirit of the defiant and beleaguered island. Even after the immediate threat receded, he remained a towering figure. In the spring of 1941 Germany invaded Yugoslavia and Greece; in June, it launched its attack on the Soviet Union; at the same time, it reinforced the Italian troops fighting the British in North Africa. Although Britain suffered severe losses, reversals and defeats during this period, Churchill continued to be looked to as a source of national inspiration. So eloquent, so pugnacious, so much larger than life, he could very easily have overshadowed the King. Not only did the Prime Minister have a more powerful personality than the monarch but he also wielded the power. Beside him, the diffident and constitutionally impotent George VI could well have become little more than a cipher.

There were, indeed, times at the start of their working relationship when the King felt slighted by the Prime

Minister. Regretting the fact that Chamberlain had been forced to resign and that Halifax had not succeeded him, he regretted, equally, the somewhat offhand manner in which Churchill seemed to treat him. Unlike Chamberlain who, in the course of their weekly meetings, had been punctilious about keeping him in touch with whatever was going on, Churchill often arrived late, stayed for just a few minutes and gave what the monarch considered to be far too little information. Even as late as 1942, by which time George VI and Churchill were on the best of terms, the royal couple sometimes felt that, unwittingly, the Prime Minister was too centre-stage. He was forever broadcasting the sort of Message to the Nation that should, by rights, have come from the sovereign.

But all this was, as the King and Queen realized, unintentional on Churchill's part. As the Prime Minister's Private Secretary, John Colville noted, not long after Churchill assumed office, the King and Queen appreciated that he was 'the man for the occasion' and that 'Winston, however cavalierly he may treat his sovereign, is at heart a most vehement royalist'.[66]

He was certainly that. Churchill had a highly romantic reverence and respect for the monarchy. Once the initial misunderstandings between the King and Churchill had been eliminated, they developed a close partnership. Not since Queen Victoria's intimate relationships with Lord Melbourne and Benjamin Disraeli had a monarch and a prime minister enjoyed such a close rapport. Although Churchill's wartime government was a coalition made up of Conservative, Labour and Liberal members (the three most important ministers concerned with home affairs were all members of the Labour Party), it was with Churchill that the King principally dealt. 'I made certain he was kept informed on every secret matter,' wrote Churchill, 'and the care and thoroughness with which he mastered the immense daily flow of State papers made a deep impression on my mind.'[67] The Prime Minister told him more, the King revealed in a letter to Queen Mary, 'than most people imagine, of his future plans and ideas, and only airs them when the time is ripe to his colleagues and the Chiefs of Staff'.[68] In his diary for the first day of 1941, the King claimed that 'I could not have a better Prime Minister.'[69]

But it was Churchill's many public tributes that made the greatest national impact. 'The whole British Empire, and most of all, the United Kingdom of Great Britain and Northern Ireland,' intoned Churchill on receiving the Freedom of the City of Edinburgh in October 1942, 'owes an inestimable debt to our King and Queen. In these years of trial and storm they have shared to the full the perils, the labours, the sorrows, and the hopes of the British nation.'[70]

An equally ringing tribute came from *The Times* on the occasion of an exchange of congratulatory telegrams between the King and the Prime Minister. 'Mr Churchill's telegram . . .', read the leading article on 18 May 1943, 'revealing the help that one of the strongest Prime Ministers has received from his Sovereign, is a powerful reminder that King George VI is doing a work as indispensable for English governance as any of his predecessors, just as he has set his peoples from the first day of the war an unfailing public example of courage, confidence and devoted energy.'[71]

4

King-Emperor

WINSTON CHURCHILL's declaration that 'the whole British Empire' owed a debt to King George VI and Queen Elizabeth was more than just a piece of rhetoric on the part of the Prime Minister. George VI was the last King-Emperor, and with Britain still regarded as the mother country by many of the inhabitants of the dominions and colonies, the King was as much the symbol of the Empire, or Commonwealth, as of the United Kingdom. On the outbreak of hostilities in 1939, almost the entire Commonwealth had declared its support for Great Britain, the Australians even adopting the unequivocal slogan of 'One King, one flag, one cause'.[1] Photographs of the uniformed King could be found tacked up in homes in the Australian outback, the South African veld and the Canadian prairie. The concept of the old Empire might have been largely replaced by a Commonwealth of equal and independent nations but the British crown remained the supreme unifying factor.

The direct link between the sovereign and the kaleidoscopic collection of peoples who made up the Commonwealth were the various governors and governors-general. Although shorn of all political power, they remained representatives of the crown. Where a governor-general of a dominion happened to be a member of the royal family, his status was greatly enhanced. The prestige and mystique of the monarchy lent an undeniable lustre to the office. Canada, as one of the most important British dominions, was fortunate in having the Earl of Athlone as Governor-General throughout most of the war years. He and his wife, Princess Alice, proved themselves to be a particularly accomplished vice-regal couple.

Lord Athlone, born on 14 April 1874 as Prince Alexander of Teck (his name and title had been changed in the general Anglicization of the British royal family in 1917), was the youngest of Queen Mary's four brothers. Princess Alice, born on 25 February 1883, was the only daughter of Queen Victoria's youngest son, Prince Leopold, Duke of Albany. This meant that Princess Alice was doubly related to King George VI: he was her husband's nephew and her own second cousin. The couple, who had been married in 1904, were known in the family as Uncle Alge and Aunt Alice.

On the outbreak of war, the 65-year-old Lord Athlone realized that he was too old for active military service (he had been a soldier in his younger days) but both he and the 56-year-old Princess Alice imagined that there must be some way in which their considerable experience and still unimpaired energies could be put to use. The opportunity came in 1940. On the sudden death of the Governor-General of Canada, Lord Tweedsmuir, the post was offered to Lord Athlone. In his discussion with George VI, he was hesitant about accepting the post: he wondered if his nephew should not appoint a younger man. But in the end he agreed to accept it for two years only. He was to stay for six. 'We both appreciate the compliment,' reported Lord Athlone to his sister Queen Mary, 'and I hope in spite of age I shall be able to carry out the work.'[2]

The couple, who arrived in Canada in June 1940, carried out the work superbly. Lord Athlone, although no intellectual, was a man of considerable presence and sound common sense. 'He had many qualities fitting him for the post,' claimed Vincent Massey, a later governor-general. 'He shared his family's ability to come down by a sort of instinct on the right side of a public issue. Like his sister Queen

Mary, he had an unbending sense of duty. He possessed an endearing nature and the engaging attributes of warmth and personal modesty.[3] In addition, Lord Athlone had all the self-assurance of an uncomplicated man born into a world of privilege. 'Totally self-confident,' claimed one of his aides, 'it would never have occurred to him that anyone might not have been happy with him.'[4]

Princess Alice was an exceptional woman. Small, attractive and elegant, with a vivacious personality and an assured social manner, she made the perfect First Lady. The long-serving Canadian Prime Minister Mackenzie King, who could be critical and who resented the fact that he was obliged to give precedence to this 'imported' royal couple, none the less admitted that the Princess was 'exceptionally clever, very charming, exceedingly intelligent and active'.[5] In later years the Queen, who knew her very well, claimed that 'she had such get-up-and-go. She was always very straight, very strong-willed, with a great natural dignity.'[6] In fact, Princess Alice's china-figurine appearance belied her true character. She was a much stronger personality than her husband. 'She was always the boss,' maintained her secretary.[7]

From their home, the sprawling Rideau Hall in Ottawa, the Athlones embarked on their new role with characteristic gusto. Having already served, from 1924 to 1930, as the Governor-General of South Africa, Lord Athlone under-stood his duties and obligations very well. He might not have any political power but, like a constitutional monarch, he could still use his influence. As in South Africa, the couple were faced with a complex racial situation: this time the division between English-speaking and French-speaking Canadians. Rendering this racial divide more serious was the fact that some French Canadians resented Canada's involve-ment in what they regarded as a British war. Nor was this resentment confined to the French. During the 1930s Canada had become increasingly isolationist, increasingly North American rather than British, in character. It had also become anxious not to become embroiled in a European war.

However, the Athlones had only to cope with vestiges of this reluctance. By the time they arrived, the majority of Canadians had ranged themselves wholeheartedly on the side of Britain. There was what one member of Lord Athlone's staff described as 'a surge of power to the centre',[8] with most local, racial and political issues being subordinated to the national war effort. Canadians, including many French-speaking Canadians, had volunteered in vast numbers to fight abroad and, by her massive wartime contribution, Canada earned for herself the title of 'the arsenal of democracy'. Throughout Lord Athlone's term of office, Canada was, above all else, a nation at war.

'The whole country', enthused Princess Alice, 'threw itself into war work and it was very inspiring to be there at that time.' Few threw themselves more unstintingly into it than the Athlones themselves. 'Our chief preoccupation', as she put it, 'was inspecting endless, endless war factories.'[9] But no matter how exhausting their daily schedule, the couple would never admit, even to their staff, how tired they were. Nor did they ever complain about anything else. On the contrary, they set their much younger staff an example. 'What are we doing tomorrow?' they would ask eagerly after a long day full of activity. 'When do we start?'[10]

In speech after speech, Lord Athlone would urge greater efforts towards winning the war. On some occasions he would feel things so intensely that he would discard his prepared text and speak from the heart. To an audience in Victoria he once declared that the winning of the war transcended any local colonial squabbling and that it was everyone's duty to rally round Britain. His impassioned outburst won him a standing ovation but the authorities insisted that reporters confine themselves to the undelivered, less controversial text.

Princess Alice felt no less strongly. She spent hours in

munitions plants, she tramped through shipyards, she clambered into aeroplanes, she rode in tanks, she comforted the wounded, she organized women's groups, she made speeches, she launched appeals, she chatted to thousands upon thousands of nurses, servicemen and voluntary workers. Yet she never allowed herself to look anything but cheerful and confident. Her common sense was one of her most notable characteristics. When, for instance, she went to inspect a new naval barracks for ratings, she proved eminently practical. Turning to the accompanying Admiral, she remarked briskly, 'There aren't enough hatches between the kitchen and the dining-room.'[11]

Added to the Athlones' concern about the general progress of the war were their worries about its more personal aspects: the plight of their various Continental relations, the fortunes of Queen Mary, and the bombing of Buckingham Palace and of their own apartments in Kensington Palace. The first news of the Kensington Palace bombing was that the building had been 'completely gutted'; only later did they hear that their apartments had not suffered too severely and that at least their pictures and furniture were safe.

Lord Athlone's reaction on first hearing the news of the 'gutting' of Kensington Palace, from his secretary, Sir Shuldham Redfern, was typical. Not only did he show no emotion; he did not even comment on it. The secretary, expecting some expression of shock or distress, was astonished to hear Lord Athlone – who was about to visit the United States – casually remark that 'Roosevelt says that we needn't bring tail coats.'[12]

'In our family,' as Princess Alice used to say, 'we never fuss.'[13]

However, life at Rideau Hall was by no means all work and no play. Despite their natural dignity, the Athlones were an animated couple, gregarious and easily amused. The atmosphere, claims a member of the household, was one of 'warmth and liveliness and conviviality'.[14] The Athlones enjoyed an excellent relationship with their staff. 'They gave us every kind of consideration,' says Neville Usher, one of Lord Athlone's aides. 'I was only twenty-five and had never seen the world at that level, but they were always on hand with guidance and advice.'

Little pencilled notes, addressed to the aides-in-waiting in Lord Athlone's neat handwriting, would draw their attention to this or that duty; and after some great occasion, such as the Opening of Parliament, His Excellency would thank them in his characteristically bluff, if oblique, fashion. 'It went very well, don't you think? It went quite well.'[15] Whenever he attended a public function or addressed an audience, Lord Athlone introduced his aides as though they were personal friends or equals.

Along with the usual royal stock-in-trade – a remarkable memory – Lord Athlone had a disconcerting tendency to assume that people knew exactly what he was talking about. Invariably he referred to someone simply as 'he' or 'she' and to the place from which they came as 'there'. A conversation with him became known, by everyone from ministers to aides, as 'playing Dumb Crambo' because one often had to guess what or who he was referring to.

One of his aides tells the story of a woman lunch guest at Rideau Hall whom Lord Athlone had last met a few years before. His Excellency opened the conversation by asking, 'How are they?'

'Oh, very well, Your Excellency,' replied the bemused woman, playing for safety.

'Yes, yes,' he barked, 'no trouble with them at all?'

Perhaps he was referring to her children? 'Never, Sir,' she answered.

'I had some difficulties at first,' he declared. To this bewildering remark, his listener could only give a noncommittal nod.

'Do you never have any trouble keeping them in in the morning,' persisted Lord Athlone.[16] Only then did the guest realize that Lord Athlone was referring to the topic of their conversation of three years before, when they had each acquired a new set of false teeth.

Princess Alice quickly established herself as a practical mistress of the house. She rearranged the furniture, she eliminated waste, she paid daily visits to the kitchen, she discussed things with the comptroller and the housekeeper, she saw to the flowers, she kept an eye on all arrangements. A small pad and silver pencil always lay beside her place at table for the jotting down of notes about the running of the household. 'She knew if a duster was misplaced,' claims one member of the staff.[17]

No more than her sister-in-law, Queen Mary, did Princess Alice approve of wasting time. Captain Tom Goff, one of Lord Athlone's aides, once sent a friend a photograph of the household at Rideau Hall 'including himself and Princess Alice knitting, and Lord Galway crocheting'.[18]

The servicemen who were invited to the Princess's regular tea dances were always delighted by the way she joined in the dancing. 'Who', one unwitting young Air Force cadet was once heard to ask, 'is the precious white-haired lamb I've been rushing all afternoon?'[19]

Adding considerably to what Princess Alice called the merriment of their first years in the house was the presence of their only daughter, Lady May Abel Smith, with her three young children. As Lady May's husband, Major Henry Abel Smith, was on active service in the Middle East, it had been decided that his family would be better off in Canada.

They were joined by Princess Alice's Dutch relations, Princess Juliana and her two daughters (Queen Wilhelmina's mother and Princess Alice's mother had been sisters), who had come to Canada to safeguard the tenuous Dutch royal line of succession. With Princess Juliana an only child and with the possibility of a German invasion of Britain, it had been decided that, as heir to the Dutch throne, she would be safer in Canada.

Princess Juliana was very much a person after Princess

Alice's own heart. Unaffected, energetic and with a keen sense of humour, she wasted no time on vain regrets. 'Juliana', said Princess Alice, 'was really magnificent. She never once complained or expressed unhappiness, but threw herself into everything that was being done for the war.'[20]

In time, Princess Juliana and her family moved from Rideau Hall into a home of their own and, in 1941, Lady May Abel Smith went back to England. With her husband having returned from service abroad and now commanding his regiment at home, Lady May was naturally anxious to join him. This turned out to be more easily said than done. It was almost impossible to get a passage back to Britain. Not even the most highly placed personages – Lord Mountbatten, Queen Mary, even the King himself – were able to secure a cabin for Lady May on the crowded troopships. Finally, in desperation, Princess Alice asked Sir Shuldham Redfern, her husband's secretary, to make one last effort. Not feeling very hopeful, Sir Shuldham went to see the military authorities who were in charge of sailing arrangements. He was directed to a lowly corporal sitting in a tiny, box-like office.

The corporal made a telephone call. Certainly, there was a cabin, with bath, available on Friday week, he said. Would that suit her ladyship? It would; and Lady May sailed back to Britain to join her husband.

'That corporal was far too valuable ever to be promoted,' claimed Sir Shuldham years afterwards.[21]

One of the spheres in which George VI felt that he could use his status as a monarch to influence events was in Anglo-American relations. His visit with the Queen to the United States in the summer of 1939 had resulted in mutual admiration on the part of the King and Franklin D. Roosevelt. In the course of two long political conversations, they had been able to discuss the international situation and the relationship between their two countries in the event of war. The King had been greatly impressed by Roosevelt. 'Why don't my ministers talk to me as the President did tonight?' he had afterwards demanded. 'I feel exactly as though a father were giving me his most careful and wise advice.'[22] The President had been hardly less impressed by the King. Expecting to meet a pleasantly mannered nonentity, he had very soon come to appreciate that George VI was a man of considerable knowledge and relatively enlightened views.

Nor was Roosevelt immune to the mystique of kingship. According to his son Elliott, the President was 'fascinated by kings and queens, half-amused, half-impressed, by the pomp and pageantry that enveloped royalty'.[23] Like Churchill, Roosevelt had a deep respect for the institution of the monarchy; in later years the President would assume that, if thwarted by Churchill, he could always go over his head to make a direct appeal to the King. For his part, George VI felt that, unlike Churchill, he could approach the President as a fellow head of state.

At the outbreak of war, the American Ambassador to the Court of St James had been Joseph P. Kennedy, father of the future President John F. Kennedy. Once a fervent supporter of Chamberlain's appeasement policy, Kennedy had remained convinced that Britain should never have gone to war against Nazi Germany. He doubted whether Britain could ever be victorious or whether war would be worth the economic cost. The King, receiving Kennedy one day early in the war, was deeply distressed by the Ambassador's defeatist attitude. He felt sure that Kennedy's pessimistic reports would influence opinion in Washington. No sooner had the Ambassador taken his leave than the worried King wrote him a letter in which he set out his own less cynical view of the coming struggle. It could not be seen in purely material and financial terms; there were deeper issues – such as the rights of smaller nations and the upholding of democratic systems – involved. 'I know that you appreciate things that are plainly expressed and that is why I do so now . . .' wrote the King. 'The British Empire's mind', he assured Kennedy, 'is made up.'[24]

But so was Ambassador Kennedy's. He continued to send his gloomy reports to Washington. In January 1940 Kennedy informed Lord Halifax that Sumner Welles, the US Under-Secretary of State, was coming to Britain: the purpose of his visit was 'to place the President in a position to judge whether there was or was not the possibility of finding the way of settlement'.[25] By 'settlement' the Ambassador meant a negotiated peace with Germany.

Roosevelt, however, remained unconvinced by Kennedy's view of the situation. As the King had discovered during his talks with the President, Roosevelt was very knowledgeable about European affairs and very sympathetic towards Britain. Since the outbreak of war, the King and the President – and the Queen and Mrs Roosevelt – had exchanged occasional letters. 'I want you and your family to know', the President had written to George VI on 1 May 1940, 'that you have very warm friends in my wife and myself over here, and you must not hesitate to call on me for any possible thing if I can help or lighten your load.'[26]

The one sure way in which Roosevelt could have lightened the King's load was by bringing the United States into the war. But faced with the powerful isolationist and neutralist elements in his country, the President dared not – in spite of his own pro-British sympathies – simply declare unprovoked war on Nazi Germany. What he was able to do, though, was to throw his weight behind what Churchill called 'the glorious conception of Lend-Lease' by which the United States supplied arms to the British.[27]

The President had also sent a personal representative to Britain with a brief to gauge both the country's ability and its will to resist the German onslaught. The man entrusted with this mission was one of his close associates, Harry Hopkins. Hopkins was 'to see whether British morale was really as bad as Kennedy pretended'.[28] Not least among the people sounded out by Hopkins were the King and Queen. He had already met the royal couple during the visit to Washington in 1939 where a typical gesture on the part of the Queen had greatly impressed him. On hearing that Hopkins's 8-year-old daughter had been bitterly disappointed to discover that the Queen, in her daytime clothes, did not look like a queen in fairy stories, the Queen had arranged for the little girl to see her setting out for a banquet in glittering crinoline, jewels and tiara. Both the King and Queen had paused to talk to the child. 'Daddy, oh Daddy,' the starry-eyed girl had exclaimed to Hopkins, 'I have seen the Fairy Queen.'[29]

After lunching with the royal couple at Buckingham Palace on 30 January 1941, Hopkins was impressed all over again, and for quite different reasons. Of their quiet courage and resolution, they left him in no doubt. 'The Queen', reported Hopkins, 'told me that she found it extremely difficult to find words to express her feeling towards the people of Britain in these days. She thought their actions were magnificent and that victory in the long run was sure, but that the one thing that counted was the morale and determination of the great mass of the British people.'[30]

Hardly had the three of them sat down to lunch than the air-raid alarm sounded. The royal couple simply ignored it until, as coffee was being served, a bell rang. 'That means we have to go to the air-raid shelter,' explained the King calmly. They retired to the cramped basement room where, for a further hour, they discussed Anglo-American affairs. Again and again, to Hopkins's gratification, the King expressed his deep admiration for President Roosevelt.

'If ever two people realized that Britain is fighting for its life, it is these two,' reported Hopkins.[31]

The King's awareness of the importance of Anglo-American relations was again evident in the matter of the exchange of ambassadors between the two countries. The death of the British Ambassador to Washington, Lord Lothian, opened the way for one of the King's favourites, the Foreign Secretary Lord Halifax, to be switched to the post. To the reluctant Halifax, the King explained that 'the post of my Ambassador in the USA was more important at this moment than the post of Foreign Secretary here'.[32] And when the new United States Ambassador, John G. Winant, who was replacing the defeatist Kennedy, came to Windsor, the King went to the station to meet him. This was 'the first time in the history of Great Britain', claimed Winant, 'that the King has gone to meet an Ambassador'.

Winant, like Hopkins, was impressed by the King. 'Then, and always afterwards,' he reported, 'I found him to be completely informed on the day-to-day progress of the armed forces, and on any other subject that concerned his people.'[33]

However, the friendship between George VI and President Roosevelt did not always run smoothly. In spite of the fact that the Battle of Britain had been won and that Hitler's attack on Russia had gained Britain a new ally, the summer of 1941 saw British fortunes at an alarmingly low ebb. With serious losses of men, equipment and warships, the British had been obliged to evacuate first Greece and then Crete. The campaign in North Africa was proving disastrous, with the British forces no match for the Germans, now commanded by the brilliant General Erwin Rommel. Masking his feelings of despair, the King again wrote a personal letter to the President in which he drew attention to the unbroken spirit of his people, the indefatigability of Churchill and, a shade optimistically, the 'wonderful coming-together of our two great countries' for 'the future betterment of the world'.[34] At the same time the Queen wrote, in equally optimistic vein, to Eleanor Roosevelt.

Neither received an answer. There was not much, in truth, that Roosevelt could say. Short of declaring war on Germany – a declaration that was unlikely to be passed by Congress – the President could give Britain no more help. The royal couple were deeply hurt by Roosevelt's silence. Both as a head of state and a friend, the King felt that he had been slighted.

But any hitch in the relationship between King and President was more than compensated for by the growing rapport between Roosevelt and Churchill. The two men met, off Newfoundland, early in August 1941, soon after the German invasion of Russia. Churchill came armed with a letter of introduction from the King. 'I am sure that you will agree that he is a very remarkable man,' wrote the King, 'and I have no doubt that your meeting will prove of great benefit to our two countries in pursuit of our common goal.'[35]

The letter which Churchill brought back for his sovereign was equally encouraging. 'It has been a privilege to come to know Mr Churchill in this way,' wrote the President, 'and I am very confident that our minds would travel together, and that our talks are bearing practical fruit for both nations.' The President had heard a recent radio broadcast by the Queen to the women of America; it had been, he assured the King, 'really perfect in every way'.[36]

Indeed, the Queen's broadcast had made a significant contribution towards the maintenance of Anglo-American accord. In that informal fashion which her American listeners appreciated, she thanked them for their generosity in sending 'Bundles for Britain'. She spoke of the heroism and hard work of the women of Britain and made a point of assuring her audience that the country was far from despairing. In spite of all the horrors and devastation, 'wherever I go I see bright eyes and smiling faces, for though our road is stony and hard, it is straight, and we know that we fight in a great cause'. The broadcast is said to have been 'ecstatically received'[37] and the Queen was enthusiastically applauded whenever she appeared on newsreels.

The meeting between the American President and the British Prime Minister resulted in the drawing up of the Atlantic Charter: a joint declaration of war aims. Its grandiosly stated objectives left the King feeling a little sceptical. 'The joint statement said all the right things,' he wrote to Queen Mary, 'but how are we going to carry them out?'[38]

The Anglo-American stalemate ended, with dramatic suddenness, on the morning of 7 December 1941. 'A bombshell arrived in the 9 o'clock News (BBC),' noted the King in his diary for that day, 'saying that the Japanese had bombed Pearl Harbour in Honolulu.' Within five days the United States and Britain were allied in a war against Germany, Italy and Japan.

'My thoughts and prayers go out to you and to the great people of the United States at the solemn moment in your history', cabled the King to the President. 'We are proud indeed to be fighting at your side against the common enemy.'[39]

With two royal homes – Buckingham Palace and Kensington Palace – already bombed, St James's Palace narrowly missed being hit one night in November 1940. The bomb fell outside York House, the part of St James's Palace recently occupied by the Duke and Duchess of Gloucester. Debris came crashing through the windows. 'Marvellous to relate,' the Duchess reported to her mother-in-law, Queen Mary, 'the house has suffered very little damage – it must be very strongly built and much more solid than we expected it to be.'[40] Indeed, on first being given York House soon after their marriage, the Gloucesters had been warned that the drawing-room floor would not stand the weight of more than twenty people. 'So we made a party list', remembered the Duchess many years later, 'of the twenty-one people whom we disliked most.'[41]

This droll remark was typical of the Duchess of Gloucester. Behind that reserved façade lay an intelligent and humorous personality. 'She was painfully shy,' wrote a member of George VI's household, 'so that conversation with her was sometimes halting and unrewarding, for you felt that she had so much more to say, but could not bring herself to say it.'[42] When she did speak, her conversation was often accompanied by a nervous twisting of her hands. This nervousness tended to obscure her beauty as well as her intelligence.

The theory that the Duchess of Gloucester was somewhat

overawed by her marriage into the royal family was not really valid. Born into one of the most illustrious families in the land, raised in some of Britain's most grandiose houses, she would not have been unduly impressed by the status of the royal family. 'I was very used to that sort of life,' she afterwards remarked.[43] The Duchess would have been no less shy had she married someone less elevated than a prince.

There was no denying, though, that her reserve was a serious handicap in the sort of life which, as a member of the royal family, she was expected to lead. But having an iron sense of duty, the Duchess forced herself to play her part to the utmost of her abilities. That she did not have the natural talent of someone like her sister-in-law, Queen Elizabeth, for public life, made her contribution all the more remarkable.

Among her many wartime duties was a harrowing visit, with the Duke of Gloucester, to Belfast in the spring of 1941. The Duchess had to wear her WAAF uniform for the flight over so that, if the plane were shot down and she fell into enemy hands, she would be treated as a prisoner of war. 'I shall never forget that visit to Belfast', recalled the Duchess.[44] It happened to coincide with the first bombing raid on the city which had taken place the night before, with most of the damage being inflicted on residential areas. This had the effect of making the royal visit seem almost providential. The Gloucesters were given, says the Duchess, 'an extraordinary, heartfelt, even hysterical' welcome.[45] Through the acrid smoke of the still smouldering buildings and the stench of damaged sewers, the couple walked amongst the cheering crowds. The Duchess was particularly moved while visiting the wounded in the hospital wards. The recently blinded men were the most heartrending casualties. She was almost overcome by emotion, she admits, 'when a young man, who had just lost his sight, would not let go when I took his hand'.[46]

A much happier and very different occasion was the confirmation, a few weeks later, that the Duchess was pregnant. After almost six years of marriage and a series of miscarriages, the Duke and Duchess were delighted. So was Queen Mary. Indeed on reading the news, she told her daughter-in-law, 'I nearly fell off my dressing-table stool in my excitement'.[47] From then on the old Queen bombarded the Duchess with advice. She was not to go to Fortnum and Mason for the cradle: 'they are *so expensive*'.[48] Happily oblivious to the complications of buying with recently introduced wartime clothing coupons, Queen Mary sent detailed instructions about the baby's layette. She was astonished to hear that the Gloucesters had been refused delivery of a present of half a dozen oranges from a friend in South Africa on the grounds that wartime restrictions forbade the receipt of any parcel weighing more than two pounds.

The Duchess of Gloucester gave birth to a son, by Caesarian section, on 18 December 1941. 'Oh what joy I felt when I heard you and Alice had got a boy,' Queen Mary wrote to her son, 'and that your great wish had been fulfilled after all these years.'[49] Queen Mary was able to attend the christening ceremony at Windsor two months later. She regretted the fact that the Duke was obliged to return, almost immediately afterwards, to his military duties. He would miss his son's first 'adorable baby days'. 'You cannot think how Papa [King George V] enjoyed our first baby,' wrote Queen Mary, referring to the son who was now languishing, as the Duke of Windsor, in the Bahamas. 'That naughty boy!!!' she called him.[50]

The Duke of Gloucester's military duties were only just, in fact, beginning to take on some sense of purpose. Ever since his return from France in the spring of 1940, he had been shunted about rather aimlessly. First as Chief Liaison Officer, GHQ Home Forces, and then as a colonel in the 20th Armoured Brigade ('If I made him a Major-General,' the King very sensibly assured the brigadier commanding the 20th Armoured Brigade, 'I can now make him a

Colonel'),[51] his days seemed to be restricted, almost entirely, to tours of inspection. These were not always an unqualified success. The Duke of Windsor, ever ready to make jokes at the expense of his slower-witted brother, called him 'the Unknown Soldier' and, with his braying laugh, blunt manner and tendency to forget faces, the Duke of Gloucester did not bring much sense of occasion to his inspections. He was tone-deaf, teased the Duke of Windsor, and only realized that the national anthem was being played when everyone stood up.

But in April 1942, he was sent on a four-month-long military and diplomatic tour which would take him to the Middle East, India and East Africa. Before setting off, he asked the King to act as guardian to his newly christened son, Prince William, in case anything should happen to him while he was away. 'I want to tell you this so that you should know that he asked me,' wrote the King to the Duchess at Barnwell Manor. 'I hope you are not too lonely and do let me know when you want to come and stay at Windsor.'[52]

The purpose of the Duke of Gloucester's mission was twofold: Britain, in the person of the monarch's brother, would be underscoring its friendship with the not always reliable countries of the Near and Middle East; and the troops, both British and Commonwealth, would be reminded that their efforts were not going unappreciated. It was yet another way in which the monarchy, standing above party or government, could fulfil its functions.

Typically, the Duke did not see his tour in such grandiose terms. 'Anyway,' he wrote to the King during the course of it, 'it might do more good than harm.'[53]

So for almost four months, often in furnace-like heat or blinding dust storms, the Duke of Gloucester carried out his official duties. Although sometimes looked down on by the top brass, he was popular with the men; they appreciated his essential honesty. The troops, he reported to the King, 'are well and cheery. Their chief grouse is that their girl friends

The uncertainties of his country's darkest hour reflected in the face of King George VI
1940

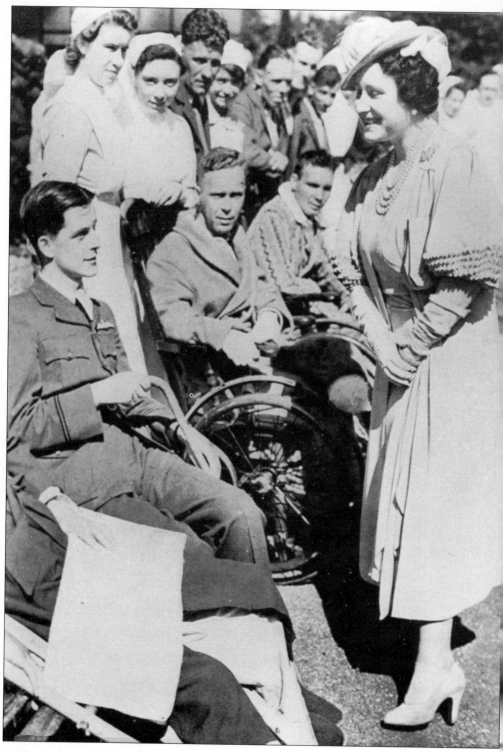

2. The Queen exercising her celebrated charm on some of the survivors of Dunkirk

Princess Elizabeth and Princess Margaret knitting for the troops in the garden of their ouse in the country'

A resplendent Queen Mary visiting the YMCA in Cheltenham

5. The Duke and Duchess of Windsor holidaying in Miami in 1940

5. Winston Churchill, the 'vehement monarchist', greeting the King and Queen at 10 Downing Street

7. The Duke of Gloucester with the Royal Observer Corps

8. The Duchess of Gloucester opening a club for service women

2. The King inspecting bomb damage at the Elephant and Castle

13. 'God Bless your Majesties!': the King and Queen being mobbed in Bermondsey

14. Princess Alice emerging from a tank in Canada

15. The Earl of Athlone with, clockwise, President Roosevelt, Prime Minister Mackenzie King and Winston Churchill at the Ottawa Conference, 1943

16. 'Looking the East End in the face': the King and Queen among the bomb damage at Buckingham Palace

have now been taken over by Canadians and Poles.' The desert, he reported in his dead-pan fashion, 'is a very healthy place except during an actual battle'.[54]

The Duke seems to have played as hard as he worked. One night, after an official dinner at the Viceregal Residence in Delhi, the Duke and four others stayed up to indulge in what he described as 'goings-on', such as trick cycling along the corridors, squirting each other with fire hoses and, one assumes, drinking. The Duke's reliance on alcohol to ease the tensions and frustrations of his days was becoming increasingly apparent. (By way of a reprimand, perhaps, for her son's fondness for whisky, Queen Mary once wrote to the Duchess of Gloucester to suggest that the Duke bring his own whisky when next he visited her at Badminton. 'We have *not* got much left and it is so expensive.')[55]

The Duke's insistence on drinking until late was not generally appreciated. 'H.R.H. had been told pretty clearly that most of us were busy men who got off to bed early,' grumbled one officer during the Duke's tour, 'but didn't leave the table until 12.15. Was I angry!'

Major-General Eric ('Chink') Dorman-Smith, that maverick figure who was Deputy Chief of the General Staff in Cairo at the time of the Duke of Gloucester's tour, had some sharp comments to make on the royal visitor. Dorman-Smith had arranged a dinner at Mena for the Duke, who had once been his pupil at the Staff College at Camberley. 'I laughed at our fantastic system', he confided to a friend, 'that he, who is created to exist in a vacuum by an intensive process of selective breeding, is a Lieutenant-General [the Duke's latest rank], while one student, a good hardworking chap, is a brigadier, another a full colonel and the rest Lieut. Cols.' The Duke of Gloucester looked, he continued, 'not unlike a dinosaur – same uncomprehending blank look, little brain in big skeleton. The world must shed its monarchs, just as it shed its dinosaurs.'[56]

Chink Dorman-Smith was, in addition to being a man of outspoken views, an ardent Irish nationalist.

It was while the Duke was away on this extended tour that he became the object of a certain amount of ridicule at home. With a succession of military defeats making Churchill's position increasingly shaky, a Conservative Member of Parliament, Sir John Wardlaw-Milne, moved a Vote of Censure. In the course of it he suggested that, in order to separate the military and political spheres – and thereby lessen Churchill's intervention in military matters – the Duke of Gloucester be made Commander-in-Chief of the British forces. 'The House', wrote Chips Channon, 'roared with disrespectful laughter, and I at once saw Winston's face light up, as if a lamp had been lit within him and he smiled genially. He knew now that he was saved . . .'[57]

Wardlaw-Milne's suggestion gave the *New Statesman* a splendid opportunity to pass judgement on the Duke of Gloucester. Calling the proposal 'fantastic' and 'preposterous' and claiming that the House of Commons had been dumbfounded, it asked how anyone could seriously imagine that 'at this grave crisis in our history the appointment as Commander-in-Chief of a Royal Duke is a suitable remedy . . .'[58]

The Duke himself made no public comment. 'What impertinence on the part of Wardlaw-Milne, without asking anybody and me in particular,' he wrote to his wife.[59]

He arrived back in Britain on 4 August 1942, having flown from Khartoum the night before. He landed at an American air force base not far from Barnwell Manor. The coded notice of his imminent arrival had simply announced that some important person was due to fly in. As it had been rumoured that the film star Cary Grant was on his way to the base, the press had gathered in force on the runway to photograph the famous actor. When they saw the Duke emerge, says the Duchess, 'they disappointedly said, "Oh, it's not him!", and vanished before he put foot on the tarmac'.[60]

5

Family Tragedy

ONE DAY IN mid-August 1942, Queen Mary was driven from Badminton to Coppins, the home of her youngest and favourite son, the Duke of Kent. The Kents' third child and second son, Prince Michael, had been christened earlier that month and the old Queen had come to spend the day with the family. Queen Mary always felt very much at home with the Kents: with the son who shared her passion for collecting ('Georgie showed me some of his interesting things')[1] and with the daughter-in-law who was part of the royal dynastic web which the Queen always found so fascinating. She appreciated how much marriage to Princess Marina of Greece and Denmark had tamed her previously wayward son. 'The women of that Danish family make good wives,' she had remarked at the time of the couple's engagement. 'They have the art of marriage.'[2] Now, after spending the day with them at Coppins, Queen Mary was pleased to note that her son 'looked so happy with his lovely wife and the dear baby'.[3]

The Baroness de Stoeckl, a relic of the world in which Princess Marina had grown up and who was now living in a cottage in the grounds of Coppins, echoed Queen Mary's comments on the happiness of the Kents' home life. 'I can still see the picture of those evenings when the Duke would be at home,' she wrote in her memoirs. 'We used to go over at about a quarter to nine, the Duchess looking a dream of beauty in an evening gown – always punctual. He would come in a little late, looking so sleek, so *soigné*, so good-looking. We would have a cocktail, and walk into the dining-room, the only light was from four long candles on the table . . . he used to give orders every night for such-and-such a centre-piece to be put on the table. I used to forget half the time to remark on the beauty of it, but the Duchess would make me a sign and I would be loud in my admiration. He would be so pleased. We used to sit at the table until a quarter to eleven o'clock. I would long to get up, but that was his special hour of relaxation. He would talk and discuss and drink several cups of coffee. After dinner we used to walk towards the Music room. After a few minutes he would seat himself before one of the pianos and play endlessly . . .'

The Duke of Kent was devoted to his infant son, Prince Michael. Each evening, recalled the Baroness de Stoeckl, 'he carries his youngest son to the nursery and lays him in his cot and stands watching and watching. Nannie told me that each night as he lays his son in his cot, she discreetly leaves the room, but she can hear the Duke talking softly to him.'[4]

On 24 August 1942, the Duke, as part of his wartime commitments, set off for Scotland. From there he was due to fly to Iceland to inspect various RAF bases.

Just after 1 p.m. on Tuesday, 25 August, the Duke left the RAF station at Invergordon in a Sunderland flying-boat. The pilot and crew – eleven men in all – were very experienced, well accustomed to this sort of mission. Half an hour later, flying through a dense mist, known locally as *haar*, at an altitude of only 700 feet, the aircraft hit a gently sloping hill below Eagle's Rock on the Duke of Portland's Langwell estate. It bounced, turned over and burst into flames. Help, in this rough, desolate and misty terrain, was a long time coming. When it did, it was too late. Of all the men on board, only one – a gunner in the rear turret – had survived. The 39-year-old Duke of Kent must have been killed instantly.

Inevitably, the dramatic death of the King's brother gave

rise to a host of theories about the cause of the crash. It has been described as 'one of the greatest mysteries in aviation history'.[5] One theory has it that he was the victim of German sabotage. An even wilder one speculates that he was killed by British Intelligence because of his involvement in a plot to reinstate the Duke of Windsor on the throne. It was, indeed, a puzzling incident. How could such an experienced pilot have descended into low cloud and mist instead of gaining altitude? Why did no other member of his equally experienced crew prevent him from doing so? Had the flight path been changed? Why were they flying over land and not, as they should have been, over the sea? For what reason was Andrew Jack, the only survivor of the crash, so reluctant to discuss it? Why are so many of the relevant files missing? It was even believed, by some members of the royal family, that 'the Duke of Kent was flying the plane himself'.[6]

The most convincing explanation – advanced by the aviation authority, Roy C. Nesbit – is that the crash was due to instrumental error. This error concerned the newly installed gyro-magnetic compass – the so-called DR compass. The setting of the compass may have been incorrectly adjusted; it may have been misread; it may have been altered during a demonstration to the Duke of Kent and his party. This, in turn, would have led to the plane being flown 13 degrees west of its intended track: over the land instead of over the sea. The pilot, reducing altitude to get out of the cloud in order to see the sea, would not have realized that he was, in fact, flying over land. It has even been suggested, by someone who had flown with the Duke of Kent, that as the royal passenger disliked flying in cloud, he had asked the pilot to drop down out of it.

That the fatal instrumental error was not noticed could have been because of poor co-ordination on the flight deck. Apart from one short flight, the four leading personnel – captain, first pilot, second pilot and first navigator – had never before flown together. They could even have been distracted, during the first few minutes of the flight, by the presence of their illustrious passenger. 'In my opinion,' sums up Nesbit, 'the crash was caused by a failure of communication, coupled with very bad luck.'[7]

The King and Queen were at Balmoral at the time of the crash. They had been joined there the night before, after a 'nightmare'[8] drive through dense fog, by the Duke and Duchess of Gloucester. During dinner on the night of the Duke of Kent's death, the King was called to the telephone. Realizing that he would only have been called from the table for some very serious reason, the rest of the company sat in apprehensive silence until he returned. He was clearly deeply distressed. The Queen, having signalled to the Duchess of Gloucester, rose and led the rest of the women out of the room into the drawing-room. They all assumed that the telephone call had been to announce the death of Queen Mary. Not until the Queen had gone to speak to the King and accompanied him back into the drawing-room did the rest of them learn that the Duke of Kent had been killed. They all left for London by special train that same night.

The Duchess of Kent, at Coppins, had gone to bed early that evening. So it was Kate Fox, one of those obligatory English nannies who had helped raise Princess Marina at the Greek court and who was now in charge of her newly born son, who took the telephone call. Hearing the nanny's approaching footsteps, the Duchess is said to have 'immediately sensed catastrophe'. The minute Miss Fox opened the door, Princess Marina cried out, 'It's George, isn't it?'[9]

The Duchess of Kent was desolate. Her life, as the King said, 'was entirely bound up with his'.[10] For days after her husband's death she refused to leave her room, alternating between bouts of uncontrollable weeping and complete apathy. 'How everything can utterly change . . .' she wrote later to a friend. 'I feel so stunned – it's all so unbelievable, yet day follows day and one goes on doing, mechanically, the same things.'[11]

Queen Mary, having spent the day of her son's death in her usual profitable fashion – listening to a lecture, visiting a gallery, arranging photographs, doing her needlework while being read aloud to – was also given the news that evening. Lady Cynthia Colville, her lady-in-waiting, was called away to the telephone where she was told, by the King's Private Secretary, of the Duke of Kent's death. As she re-entered the sitting-room, Queen Mary asked, 'What is it? Is it the King?'

'No, Ma'am, I am afraid it is the Duke of Kent,' answered Lady Colville.

'The blow to Her Majesty was catastrophic,' she afterwards wrote, 'but I have never had more cause to admire wholeheartedly the Queen's heroic courage and unselfish thought for others. "I must go to Marina tomorrow," she said.'[12]

'I felt so stunned by the shock I could not believe it,' wrote Queen Mary.[13] But exerting that phenomenal self-control which had seen her through so many crises, she suppressed her own grief and drove, the next morning, to Coppins. No one knows exactly what she said to Princess Marina but the old Queen later revealed that she had spoken of the indulgence of 'self-pity' and the imperatives of 'duty'.[14] Queen Mary would have made it clear that the Duchess of Kent was more than just one of those many women who had lost a husband on active service. As the widow of a prince of the reigning house and as the mother of princes, she had special obligations: she had an all-transcending duty to the royal family, and to that most sacrosanct of institutions, the British monarchy.

The Duke of Kent's funeral service was held in St George's Chapel, Windsor, on 29 August 1942. 'I have attended very many family funerals in the Chapel,' wrote the King, 'but none have moved me in the same way ... Everybody there I knew well but I did not dare to look at any of them for fear of breaking down.'[15]

The Duke of Windsor had always been very attached to his brother and, during the memorial service to the Duke of Kent in Nassau Cathedral in the Bahamas, he 'broke down and wept like a child all the way through'. It was, claims an aide, 'the only time I saw him lose his self-control like that'.[16]

'It really is a tragedy,' the King afterwards wrote to Edwina Mountbatten, that the Duke of Kent, 'of all people, just when he was coming into his own, should have been taken from us. I shall miss him terribly . . .'[17]

Knowing how attached Princess Marina was to her Continental family, and how apart she felt herself to be from the rest of the British royal family, the King made a characteristically kind gesture. He sent for the Duchess's sister Olga, the wife of Prince Paul of Yugoslavia. In this, the King was risking possible repercussions from the press and Parliament, because Prince and Princess Paul were then living under house arrest in Kenya – the result of what were regarded as Prince Paul's pro-German leanings during his period as Regent of Yugoslavia. But with Churchill's approval, the King went ahead. Only when Princess Olga was on her way did the King tell the Duchess that her sister would soon be arriving. Princess Olga's presence was of inestimable comfort to the grieving Princess Marina.

Of them all, Queen Mary showed the greatest fortitude. Driving back from her son's funeral in 'a fearful thunderstorm', she gave a lift to two servicemen whom she described as 'a charming young American parachutist, most friendly' and 'a nice Sergeant Observer (Air Force)'. Neither of these young men would have guessed, from the Queen's amiable conversation, that they were travelling with a mother who had just seen her favourite son laid to rest. Three days later, Queen Mary renewed her 'wooding'.

'I am so glad', she wrote, 'I can take up my occupations again – Georgie would have wished me to do so.'[18]

A fortnight after the Duke of Kent's funeral, the King paid what he called 'a pilgrimage' to the place where his brother had been killed. 'The impact must have been terrific', he noted in his diary, 'as the aircraft, as an aircraft, was unrecognisable when found.'[19] The King's only consolation, as he stood on that wind-swept slope, was that the Duke of

Kent 'was killed on Active Service'.[20] The tragedy linked him to all those others who had lost their loved ones.

'Once again,' as one historian put it, 'this time in the fullest possible sense, the Royal Family identified itself with the people and their war effort.'[21]

The Duke of Kent's death could hardly have come at a worse time for King George VI. Throughout that year, 1942, one disaster had followed another. In spite of the fact that both Russia and America were now allied to Britain, the military situation was as bad as ever. The relentless advance of the Japanese through Malaya ended in the humiliating surrender of the vast British naval base of Singapore. The abandonment of Malaya was followed by that of Burma. In North Africa came the equally humiliating surrender of Tobruk, and by late July the Eighth Army had been forced back to a defensive position at El Alamein, a mere sixty miles from Alexandria. There were serious losses in the air and at sea, and of confidence in both the Royal Navy and the Royal Air Force, when three German battleships sailed boldly up the Channel to the safety of their home waters.

In Britain, this series of disasters led to mounting criticism of Churchill's leadership. 'I do wish people would get on with the job and not criticise all the time,' wrote the King to Lord Athlone about these attacks on Churchill.[22] He took them seriously enough, though, to have his secretary investigate the accusations.

This year, too, brought that series of so-called 'Baedeker Raids' in which the Luftwaffe bombed historic but strategically unimportant cities such as Exeter, Bath, Norwich and York. Tirelessly, the King and Queen toured the devastated cities, listening to stories of civilians killed and homes wrecked. When, in Exeter, the King suggested that a piece of bomb be sent for scrap, the Queen had a better idea. 'Let's send it back to the Germans,' she said.[23]

The King's last entry in the fifth volume of his wartime diary was especially despondent. 'I cannot help feeling depressed at the future outlook. Anything can happen, and it will be wonderful if we can be lucky anywhere.'[24]

And all the while, the King was having to give his attention to the day-to-day business of monarchy. His multitudinous wartime commitments were additional to his usual duties. There was the desk work, in which he had to attend to the 'boxes'. These contained Cabinet minutes, memoranda, dispatches and reports; department statements and letters from ministers, ambassadors and governors-general; documents for signature, programmes for forthcoming functions, petitions, appeals, messages and protests. All these had to be read and digested; many demanded written replies; some had to be commented on and discussed with his secretaries or the relevant ministers.

Then there were the audiences to be granted to distinguished visitors – churchmen, holders of various offices, foreign ambassadors and, more especially now, military personnel. In addition to his weekly meeting with the Prime Minister, the King had to preside over Privy Council meetings and to receive departmental ministers and other political figures.

For a well-trained, fully experienced, self-confident man these private and public obligations would have been taxing enough; for the King, they must sometimes have appeared overwhelming. After all, he was still obliged to contend with his many personal inadequacies. His stammer remained an embarrassment. Although, under the sympathetic treatment of the Australian speech therapist, Lionel Logue, it had been all but cured, his delivery remained far from fluent. In private conversation, among his family, friends and members of the royal household, his defect was hardly noticeable. 'With others,' wrote one of his later wartime equerries, 'he stammered occasionally, but the stammer was not a "stutter" with visible movements of the head or lips. It took the form of a silence during which he tried to emit, pronounce, the offending word or a synonym . . .'[25] Lady Hambleden who, as Lady of the Bedchamber, was with the King and

Queen throughout the war years, claimed that the King's stammer was 'always worse indoors. Once he was in the open air, it seemed to disappear.'[26]

It bothered him most seriously, of course, when he had to broadcast. Lionel Logue and Robert Wood, the BBC's engineer in charge of outside broadcasts, would scour the script for words that might give the King difficulty: 'often another word would be inserted or an entire phrase changed'.[27] During the war years, the King still had trouble with initial 'c's and 'g's, and with words containing double 's's, such as 'oppression' and 'suppression'; words which, not unnaturally, were always cropping up in wartime speeches. But the King struggled on, says Wood, 'without let-up. I was full of admiration for his perserverance, his resolution.'[28] And Logue described him as 'the pluckiest and most determined patient I ever had'.[29]

His hesitation apart, the King had a good voice, manly and resonant, with an endearing inability to pronounce his 'r's: they sounded like 'w's or even rather guttural 'g's. The truth was that, far from diminishing the King's stature in the eyes – or ears – of his listeners, his dogged delivery aroused their admiration. They appreciated how much it cost him. 'His little impediment of speech endears him to us,' wrote one listener. 'We grow anxious for him if he falters and rejoice when he overcomes his difficulty of enunciation.'[30]

Invariably, the monarch's broadcast speech would be followed by the playing of the national anthem. As often as not, listeners – even in the privacy of their own homes – would rise to their feet and stand to attention. 'We all stood rigidly to attention, looking and perhaps feeling rather foolish in the small, low-ceilinged lounge,' admitted one listener. A 'spinster in Essex' proudly claimed that she 'stood up for "God Save the King" and my little dog got out of her basket and stood beside me'.[31]

Another of the King's personal battles was against a curious phobia for taking reviews. He dreaded having to stand up, the cynosure of all eyes, to review troops. 'Even when he had to review the guard in the quadrangle at Windsor he would get into a nervous state beforehand,' says one commentator.[32] For a man in his position, particularly in wartime, this was a most devastating drawback. A mayoress, standing behind the King at a review which was a little late in starting, noticed that 'he was getting more and more agitated. The Queen put out her hand and very gently stroked his arm, just up and down, and kept saying something to him. I don't know what it was, but it helped calm him down.'[33]

The writer Sarah Bradford, in her biography of the King, describes the occasion when he was due to review Eighth Army troops in North Africa in 1943. 'When the time came for the King to leave his tent and take the review,' she writes, 'he suddenly began to grit his teeth and mutter, "I can't, I can't . . . I'm not going to do it." The equerries were ashen as Joey Legh [Sir Piers Legh, the King's most trusted equerry] told him calmly, "Well, Sir, I'm afraid you've got to do this. You've come all this way and you've got to . . ." Still gritting his teeth, the King repeated, "No, I'm going home, I'm going home . . ." Legh said, very quietly, "Well, all right, Sir, you'll have to swim." There was a dreadful pause, then suddenly the King smiled, seeing the humour of the situation. "Give me my cane," he said and got up, went out and did it perfectly.'[34]

Yet he never cut down on reviews or inspections. On the contrary, knowing how much even a glimpse of their sovereign meant to the men, he instituted a new kind of inspection so designed that as many as possible could see him. 'Long lines of men would be paraded along each side of country roads and the King, leaving his car, would walk for mile after mile between their ranks, pausing at the end of each company or battalion while the men gave three cheers for him.'[35] He even ordered those usually left out of formal inspections, such as cooks, to be included in these informal parades.

The King was responsible, too, for enlarging investitures. Whereas, before the war, primarily officers had received their decorations from the sovereign's own hand, George VI extended the privilege to all ranks, to the women's services and to the recipients of civilian awards. A further extension included the next-of-kin of those due to be decorated who had been killed on active service. As each recipient was allowed a couple of guests, this meant that well over 100,000 people filed through the crimson and gold splendours of the Grand Hall of Buckingham Palace during the course of the war.

These investitures, taking place week after week, could be tiring and monotonous occasions for the King. For over two hours at a time he would stand on a raised dais to award honours to some 300 people. On either side would be two immobile gentleman ushers and, at his elbow, would be an equerry, whose duty it was to hand the monarch a sword if someone were to be knighted, or a medal on a velvet cushion if they were to be decorated. His name having been read out by the Lord Chamberlain, the recipient would march up a ramp and halt before the King. His Majesty would pin on the medal, say a few words and shake hands. The gratified recipient would then march down the opposite ramp. Sometimes the King could be heard humming one of the musical comedy tunes played by a string ensemble in the gallery opposite; at others he might turn to his equerry and say, far too loudly, 'For God's sake tell them not to make such a ghastly noise.'

Normally, the ceremony went like clockwork but there were occasional mishaps. Once an Indian sepoy, up for the Victoria Cross, 'marched smartly up the ramp, eyes to the front, straight past the King and down the other side. He made it the second time round.'[36]

The King also suffered from a fear of heights. This was obviously a family failing: his brother, the Duke of Gloucester, was always having to force himself up ladders and towards parapets. Once the King had to inspect a lighthouse. He could have refused to do it but, having whispered to his entourage that 'I can't say no', he braved the night-marish feeling of vertigo and climbed to the top. 'He *just* managed it,' said Lady Hambleden. 'He never shirked anything like that.'[37]

Impatience was another of the traits which the King had to try to control. All monarchs, so accustomed to the precision with which their public lives are ordered, tend to be put out by delays or last-minute changes. This monarchal obsession with punctuality was heightened by the King's nervous temperament; he would become agitated at some quite trivial change of plan or hitch in an arrangement. Only with the Queen, whose lack of punctuality was notorious, was he forebearing.

At times, his impatience could be positively dangerous. One day, when he was on the point of leaving the Palace to drive to Liverpool Street Station, an air-raid warning sound-ed. The King and his entourage duly trooped down to the shelter. But after they had been there for about ten minutes, he began to fret. Finally, instead of sending someone else to find out what was happening, the King darted upstairs himself. The rest of the company, of course, were obliged to follow and, without waiting for confirmation that it was safe to do so, the King insisted that they drive to the station. Through the bombed and smoking streets they careered and when they reached Liverpool Street 'the King got into the train quite calmly, as though nothing unusual had happened'.[38]

George VI's most serious fault, though, was his tendency to lose his temper. The explosive temper inherited from his father and grandfather – George V and Edward VII – was made worse by the insecurities of his own personality. This, in turn, was aggravated by the strains of the war. The disruption of everyday life, the horrors of the bombing, the worrying casualties, the almost unrelieved bad news from every front rendered him tetchier than ever. Quite suddenly he would lose control, and for several minutes his entourage would be subjected to a flow of noisy invective. At other times he might bark out a single, irascible sentence. On many occasions Ainsley, the immensely dignified Palace steward, who had been in royal service for many years, would stand, apparently unperturbed, while his master raged on. Only afterwards would the steward be seen to be pale and quivering. What were called his 'gnashes' never lasted long but, for a man in his position, they could cause considerable embarrassment.

When all these handicaps were added to the others – his persistent shyness, his distaste for public appearances, his preference for a quiet family life – one can appreciate why the King once exclaimed, even if in mock exasperation, 'Oh my God! How I hate being King! Sometimes at ceremonies I want to stand up and scream and scream and scream.'[39] It made the doggedness with which he carried out his duties all the more admirable. One can also appreciate why Winston Churchill, on King George VI's death in 1952, wrote just two words on the card which accompanied his wreath: 'For Valour'.

As if George VI did not have enough to contend with, his eldest brother, the Duke of Windsor, continued to make a nuisance of himself. Or, as the Duchess of Windsor herself put it, 'we had two wars to contend with, the big war . . . in which everyone was caught up, and the little war with the Palace, in which no quarter was given'.[40] Once the Windsors had reached the Bahamas, it was with the waging of this 'little' war that their emotions seem to have been most intensely involved.

The opening salvo came from the Palace. The Duke of Windsor arrived at Government House, Nassau, to discover a telegram of instruction to the previous governor on the etiquette concerning the Duchess. She was to be addressed merely as 'Your Grace' and not 'Your Royal Highness', and she was not entitled to a curtsey. The Duke was incensed. In this, as in all such humiliations, he saw the hand of the

Queen. But if the Queen was indeed concerned about the Duchess's social position, she shared the King's worries about the Duke's political activities. Churchill's sternly worded warning to the Duke – that as Governor of the Bahamas he must act and speak with circumspection so as not to appear to be in conflict with 'His Majesty's Government' – was not being taken very seriously. The Duke of Windsor continued to cultivate politically suspect friends, to give indiscreet interviews to the American press and to air his defeatist opinions. 'David', wrote the worried King about his brother to Queen Mary, 'really can do a lot of harm if he is not careful.'[41]

There was a flurry of family alarm when, in the summer of 1941, the Duke decided to visit the ranch which he had owned for many years in Canada. 'Please stop any nonsense about David's paying a visit to his ranch,' wrote Queen Mary to her brother Lord Athlone, by then Governor-General of Canada.[42] Lord Athlone was no less dismayed by the idea. Things had been bad enough when the Duke of Windsor, as Prince of Wales, had stayed with the Athlones in South Africa ('He was very naughty indeed,' remembered Princess Alice),[43] but now the situation would be infinitely worse. However, as there was no way, short of a public scandal, by which Lord Athlone could prevent the Governor of the Bahamas from visiting his own ranch, he could only hope that his nephew and wife would not want to come and stay with the Athlones at Rideau Hall in Ottawa. 'What trouble the dear boy continues to give wherever he goes,' sighed Princess Alice.[44]

But the King was reassuring. Churchill, he explained to Queen Mary, had warned the Duke that he was not to include Ottawa in his visit, 'as Aunt Alice won't, and cannot from my point of view, receive *her*. How I dislike the perpetual troubles over David . . . but it will make him realize, or rather *her*, that they cannot do as they like.'[45] For the rest of her long life, Princess Alice always spoke of 'the Duke of Windsor and that woman'.[46]

The Duchess of Windsor, who was never quite the Jezebel of the royal family's imaginings, then turned her hand to a little peace-making. Without her husband's knowledge, she wrote to Queen Mary. The Bishop of Nassau was returning to Britain and as the Duchess felt sure that he would be received by Queen Mary, she gave him a letter to present to her mother-in-law. The letter could hardly have been more self-effacing or respectful. The Duchess mentioned her regret at being the cause of the coolness between mother and son; she assured the Queen that the Bishop would be able to give her news of the Duke; she said something about the importance of family ties in wartime.

In due course, the Bishop of Nassau presented the letter. Queen Mary asked several questions about her son but none about his wife. Nor did she reply to the letter. But several weeks later, in a letter to the Duke of Windsor after the death of the Duke of Kent ('My thoughts go out to you, who are so far away from us all, knowing how devoted you were to him . . .'), Queen Mary actually acknowledged the Duchess's existence. 'Please give a kind message to your wife . . .' she wrote.[47]

'Now what do you suppose', asked the astonished Duke, 'has come over Mama?'[48]

Not a great deal, was the answer to that particular question. Queen Mary's message indicated no breach in the family's defences. When late in 1942, the Duke, through Churchill, asked the King to 'restore the Duchess's royal rank' in the New Year's Honours List, George VI refused. In a memorandum to Churchill he made his position quite clear. There was no question of 'restoring' to the Duchess a rank which she had never held. And the reasons for refusing her that rank were as valid now as they had been at the time of her marriage. 'I know you will understand how disagreeable this is to me personally,' wrote the King, 'but the good of my country and my family comes first . . . I have consulted my family who share these views.'[49]

They – in the persons of Queen Elizabeth and Queen

Mary – certainly did. What were the reasons for their unyielding attitude, an attitude which, from this distance, can look petty and sanctimonious? As the King had once pointed out to a previous prime minister, Stanley Baldwin, a Royal Highness remains a Royal Highness for life; there is no means of depriving someone of the title. Knowing very little about Wallis Simpson, the royal family probably assumed that this third marriage of hers would last no longer than the others; that having failed in her plan to become Queen of England, she would drop her new husband as airily as she had dropped her previous ones. This would leave a Royal Highness floating about, not so much the world, as the *demi-monde*.

To Queen Mary, so conscious of the sanctity and mystique of the monarchy, the idea of this twice-divorced woman of doubtful reputation being received into the family remained as repugnant as ever. But why did Queen Elizabeth, so renowned for her generosity of spirit, remain so implacably opposed to any acceptance? For one thing, she shared Queen Mary's low opinion of the Duchess; during Edward VIII's brief reign, she had disapproved of the way in which this flashy parvenue had assumed the role of the King's hostess. For another, she deeply resented the fact that, because of King Edward VIII's infatuation with Mrs Simpson, her own husband was now being subjected to such intolerable strains. But there was another reason for the Queen's attitude. It was strongly suspected, in court circles, that the Duchess of Windsor might even resort to treason in her determination to avenge herself on what she considered to be her unfair treatment by the royal family. It was known that she shared the Duke's reactionary political views, that she had been friendly with various leading Fascists, that, even in the Bahamas, she associated with rich Fascist sympathizers who were anxious for a negotiated peace. Perhaps the Queen's apprehensions were exaggerated but, in the dangerous climate of wartime Britain, they were understandable.

That it should have been these two women who had set their faces so resolutely against the Windsors' acceptance came as no surprise to the Duchess. Their banishment was entirely due, she once exclaimed, to 'a woman's jealousy'.[50] 'The reign of George VI', she said bitterly, 'is a split-level matriarchy in pants. Queen Mary runs the King's wife, and the wife runs the King.'[51]

How much truth was there in the Duchess of Windsor's assertion that the Queen 'ran' the King? Because of Queen Elizabeth's stronger public image – her assured social manner, her dignified bearing, her wider-ranging interests, even her gift for the memorable phrase – it was often assumed that she was the power behind her husband's throne. To see them together in public, with the Queen moving forward to initiate every conversation while the King hung back, was to believe that she was the more forceful personality. Her pretty, pastel-coloured, ultra-feminine image was known to be slightly misleading: the Queen was tough, very conscious of her royal status. If ever the King seemed to be acting in a less than regal manner, she would – as unobtrusively as possible – ensure that he behaved with more dignity. It is said that when the historian John Wheeler-Bennett later came to write the official biography of King George VI, Queen Elizabeth – by then Queen Mother – asked him to tone down the many references to the importance of her role in the King's life.

'The King', wrote Oliver Harvey, secretary to Anthony Eden, the Foreign Secretary, is 'fundamentally a weak character and certainly rather a stupid one. The Queen is a strong one out of a rather reactionary stable.'[52] Another observer accused her of being an 'obstructive influence in all that touched the Sovereign'.[53] Ministers and secretaries, accustomed to dealing with that male-chauvinist King George V and that irresponsible bachelor King Edward VIII, now found that they were having to deal with King George VI and Queen Elizabeth; that the King invariably consulted the Queen before giving an answer or making a decision.

On the other hand, those who were close to her always denied that she was the dominant partner. 'The King was a rock to her . . .' claimed one of the Queen's sisters. 'In fundamental things she leant on him; I have always felt how much the Queen was sustained by the King.'[54] And Lady Hambleden maintained that it was the King who made all the important decisions. 'He was a man of very sound judgement,' she said. 'The Queen always relied on him. Before coming to any decision or even before accepting an invitation, she would always say, "I'll have to ask the King." '[55]

The truth was that the King and Queen were a part-nership. Not since the days of Queen Victoria and Prince Albert had a royal couple been as close – emotionally, domestically and politically – as George VI and Queen Elizabeth. Except when the King's wartime duties took him away from her, they were seldom apart. She was the only person he really trusted. There was almost nothing they could not, and did not, discuss. Her interest in political issues was as keen as his. It was the Queen who, during the war, read Hitler's *Mein Kampf* and who sent a copy of it to Lord Halifax, at that stage still Foreign Secretary. 'I do not advise you to read it through, or you might go mad . . . Even a skip through gives one a good idea of his mentality, ignorance and obvious sincerity,' she wrote.[56] That the Queen had read *Mein Kampf* is not surprising; that Lord Halifax had not is astonishing.

The King's burdens, so much heavier during the war, were lightened by his being able to share them with the Queen. For instance, he was one of the very few people to know the true extent of the wartime casualties: the know-ledge was somehow less horrific when shared with his wife. 'The King was told everything,' said the Queen in later years, 'so, of course, I knew about everything as well. That's when I learned to keep things to myself. There were so many rumours going round at that time; one heard so many stories. I became very cagey. And I've been very cagey ever since.'[57]

There was no denying, of course, that the Queen was an astute and strong-willed woman but she was never aggressive or domineering. Whatever she achieved was by way of tact and good humour. 'She was the greatest possible fun to be with,' said one of her ladies-in-waiting.[58] Mrs Churchill, having entertained the royal couple to lunch at 10 Downing Street, reported the Queen as being 'so gay and witty and very, very pretty close up . . .'[59] In the most decorous possible manner, the Queen was something of a flirt: she had a way, in conversation, of tilting her head, of smiling a mock-rueful smile, of employing a teasing tone. More than one Palace official, misled by her mildly flirtatious manner, talked in terms of romantic friendship.

The Queen knew exactly how to handle her often fretful husband. 'One evening,' remembers a young Guardsman at Windsor Castle, 'she returned late from London after a *dreadful* day. Hundreds of houses down, streets up, people crying. The lot. But she came down to see us . . . as she always did, and laughed and joked with the children. And *what* she was like with the King! For ever loving and soothing . . .'[60]

During her husband's frequent bursts of temper, she would, testifies an equerry, 'mollify him with a soothing word or gesture'. Once, as he raged on about something, the Queen held his pulse and 'with a wistful smile, began to count – tick, tick, tick – which made him laugh, and the storm subsided'.[61]

There was a curious telepathy between husband and wife. It was as though she could transmit some of her tranquillity to him. On one occasion, when the King was opening Parliament, he faltered in the course of his address. Although he could not possibly have seen the Queen's face as she sat beside him, she gave a barely perceptible nod. On this, he took courage and continued.

Yet, in many ways, their tastes and interests were very

different. The King had a liking for practical jokes, salty stories, knock-about comedy. He would guffaw at The Crazy Gang and hated missing that famous wartime radio show ITMA. The celebrity concerts organized at Windsor Castle during the war very much reflected the King's somewhat philistine tastes. When the ukelele-playing George Formby arrived to do his act, his intention of toning down his *risqué* lyrics was firmly scotched by royal command. 'By the way,' said an official to the comedian, 'Their Majesties have especially asked that you give *exactly* the same show as you would to the troops.' He did, and the King laughed heartily at Formby's famous *double entendres* in 'When I'm cleaning windows'.

Another of the King's favourites was Tommy Trinder. The first time that Trinder appeared before George VI as King, the comedian reminded His Majesty that he had performed for him when he was Duke of York.

'Yes, I remember,' answered the King. 'You've reached great heights since those days, haven't you?'

'You haven't done so badly yourself, Sir,' quipped the irrepressible Trinder.[62]

(Another quick-fire theatrical riposte concerned the Queen. Gertrude Lawrence and Noël Coward were once watching her take her seat in the royal box at the theatre.

'What an entrance!' exclaimed the admiring Gertrude Lawrence.

'What a part,' snapped Coward.)[63]

On one occasion Tommy Trinder entertained the royal family at a concert on the lawns of Windsor Castle. Invariably, and to his increasing exasperation, the tag-lines of his jokes were drowned out by low-flying RAF planes.

'Can't you do anything about them, Sir?' he finally shouted to the King. 'After all, you're the governor.'

Some years after the King's death, Trinder was presented to Princess Margaret at a cabaret performance. 'My Papa loved you,' she said.[64]

A frequent wartime guest at Windsor, while describing

the King as 'a simple man', claimed that the Queen was 'intelligent and *au fait* with everything, including books'.[65] Edith Sitwell agreed. The Queen, she told the young Denton Welch, 'has a real interest in books'.[66] To an expert who once came to Buckingham Palace to attend to the famous Handel harpsichord, the Queen said wistfully, 'You are a lucky man to be able to do what you like.'[67] She was to be seen at the wartime recitals given by Dame Myra Hess in the National Gallery; she attended public poetry readings to listen to the likes of Edith Sitwell and T. S. Eliot; she started a collection of modern paintings and commissioned John Piper to do a series of watercolours of Windsor. On viewing Piper's finished studies with their typically lowering, atmospheric skies, the King is said to have commiserated with the artist for not having had better weather during his stay.

'The King frankly admitted to having only a small knowledge of art,' wrote Wilfred Blunt, at that time drawing-master at Eton, 'confessing once . . . that when he saw a name under a portrait he was not always sure whether it was that of the artist or the sitter.'[68]

The Queen always knew. Kenneth Clark, who had been appointed Surveyor of the King's Pictures by George V, soon discovered that the Queen's knowledge of, and interest in, paintings was considerable. One day, the Queen telephoned the Duchess of Wellington to ask if it were true that 'the treasures' of Apsley House had not been evacuated. As 145 Piccadilly, the house in which the King and Queen, as Duke and Duchess of York, had lived before the accession, had been bombed, and as it lay close to Apsley House, the Queen was understandably concerned. The Duchess had to admit that the treasures had not been safely stored.

'Well then,' said the Queen, 'I am coming round at eleven with a van to take them to Frogmore.'

Accompanied by the King, she arrived punctually at eleven. Armed with pencil and paper, she made lists of what had to be removed and what left behind. Only the most valuable pictures needed to go. 'You mustn't be sentimental, Duchess,' said Her Majesty briskly.[69]

These differences in tastes and temperament were never allowed to affect the close relationship between the King and Queen. General Sir Alan Brooke, dining one night at Buckingham Palace, was deeply impressed by the rapport between them. 'The King and Queen were as usual quite extraordinary hosts and made us forget at once the regal atmosphere of the meeting. The King thrilled about the new medal ribbons he was devising and had an envelope full of them in his pocket; the Queen charming and captivating, interested in everything, full of talk and quite devoid of any stiffness.'[70]

One taste the couple did share was for outdoor activities: she for racing and fishing, he for stalking and shooting. They were both passionately interested in gardens. Not even the war could prevent them from paying short visits to Balmoral and Sandringham. Picnicking in the heather in the Highlands, driving in a dogcart in the Fens, even strolling in the King's famous rhododendron garden at the Royal Lodge, this devoted and attractive couple, still in their forties, were able to recapture something of the happiness they had known before the King was forced to ascend the throne; before he embarked on what the Queen was afterwards to describe as 'those anguished years'.

'I longed for him to have some peace of mind,' wrote the Queen to a friend after the King's sudden death in 1952. 'He was so young to die, and was becoming so wise in kingship. He was so kind too, and had a sort of natural nobility of thought and life, which sometimes made me ashamed of my narrow and more feminine point of view . . .'[71]

To him, she was, quite simply, 'the most marvellous person in the world'.[72]

6

Family Matters

THE LEAST well-known member of King George VI's immediate family was undoubtedly his only sister, Princess Mary, the Princess Royal. This was partly due to the fact that, as the wife of the 6th Earl of Harewood, she spent much of her time at the palatial Harewood House in Yorkshire. But another reason was her retiring nature. Princess Mary, born on 25 April 1897, had inherited her full share of the family reserve. 'Shyness . . .', as her eldest son once wrote, 'was one of the first things people noticed about my mother . . . she was conditioned to communicate only on as uncontroversial a level as possible; I have always believed that this was the result of an upbringing which discouraged direct discussion or any display of emotion.'[1] Even amongst themselves, he claimed, the children of King George V and Queen Mary spoke 'in commonplaces'.[2]

Marriage, at the age of 24 in 1921, to Viscount Lascelles, eldest son of the 5th Earl of Harewood, had in no way lessened Princess Mary's shyness. Her husband was hardly the sort to encourage the casting off of inhibitions. Fifteen years older than his wife, thin, gaunt and unattractive, the 6th Earl of Harewood was equally incapable of showing his emotions. But he was extremely rich and, in addition to his interest in the conventionally aristocratic pastimes of riding, hunting and horse-racing, was a celebrated collector of pictures, furniture and china.

The marriage seems to have been happy enough. To the

outside world, Lord Harewood appeared to be a cold, unsympathetic man but he and his wife had many friends and interests in common and, according to their eldest son, his mother was 'never so happy . . . as when she and my father were embarked on some scheme together'.[3] In their undemonstrative way, the couple were very fond of one another. They had two children: George, born in 1923, and eighteen months later Gerald. Her sons remembered their mother as a kind but curiously detached figure. As a family, explains one of them, 'we did not talk of love and affection and what we meant to each other, but rather – and even about that not easily – of duty and behaviour and what we ought to do . . .'[4]

In the years leading up to the Second World War, Princess Mary, who was created Princess Royal on the death of her aunt, Princess Louise, in 1931, led a relatively uneventful life. She confined herself, very largely, to such pursuits as gardening, letter-writing and, above all, race-going. Dutifully she played her part in all the great royal ceremonies of the period, where she was notable for the beauty of her complexion and the stoniness of her expression. But, in the main, the Princess Royal's official obligations were of the Lady Bountiful variety: ribbon-cutting, foundation-stone laying, fête-opening.

With the war, things changed. Unhesitatingly, the Princess Royal emerged to play her part in the royal war effort. Although she could hardly be counted as one of those whom the Queen admiringly referred to as 'the afternoon bridge-playing ladies who suddenly found themselves driving trucks',[5] the Princess Royal took on a host of new duties. Fortunately, during the First World War, the young Princess Mary had carried out many unconventional tasks; and, before her marriage, she had blazed a royal trail by working for two years as a nurse in the Hospital for Sick Children in Great Ormond Street. Now, at 42, she was able to put this experience to good use.

As her chief wartime duties concerned the ATS (of which

she became Controller-Commandant), the British Red Cross Society and the RAF Nursing Service, the Princess Royal did her full share of canteen-visiting, troop-inspecting, hospital-comforting and appeal-launching. Between thirty and forty times each year she would leave Harewood House (part of which had been turned into a convalescent hospital) to travel, in cheerless wartime conditions, to wherever she was needed.[6] Such was the aura of monarchy that even a visit from this ordinary-looking, often tongue-tied member of the royal family could bring a tremendous lift to the spirits of wounded men or exhausted workers.

The Princess Royal had always been very close to her mother, Queen Mary, and as often as she could get away from her commitments, she would travel to Badminton to visit her. Even she, though, could not escape being dragooned into the old Queen's 'wooding squad'. When she was not visiting her mother, the Princess Royal would be writing to her. The Princess was an almost obsessive letter-writer (and, in spite of being married to one of the richest men in the land, a string and brown paper hoarder) and only by pretending that the post left Harewood House at five in the afternoon, rather than the actual time of five-thirty, could Lord Harewood ensure that the family were able to enjoy their tea at a reasonable hour. They all blessed the day, says her eldest son, when 'during the war the afternoon post from Harewood was altered to leave at four-thirty'.[7]

Another member of the family with whom the Princess Royal kept in contact was her errant brother, the Duke of Windsor. Of all his relations, she proved the most sympathetic. After his abdication, she and her husband had been to stay with the Duke in Austria and, during the war, brother and sister kept in touch. It was not until after the war that the Princess Royal met the Duchess of Windsor. 'She was really quite nice,' said the Princess in her understated fashion. 'No cloven hooves or horns', was her eldest son's wry comment on his mother's reaction to the Duchess.[8] Allegedly resenting the fact that the Duke of Windsor had not been invited to the post-war wedding of Princess Elizabeth to Prince Philip of Greece, the Princess Royal stayed away. A 'chill' was given as the reason for her absence. She was able, nevertheless, to attend a public function a couple of days later.

For the Princess Royal the anxieties of the war were brought closer to home when, in 1942, her 19-year-old son George, Viscount Lascelles, joined the Grenadier Guards. His enlistment was followed, not long after, by that of her second son Gerald who joined the Rifle Brigade. Those who imagined that membership of the royal family automatically meant a cushioned military career were proved very wrong in the case of Viscount Lascelles. Far from easing his path, the fact of his being the nephew of the King of England was to land him, before the end of the war, in an extremely hazardous situation.

In October 1942 Eleanor Roosevelt was the guest of the King and Queen at Buckingham Palace. 'The feeling I had about them during their visit to the United States – that they were simply a young and charming couple, who would have to undergo some very difficult experiences,' wrote Mrs Roosevelt during her stay at the Palace, 'began to come back to me . . .' For by now the royal couple had undergone those 'very difficult experiences'. From them, Eleanor Roosevelt soon appreciated, they had emerged with their stature greatly enhanced. Whereas, in the summer of 1939, she had admired them for their professionalism and grace, she was now deeply impressed by their maturity. A perceptive and highly intelligent woman, unlikely to be dazzled by the magic of monarchy, Eleanor Roosevelt claimed that 'the fact that both of them are doing an extraordinarily outstanding job for their people in the most trying times stands out when you are with them, and you admire their character and their devotion to duty'.[9]

Mrs Roosevelt, who had come to Britain on the Queen's invitation to study the part played by British women in the war effort (and to check on the conditions of United States troops stationed there), spent two nights at Buckingham Palace. Any notion that the royal couple might not be sharing the hardships and austerities of their subjects' lives was quickly dispelled. The guest was given the Queen's own suite. The rooms were huge but freezing. When the bombing of the Palace had shattered the window panes, the glass had been replaced with wood and isinglass. The wartime restrictions on heat, water and food were as strictly observed in the Palace as in the humblest home in the land. One bulb only was allowed in each bedroom; the central heating was switched off. Mrs Roosevelt was permitted a small fire in her sitting-room; in every other room was 'a little electric heater'.[10] A black line painted round the bathtub indicated the amount of water to be used.

For one purpose only, it appears, did the King use his personal influence to obtain supplies not readily available to his subjects. In a letter to Lord Halifax, the Ambassador in Washington, he once added a postscript. 'We are getting short of a certain type of paper which is made in America and is unprocurable here. A packet or two of 500 sheets at intervals would be most acceptable. You will understand this, and its name begins with B!!!'[11]

Cecil Beaton, summoned to the Palace to record Mrs Roosevelt's visit, was struck by the air of austerity. The temperature was little above freezing; the fireplace was empty; the glass cupboards were bare of china; there were no flowers in the vases.

Beaton was given another assignment. The Queen, with her strong sense of history, was anxious to have a visual record of the wartime appearance of the Palace, so she commissioned him to take a series of photographs. Beaton photographed not only the bomb damage but also the curiously empty State Apartments. Although it would have been impossible to have stripped the Palace of all its furniture, paintings, sculpture, china and silver, the more valuable possessions had been taken away for safe-keeping. The great Picture Gallery, with its masterpieces by Rubens and Rembrandt, was emptied and, under the direction of Kenneth Clark, the paintings sent to Wales. First they were stored in Penrhyn Castle near Bangor but, as the bombing became more severe, they were moved – together with pictures from the National Gallery – into an abandoned slate quarry in North Wales.

Other valuables were dispatched to the cellars at Windsor Castle and five large crates of china were stored in the London Underground, at Knightsbridge and Aldwych. It was not until five years after the end of the war that the famous Royal Worcester service was unearthed and sent back to the Palace.

As a result of all this, Beaton's photographs were a record of bare, carpetless rooms whose walls were hung with empty frames. Strategically placed buckets caught the drips from leaking roofs. Inevitably, with only a minimum of maintenance work being undertaken, the fabric of the Palace deteriorated. By the end of the war the building was teeming with rats, remembered the Queen.

Food at Buckingham Palace, although served from gold and silver dishes, was simple in the extreme. All the obligatory wartime fare – dehydrated and reconstituted eggs, puddings and jams made of root vegetables, rissoles consisting mostly of mashed potato, the famous 'Woolton Pie' (named after the Minister for Food) – were served at the royal table. 'Probably sawdust', was the Queen's blithe description of the ingredients of one dubious-tasting confection.[12] 'If ever we went anywhere to stay,' remembered the Queen, 'we always took our two pats of butter with us.'[13]

When, faced by a surprisingly lavish civic luncheon in Lancashire, the Queen explained to the mayor that rationing was strictly adhered to in Buckingham Palace, His Worship was very sympathetic. 'Ah well then,' he replied cheerfully, 'thou'll be glad of a bit of a do like this.'[14] The Queen was highly amused.

One suspects, though, that this strict adherence was an exercise in royal example-setting. It is difficult to believe that, in private, the royal family did not enjoy the occasional treat. The royal estates – Balmoral and Sandringham – on which the King was still able to shoot, boasted plenty of game, and it is claimed that something like eighty rabbits were sent to Windsor each week. Even allowing for the size of the household and staff, the supply of birds, rabbits and larger game, added to the fruit and vegetables grown on the extensive allotments at Windsor and Sandringham, and to fish from the royal hatcheries, would have helped alleviate any serious shortages. Frederick Corbitt, in charge of the Palace catering, even lists *mille-feuille* among the delicacies created by an inventive chef.

Conditions on the royal train have been described as 'spartan'. Although the carriages themselves, some of which dated back to the Victorian or Edwardian era, were luxuriously appointed, wartime restrictions were rigorously applied. The five-inch water-line was painted round all the baths and food was rationed. 'My dear, we simply starved,' remembered one of the Queen's ladies. 'I always took along a packet of biscuits to eke out the meagre rations.'[15] The royal couple travelled for tens of thousands of miles by train in the course of their official duties. As the train had to serve as the monarch's headquarters, it would be connected up, wherever it rested for the night, with the national telephone system. This allowed the King to keep in touch with his private secretaries at Buckingham Palace and, through them, with his ministers. Invariably, to avoid inconveniencing the local authorities or the owner of some country house that the King might be visiting, the royal couple would eat and sleep on the train. Sometimes, after dinner, the King and Queen might be glimpsed going for a walk beside the track.

On one occasion, the Queen was unwittingly involved in

a serious breach of wartime regulations. She had gone to visit her father, the Earl of Strathmore, at Glamis Castle in Scotland. Although before, and even after, his daughter's marriage to the Duke of York, the Earl had never allowed himself to be unduly impressed by the royal family, he felt that this visit by his daughter, now Queen of England, should be appropriately celebrated. So as lavish a banquet as rationing would allow was held in the little-used great dining hall of the castle. Not until the anguished local police arrived was it suddenly realized that, in defiance of blackout regulations, all the windows of the dining hall were 'ablaze with light'.[16] The castle was making a dazzlingly lit target, in the heart of which was sitting the Queen of England, for enemy bombers.

Although the King and Queen were allowed some extra clothing coupons, they adhered to the general restrictions. One day, while the royal couturier Norman Hartnell was in consultation with the Queen, the King called him into another room. 'Look at that!' he commanded. In the interests of austerity, the King had had an old military greatcoat cut up and refashioned into a pair of trousers. But the fabric was so heavy that the trousers were able to stand up, unsupported, on the floor. 'What do you think of that for a pair of fine upstanding trousers?' asked the grinning King.[17]

The Queen, in spite of her penchant for pretty, romantic clothes, 'adhered strictly', says Hartnell, to the 'limitations in dress, which stipulated how much material, how many seams a dress could comprise, how much adornment and how wide the collar or belt of a dress might be'.[18] 'Suddenly,' remembered the Queen, 'one would be told that one could only have so many buttonholes, because if one didn't it would affect the war effort!'[19] Photographs of those war years show the Queen wearing the same dresses time after time.

She once told a member of the family that many of her dresses were being altered for Princess Elizabeth. 'Margaret gets Lilibet's clothes then, so with the three of us we manage in relays.'[20]

There were occasions, though, such as diplomatic receptions, when she needed to wear something more impressive. With Hartnell's trademark – elaborate embroidery – being forbidden, he was obliged to refashion pre-war trimmings or simply to handpaint garlands of flowers on to her satin crinolines.

On one occasion during the war the Queen attended an exhibition of Latin American costumes made by Hartnell. On describing a Nicaraguan peasant costume to her, he explained that, in order to capture the extreme simplicity of the dress, he had used an old scrap of stuff of very ordinary quality.

'Indeed,' observed the Queen serenely, 'I see you used a piece of my last year's evening wrap.'[21]

If Buckingham Palace was bleak, Windsor Castle was hardly better. Over 1,500 acres of beautiful parkland had been ploughed up and given over to the cultivation of cereal crops. The huge herd of deer had been drastically reduced. Even horses from the Royal Mews – the famous Windsor Greys – were being used for such ignoble tasks as drawing ploughs and mowers. With Hitler, according to Princess Margaret in later life, having decided 'that he would use Windsor Castle as his headquarters once Britain had been conquered', the castle was very well guarded. It was surrounded not only by troops but also by slit trenches and barbed-wire entanglements. 'They would never have kept the Germans out,' Princess Margaret went on to say, 'but they certainly kept us in.'[22]

In fact, one intruder did manage to get through all these defences and right into the Queen's apartment. One evening, as she was dressing for dinner, she went into an adjoining room to find herself faced by a stranger. The Queen remained admirably calm. 'Putting on my best nanny voice,' she said, 'I told him that he had no business there and

that he was to go away immediately. And he did.' What had
he wanted? 'Oh, he just wanted to speak to me,' she recalled
airily. 'People were always wanting to speak to one about
something or other.'[23]

As at Buckingham Palace, almost all traces of pre-war
grandeur had been obliterated. Pictures had been removed,
chandeliers taken down, glass-fronted cabinets turned to the
wall, the furniture in the State Apartments shrouded in
dust-sheets. To cut down on the laundering of shirts and
collars, the King decreed that the livery worn by the male
members of staff should be replaced by navy blue battledress
with GR VI embroidered on the breast pocket. The
thousands of windows presented another problem. 'By the
time we've blacked out all the windows here,' grumbled one
servant, 'it's morning again.'[24] Having reduced the number
of boilers in operation, there were days when hot water had
to be lugged from the distant kitchens to the bedrooms. The
staff – an assortment of chefs and chauffeurs, footmen and
gardeners – was obliged to form a sort of Castle Home
Guard and to join the regular troops in rifle drill. Their
efforts seem not to have been conspicuously impressive.

One day the King's Librarian, Sir Owen Morshead, asked
the two princesses – who lived permanently in the castle – if
they would like to see something interesting. He then led
them into the vaults where he showed them a pile of
ordinary leather hatboxes which seemed, at first sight, to be
stuffed with old newspaper. Only on closer inspection did
the princesses discover that the hatboxes were crammed
with the Crown Jewels.

In an effort to enliven the bare walls of the great picture
galleries, the young Princess Margaret inserted her own
drawings into the ornate gilt frames which had once
accommodated famous portraits of Britain's kings and
queens. 'There was Dick Whittington with his cat gazing
down from a frame marked Charles I,' noted Marion
Crawford, the children's governess. 'Mother Goose
appeared as Queen Henrietta Maria and so on all round the

room.' The governess had wondered whether the King would mind this *lèse-majesté*. She had no need to feel apprehensive.

'What do you think', the King once asked a guest, 'of my ancestors?'[25]

In spite of all its gloom, Windsor Castle was regarded as home by the royal family during the war years. For the King and Queen, it presented an oasis of cheerful domesticity; for their two daughters, it was the only place they really knew. Except for short breaks at Balmoral and Appleton House on the Sandringham estate (the big house had been closed), or the odd day in London, the princesses remained at Windsor for over five years. Watched over by their governess Marion Crawford ('Crawfie'), their nanny Mrs Clara Knight ('Allah') and their nursemaid Margaret MacDonald ('Bobo'), they lived as normal a life as possible.

But, of course, the circumstances were such that their lives were far from normal. At night, when the bombing was bad, they would scramble into their siren suits, pick up their gas-masks and Iron Rations, carry their ready-packed suitcases and make their way along dark, damp passageways to their dungeon shelter. Only in later years was a more permanent, more convenient shelter organized. Every night before going to sleep, no matter how alarming the bombing, the two princesses would fill in their diaries; on this, the Queen insisted.

Like children all over the country, the princesses cultivated their vegetable gardens, collected tinfoil, rolled bandages and knitted scarves and socks for the troops. Rationing applied no less to them and they looked forward to their Sunday morning egg. It has been claimed that, unlike the majority of children, they were able to enjoy bananas; these were supplied, apparently, by the 'tropical house in Kew Gardens'.[26] On one occasion, the princesses received bananas from another source: Lord Louis Mountbatten brought them a large bunch from Africa. With Princess Elizabeth suggesting that the fruit be given to less privileged children, the Queen took the bunch to a hospital in Lewisham, South London, where she was visiting a group of children who had been injured in an air-raid on their school. One 4-year-old girl was very suspicious of the unfamiliar fruit presented to her by the Queen. 'Do I *have* to eat it?' she asked plaintively.[27]

As girl guides, the two princesses continued their activities throughout the war years, even camping out with their troop overnight. Although the younger, more extrovert Princess Margaret enjoyed sleeping under canvas, Princess Elizabeth did not. 'She was getting older', commented Crawfie, 'and had been brought up so much alone, I could understand why she did not want to undress before a lot of other children all of a sudden and spend the night with them.'[28]

The princesses played hostess to groups of officers stationed at the castle, sometimes entertaining them to tea or lunch. 'If you sat at Princess Margaret's end of the table,' remembered one young officer, 'the conversation never lapsed for a moment. She was amazingly self-assured, without being embarrassingly so.'[29] After the meal there would be guessing games and charades.

In October 1940, during *Children's Hour* on the BBC, the 14-year-old Princess Elizabeth made a five-minute broadcast to 'the children of the Empire'. She approached the nerve-racking task conscientiously, adding phrases of her own to the prepared script and following her mother's advice on breathing and timing. The Queen herself broadcast several times during the war – to the women of France, the United States and, of course, Britain – and in this, as in so much else, revealed a real talent. The Queen's voice, unlike the King's, was light and melodious and she always insisted on delivering a 'human' as opposed to an official speech. Although Princess Elizabeth was not able to match her mother's apparent spontaneity on the air, she acquitted herself very well on this first occasion. Churchill's secretary, although 'embarrassed by the sloppy sentiment she was made to express', claimed that 'her voice was most impressive and, if the monarchy survives, Queen Elizabeth II should be a most successful radio Queen'.[30]

At the end of her broadcast the Princess suddenly said, 'My sister is by my side, and we are both going to say goodnight to you. Come on, Margaret.' At this the 10-year-old Princess Margaret piped up: 'Goodnight and good luck to you all.'[31]

A celebrated feature of these years at Windsor were the annual Christmas pantomimes. They originated in a nativity play put on in December 1940, with Princess Elizabeth as one of the Three Kings and Princess Margaret as the Little Child, heading a cast of local schoolboys. The King was deeply moved. 'I wept through most of it,' he noted in his diary.[32] From then on, each Christmas, a pantomime was staged in the Waterloo Chamber. They did *Cinderella*, *The Sleeping Beauty*, *Aladdin* and *Old Mother Red Riding Boots*, with Princess Elizabeth usually revealed, in stockings and tunic, as the Principal Boy, and Princess Margaret, in wig and long skirts, as the leading lady.

Even the King was caught up in the excitement. It all made such a wonderful distraction: the rehearsals, the painting of the scenery, the making and borrowing of costumes, the printing of programmes, the putting up of posters, the hoary old jokes, the topical allusions (*Aladdin* was a particularly fertile field for anti-Japanese digs) and the inevitable mishaps. As these pantomimes were staged for the public, with the proceeds going to the Queen's Wool Fund, an entrance fee had to be decided upon. Princess Elizabeth thought that the initial ticket price of seven and sixpence would be too much. 'No one will pay that to look at *us*!' she protested.

'Nonsense!' countered Princess Margaret. 'They'll pay anything to see us . . .'[33]

One of the chief advantages of these productions was that they gave the princesses the opportunity of meeting and working with children of their own ages and different backgrounds. But in the main, these wartime years at Windsor strengthened the already strong bond between parents and children. General Sir Alan Brooke, spending a weekend with the royal family during this period, was particularly struck by this family solidarity. 'The main impression that I have carried away', he wrote, 'is that the King, Queen and their two daughters provide one of the very best of examples of English family life. A thoroughly close-knit and happy family all wrapped up in each other. Secondly, I was greatly impressed by the natural atmosphere, entirely devoid of all pomposity, stiffness or awkwardness. They both have a gift of making one feel entirely at home. The Queen, I think, grows on one the more one sees her and realizes the wonderful qualities she possesses.'[34] Looking back, Princess Margaret claimed that 'We were very lucky in that we all got on so well together.'[35]

They were full of family jokes. Their favourite standing joke – which they would use for years afterwards – was the question the princesses would ask their parents whenever they were in gala dress: 'Is this a special occasion?' The joke had its origins in the 1939 royal tour of Canada when the King once noticed that a local mayor was not wearing a mayoral chain. The King, thinking that he might present him with one, asked him whether or not he had a chain.

'Oh yes, Sir,' answered the mayor, 'I have.'

'But I notice you're not wearing it,' said the King.

'Oh,' explained the mayor, 'but I only wear it on special occasions.'[36]

Devoted to both daughters, the King could see many of his own characteristics in Princess Elizabeth. She was reserved, steady, conscientious, happiest in the open air. Like him, she did not shine in society; she could look awkward in public; she smiled her dazzling smile only when she was genuinely amused. But already she was showing the dignity and devotion to duty that were to be essential for her future role as Queen-Regnant. Mrs Roosevelt, meeting her in

1942, when the Princess was 16, described her as 'quite serious and a child with a great deal of character and personality. She asked me a number of questions about life in the United States and they were serious questions.'[37]

Princess Margaret was different. In her, the King could see much of his wife's wit and sparkle. There were times when it seemed almost impossible for him to believe that this high-spirited, talented and already socially accomplished girl was his daughter. There was nothing like one of her pert imitations to bring a smile to the King's often careworn face.

Queen Mary, coming up from Badminton to Windsor for Princess Elizabeth's confirmation in March 1942, was very struck by the difference between the two girls. To her sister-in-law, Princess Alice in Ottawa, Queen Mary reported 'Lilibet much grown, very pretty eyes and complexion, pretty figure. Margaret very short, intelligent face, but not really pretty.'[38] The old Queen later described Princess Margaret as *espiègle* – mischievous, roguish – but admitted that 'all the same she is so outrageously amusing that one can't help encouraging her'.[39]

Princess Margaret, for her part, always found her grandmother '*absolutely* terrifying'. She 'didn't really like children and made no sort of effort with them', she remembered.[40]

In Princess Elizabeth, Queen Mary might have recognized some of her own character traits. Indeed, as Queen Elizabeth II has aged and matured, so has she gradually come to resemble her grandmother, both in features and in a certain unsmiling stiffness of public demeanour. But to Queen Mary, in 1942, the Princess – then on the eve of her sixteenth birthday – seemed to be showing unmistakable signs of developing into another Queen Victoria. With this assessment Queen Mary's lady-in-waiting, Lady Airlie, agreed.

'I saw a grave little face under a small net veil, and a slender figure in a plain white woollen frock,' wrote Lady Airlie. 'The carriage of her head was unequalled, and there was about her that indescribable something which Queen Victoria had. Although she was perfectly simple, modest and unselfconscious, she gave the impression of great personality.'[41]

On the afternoon of 4 November 1942, the King and his speech therapist, Lionel Logue, were rehearsing the address which he was to make at the Opening of Parliament a week later. Although the glittering pre-war pageantry of the occasion had been dispensed with, and the King and Queen drove to the Palace of Westminster in a closed car instead of a horse-drawn landau, the King was still obliged to deliver his annual Speech from the Throne. These periods of rehearsal, as the King painstakingly worked on his speech, were regarded as sacrosanct. They were to be interrupted only by matters of the utmost urgency. So when the telephone rang that afternoon, the King gave Logue a quizzical look before going to answer it.

'Well, read it out, read it out,' Logue heard the King exclaim. A few minutes later, having listened intently, the King said, 'Good news, thanks.'[42] With a broad grin, he turned to face Logue.

What had been read out to the King over the telephone was a telegram from General Alexander, Commander-in-Chief Middle East, giving news of a severe defeat of the German and Italian forces at El Alamein in North Africa. The British Eighth Army under the command of General Montgomery had routed the hitherto invincible General Rommel and his Afrika Korps.

'A victory at last,' wrote the King in his diary that night, 'how good it is for the nerves.'[43]

George VI had been very concerned with North African affairs during the previous months. Churchill, who always took care to keep him informed on all aspects of the war, had recently been involving the King in actual high-level military discussions. At Buckingham Palace, at Windsor and at 10 Downing Street, the King sat in on talks between British and American military personnel. By July 1942 it had been decided that an Anglo-American landing in North Africa, known as Operation Torch, would be staged later that year.

That the King was very much 'in the know' as to current and prospective plans for Allied Operations was immediately apparent to General Dwight D. Eisenhower when, in the course of the planning of Torch, he was received at Buckingham Palace that summer. During a forty-five-minute meeting with the King, Eisenhower found the British monarch to be a well-informed and amiable person.

As he was also an amusing one, the King told the unsuspecting Eisenhower about an incident which had happened earlier that year. One Sunday, as a special favour, Eisenhower and his deputy, General Mark Clark, were being shown over Windsor Castle. On being told that the sightseeing visit was to take place, the King had volunteered to keep to his apartments, so as not to embarrass the American visitors. But, having forgotten his promise and as it was such a lovely day, the King – accompanied by the Queen and the two princesses – decided to have tea in a certain part of the garden. Hearing voices and then seeing four distant heads, the King suddenly remembered his promise. 'This is terrible,' he hissed, 'we must not be seen.'[44] So on their hands and knees the royal family crawled across the lawn to the garden wall and escaped through a door into the castle.

Operation Torch was staged on 8 November 1942. These Anglo-American landings in North Africa constituted the first major offensive to be undertaken on the initiative of the Allies and not simply as a response to enemy action. Their success – coming on the heels of the great victory at El Alamein – was, claims the King's official biographer, 'of the greatest psychological, political and strategic importance'.[45]

In his elation at what at last seemed to be a turning of the tide, the King wrote a generous tribute to Winston Churchill. 'When I look back and think of all the many arduous hours of work you have put in, and the many miles you have travelled . . .', he wrote, 'you have every right to rejoice;

while the rest of our people will one day be very thankful to you for what you have done. I cannot say more.'[46]

The Prime Minister's reply was equally heartfelt. 'No Minister in modern times . . .', wrote Churchill, 'has received more help and comfort from the King, and this has brought us all thus far with broadening hopes and now, I feel, to brightening skies.

'It is needless to assure Your Majesty of my devotion to Yourself and Family and to our ancient and cherished Monarchy – the true bulwark of British freedom against tyrannies of every kind . . .'[47]

Part Two

THE KING AMONG HIS SOLDIERS

7

'I know I shall be doing good'

'HE FEELS SO much not being more in the fighting-line,' wrote the Queen to Queen Mary about the King's constitutionally enforced military inactivity.[1] For over three years, since his visit to the British Expeditionary Force in France in December 1939, George VI had been obliged to remain in Britain. Those hours spent at his desk or in granting audiences, attending meetings, holding investitures and travelling for what has been calculated to be equivalent to twenty times the circumference of the globe on his various tours of inspection, could not compensate for the fact that he had spent no time at the battle-front. As a man of action, the King felt this keenly.

His opportunity came in the spring of 1943. The combined Anglo–American operations in North Africa ended triumphantly, on 13 May, with the surrender of the last Axis forces. 'It is an overwhelming victory,' wrote the King in his diary that night.[2] The lull between the conquest of North Africa and the Allied invasion of Sicily, planned for July, gave him his chance. Already, in March, with the Allied victory in sight, the King had told Churchill of his eagerness to visit the troops. For, in spite of his personal modesty, George VI was fully alive to the prestige of his office. He appreciated how much a visit from the sovereign would mean to the fighting men.

The Prime Minister was all in favour of it. An unquestioning believer in the inspiriting and ameliorating powers of the monarchy, Churchill hoped that a North African visit from the King would both invigorate the British and Commonwealth troops and sweeten the not always harmonious relationship between the British, American and Free French commanders. The King's departure was set for the night of 11 June 1943.

On the day before he flew off (the King hated flying) he was assailed by the inevitable last-minute reservations. 'As the time draws nearer for my departure on my journey, I wonder if I should go,' he wrote to Queen Mary, 'but I know I shall be doing good in visiting those men who have done such wonderful deeds for this Country, and who will shortly be going into action again.' As the journey could prove hazardous, the King summoned his solicitor so as 'to leave nothing to chance',[3] and appointed five Counsellors of State, among whom were the Queen, the Duke of Gloucester and the Princess Royal.

Secrecy, of course, was an essential element of the King's departure. 'We were never told *anything*,' remembered Princess Margaret. 'When my father flew off to North Africa he came to say goodbye to us and, as he was leaving, he turned round, put a finger to his lips and said "Not a word to anyone". But we had no idea *where* he was going.'[4]

Travelling as 'General Lyon' and accompanied by, among others, his Private Secretary, Alexander Hardinge, the King flew off in the York bomber normally used by Churchill. The plane was meant to land for refuelling at Gibraltar but because of dense fog was obliged to fly on to North Africa. The change of plan alarmed the Queen considerably. 'Of course, I imagined every sort of horror,' she reported to Queen Mary the next day, 'and walked up and down my room staring at the telephone.'[5]

For the following two weeks the King was subjected to a gruelling round of inspections, reviews, conferences, lunches, dinners and receptions. In stifling heat, often suffering from 'desert tummy', obliged to fly for long distances, accommodated, in Algiers, in a rich French wine merchant's home where 'the plumbing was defective and erratic',[6] and, in Tripoli, in a captured German caravan, the King carried out his duties. He held discussions with General Eisenhower in Algiers and with General Montgomery in Tripoli. He inspected the American forces, under General Mark Clark, in Oran. He lunched between the two rival French generals, Giraud and de Gaulle. He hosted a garden party at his Algerian villa for 180 British and American soldiers and civilians. It was, reported Harold Macmillan, the newly appointed Minister Resident to Allied Forces Headquarters, 'a *tremendous* success . . . H.M. did very well and was most gracious to everybody. The Americans were really delighted, and letters about it will reach every distant part of the U.S.A.'[7] As with everyone who met George VI on this tour, Macmillan found him to be very well-informed, very interested and very natural. 'He is a most delightful person,' agreed Montgomery, himself gratified at this opportunity of playing host to the monarch, 'and he likes people to be quite natural with him . . .'[8]

The celebrated comedienne, Beatrice Lillie, on a North African tour with ENSA, was due to have attended a reception for the sovereign but was forced, because of an attack of dysentery, to miss it. The King, a fellow sufferer, would have appreciated this only too well. Some years later, on being presented to him at a Buckingham Palace garden party, Beatrice Lillie spent several minutes in animated conversation with the monarch. What, demanded her envious companions, had the two of them spoken about? 'Diarrhoea,' answered Miss Lillie.[9]

An actress whom the King did meet in North Africa was another member of the ENSA troupe, Vivien Leigh. She was one of the cast performing before him on the white marble terrace in the grounds of a villa at Hamamet, near Tunis. 'It was a night of perfect beauty,' reported Vivien Leigh, 'with a huge moon which shone on the sea only about 30 yards behind where the audience was sitting.' At a reception after the performance, the troupe was presented to the King. 'He was looking extremely well and never stuttered once the whole time,' noted the actress.[10]

The King told Vivien Leigh how much he had enjoyed her 'Ode to Plymouth', written by Clemence Dane. A man of conventional literary tastes, he suggested that she extend her repertoire to include his favourite poem: that patriotic paean by Alice Duer Miller, 'The White Cliffs'.

But the King was not always as amiable as this. His habitually short temper, aggravated by the heat and his upset stomach, manifested itself on several occasions. Macmillan complained of his being difficult and uncooperative, and Field Marshal Lord Carver, then a brigade commander, has an anecdote about the King's irascibility. While driving in Montgomery's open car along a road lined with troops, the King stopped to speak to a party of brigade commanders. On having Brigadier Robert Hinde (always known as Loony Hinde) presented to him, the King asked if they had met before.

'I don't think so,' answered Hinde.

The King was furious. 'You b-b-b-bloody well ought to know,' he spluttered.[11]

Two occasions – one informal, one formal – imprinted themselves on the King's mind during this North African tour. While visiting a convalescent camp for Eighth Army soldiers along the shore outside Algiers, he suddenly came across about five hundred half-naked soldiers bathing in the sea. Recognizing him, they gave him a tremendous ovation, crowding round and lustily singing, 'For he's a jolly good fellow'. The King was very touched.

The second occasion was what he afterwards described to Queen Mary as 'the real gem' of his tour.[12] This was his visit to the island of Malta. The fortunes of this Mediterranean island had preoccupied him for several years. Because of its strategic importance – a lone British outpost in what Mussolini grandiloquently referred to as *Mare Nostrum* – Malta had been mercilessly besieged and bombarded by enemy forces for months on end. Stirred by the epic gallantry of its defence and by the suffering of its civilian population, the King, on his own initiative, had conferred his personal decoration – the George Cross – on the people and garrison of the island. This honour had been awarded in the spring of 1942. Since then, after further attacks and privations, the siege had been lifted, but the Battle of Malta remained, in the King's mind, as 'one of the most valiant and glorious episodes' of the war.[13] Because of this, he was anxious to pay a personal visit to the island.

Although he had already discussed the possibility of such a visit with Churchill, it was not until the King was in North Africa that the plan was finalized. It would be a risky business. Sicily, a mere sixty miles to the north of the island, remained in Axis hands and Malta was still being subjected to enemy air-raids. Nevertheless, on the night of 19 June, in strict secrecy, the King embarked from Tripoli on the cruiser *Aurora*. Not one of the anxious naval officers aboard the cruiser got a wink of sleep that night. Soon after eight the following morning, in brilliant sunshine, the King mounted a special platform constructed in front of the bridge of the *Aurora* and stood there, for almost an hour, as the cruiser slowly made its way into the Grand Harbour at Valletta.

The arrival of King George VI off Malta remains one of the most unforgettable spectacles of his reign. There he stands, a slim, suntanned figure in his immaculate white naval uniform, lifting his hand in salute to those thousands upon thousands of wildly cheering people who had clambered on to the rooftops and ramparts of the town. 'I have never heard such cheering,' wrote one witness, 'and all the bells in the many churches started ringing when he landed.'[14]

The King was deeply moved. 'I shall never forget the sight of entering the Grand Harbour at 8.30 a.m. on a lovely sunny day and seeing the people cheering from every vantage point while we were still some way off,' he afterwards admitted to Queen Mary. 'Then later, when we anchored inside, hearing the cheers of the people which brought a lump to my throat, knowing what they had suffered from six months constant bombing . . .'[15]

Throughout that day, he toured the island. Everywhere he drove he was greeted by vociferous crowds. 'Flowers, flags, confetti . . .', wrote the accompanying Harold Macmillan. 'Considering that many had only been told in the early morning, I don't know where they found the flags or how they had time to decorate the streets . . .'[16]

For the war-weary King, it was a wonderfully uplifting experience. It did not matter that the day's non-stop touring and repeated public appearances had exhausted him or that his once-pristine uniform had been soiled by the rain of flowers. 'You have made the people of Malta very happy today, Sir,' said the Lieutenant-Governor as the monarch was about to embark on the *Aurora* that night.

'But I have been the happiest man in Malta today,' answered the King.[17]

In addition to their multifarious wartime duties in Canada, the Athlones were obliged to play host to a constant stream of exiled or visiting members of Europe's royal houses. These ranged from that redoubtable symbol of anti-Nazi resistance, Queen Wilhelmina of the Netherlands, to a German prisoner-of-war, Prince Friedrich of Prussia, grandson of Kaiser Wilhelm II, who happened to be – such were the dynastic entanglements of royalty – Princess Alice's godson. Whenever the Athlones were staying in the Citadel, the Governor-General's official residence in Quebec City, the captive German prince would be allowed out from Camp L on the Plains of Abraham to have tea with his godmother. There they would sit, chatting happily away in German – the native tongue of Princess Alice's mother and of Lord Athlone's father.

One of the most curious members of Princess Alice's family to stay at Rideau Hall in Ottawa, and about whose death there hangs an intriguing air of mystery, was the

28-year-old Alastair, 2nd Duke of Connaught. He was the grandson of Queen Victoria's long-lived son Arthur, 1st Duke of Connaught. As his father had died before his grandfather, the young man had become the 2nd Duke on his grandfather's death in 1942.

Periodically, royal families throw up a member such as he: a pleasant enough but vapid and ineffectual young man, to whose amorphous personality no amount of training can give shape. Alexander Hardinge described him as 'a nice boy without any vice, but the combination of a bad upbringing and uncertain health has imposed severe limits on his capabilities'.[18] Others were less circumspect. 'He was soft in the head,' was the frank opinion of the Duchess of Gloucester.[19]

On the outbreak of war, as a Lieutenant in the Royal Scots Greys, the young man had been posted, in some ill-defined capacity, to the Middle East but, 'in consequence', as Hardinge tactfully put it, 'of adverse reports on his reliability for command in active operations' he had been recalled to Britain. Back home, the Duke's main concerns seem to have been about the possibility of renouncing his recently inherited title of Duke of Connaught and Strathearn for that of Strathearn only and of obtaining extra clothing coupons so as to replace the clothes eaten by moths during his absence in the Middle East.

Although the second request may well have been granted, the first was not and it was as the 2nd Duke of Connaught that he was shunted on to a Brigadier Bruxner-Randall at Sandhurst. He was to act as his ADC and 'run odd jobs'; he would 'certainly not be doing any teaching'. Poor Bruxner-Randall was entrusted with the giving of a 'new opinion' of the Duke. Alas, the new opinion proved to be no different from the old.

In the meantime the young man's widowed mother, Princess Arthur of Connaught, had been badgering the King about her son. In desperation he advised the customary remedy in these cases: perhaps the Viceroy of India could take him on as an extra ADC for a trial period of a few months. 'The boy', warned the King, 'would require close supervision' by His Excellency's Military Secretary.[20]

His Excellency, apparently, was not prepared to take on the responsibility and so, in the hope that blood would prove thicker than water, the King turned to his uncle, the Earl of Athlone. Would *he* possibly take on the Duke (who was Princess Alice's second cousin) as an extra ADC? Lord Athlone agreed, and to Rideau Hall came the 2nd Duke of Connaught.

Any hopes that the example of devotion to duty set by the Athlones would have any effect on the Duke were short-lived. He remained as vague and feckless as ever. 'He was a real handful,' claimed Princess Alice. 'Nice enough but, you know, not really much up top.'[21] The Duke's irresponsibility was such, in fact, that it killed him. On the morning of 26 April 1943, he was found dead on the floor of his room at Rideau Hall. He had died, it was claimed, of hypothermia. It was generally believed in the royal family that the Duke had come home drunk and that in his befuddled state he had opened the window, possibly to be sick out of it, and had fallen asleep on the floor. The night air, coming through the open window, was apparently cold enough to freeze him to death.

The 2nd Duke of Connaught had died, it was dutifully reported, on active service.

Of more significance than their relationships with their various royal connections were the Athlones' encounters with important wartime political figures such as Churchill, Roosevelt, de Gaulle, Smuts, Eden and the inimitable Madame Chiang Kai-shek, who was fondly remembered by the staff at Rideau Hall for the size of the tips she doled out on leaving.

Not long after their arrival in Canada in 1940, the Athlones travelled to the United States to pay a private visit to the Roosevelts at their home, Hyde Park, on the Hudson

River. Princess Alice was fascinated by the Roosevelt house-hold. She found the interior of the house to be a 'delightful old-fashioned muddle'. President Roosevelt she thought utterly charming and possessed of 'real greatness of charac-ter'; 'we both fell completely under his spell'. At the wheel of his own car, the President drove them through the autumn woods of his Hyde Park estate. As usual, there was strict security. They were accompanied by two police cars and at every bend of the road stood yet another plain-clothes policeman. Security, sighed the President, was the curse of his office.

The Princess was equally taken with the gaunt, toothy, dynamic Eleanor Roosevelt. She arrived from Seattle 'like a whirlwind' and made so much noise at luncheon that Lord Athlone complained of being deafened. (Cecil Beaton, on photographing her during her stay at Buckingham Palace, had the same complaint. 'I haven't put a comb through my hair since New York. I haven't had any powder on my face since leaving Washington,' she shouted.)[22] But the most notable character of all was the President's mother, Mrs Sara Roosevelt. Plump and domineering, old Mrs Roosevelt had an energy which belied her eighty-four years. 'She was a great dear, but such a matriarch,' remarked the Princess.[23]

A couple of years later, after America had entered the war, President Roosevelt invited the Athlones to visit Alaska. He was anxious for Lord Athlone to see the American planes being ferried across the Bering Strait to the Russian allies. It was, recalled Princess Alice, 'a very interesting experience.'[24] Through an interpreter, they were able to chat to the various Russian pilots who had come over to fetch the planes. To the astonishment of his American hosts, the royal Earl of Athlone, in his straightforward way, established an immediate rapport with the Russians, something which the republican Americans were having great difficulty in doing.

Allies or not, Princess Alice simply could not reconcile herself to the Russian regime. She had, after all, been 34 at the time of the Russian Revolution and the murder of so many members of the imperial family, including her first cousins the Empress Alexandra and the Grand Duchess Elizabeth. Nevertheless, the Russian Embassy in Ottawa was famous for its parties, and the Athlones were frequently obliged to attend them. 'These people killed my relations,' she would mutter as the viceregal car drew up outside the spotlit hammer and sickle on the Russian Embassy.[25] But once inside, according to Lord Athlone's secretary, Sir Shuldham Redfern, the Princess was her usual charming self.

The most internationally significant events to take place in Canada during the Second World War were the Quebec Conferences of 1943 and 1944. In the summer of 1943 Churchill let the Canadian Prime Minister, Mackenzie King, know that he would like to have a formal meeting with President Roosevelt in order to discuss the conduct of the war. He suggested that a meeting take place in the Citadel, Quebec. Lord Athlone, on being told of Churchill's plan, was immediately 'struck by the idea'.[26] The holding of the conference in Quebec would do wonders for Canadian prestige. It was agreed that the conference would take place between 17 and 24 August and that the Athlones would act as hosts to the delegates. Churchill (with his wife and daughter, Mary), Roosevelt and Mackenzie King, with their immediate staff, would all be accommodated in the Citadel.

When the Athlones arrived at the Citadel from Ottawa to welcome President Roosevelt they discovered that security was expected to be even stricter here than it had been at Hyde Park. An American president, explained Roosevelt's chief detective earnestly to Princess Alice, was assassinated every forty-five years. As the next assassination was due that year, extra precautions had to be taken. So the detective insisted on stationing one of his own men on each landing. The weather being hot, these American security men appeared in their shirtsleeves. This was too much for the punctilious Lord Athlone. That security, in the Governor-General's Quebec home, should be entrusted to the Americans was bad enough; that the security men should appear in shirtsleeves was beyond reason. As the Americans refused to dress more appropriately, Lord Athlone stationed a scarlet-tunicked, immaculately turned-out Mountie beside each one of them. He won his battle. The security was left to the Mounties.

Nor was this the end of the Athlones' troubles with American detectives. Princess Alice, expecting President Roosevelt to arrive at any moment, had just left the drawing-room tidied to her satisfaction when two of the President's 'toughs' flung themselves on the sofa, tossed their legs over the arms and lit up their cigars. To crown this, they forbade her – as 'a security risk' – to go out on to the terrace to welcome the President. Only the appearance of Churchill, who had already been at the Citadel for a couple of days, saved the situation. 'Come along with me,' he growled and led her out.

Although the Athlones played no part in the official business of these conferences (the second Churchill–Roosevelt conference was held from 10 to 15 September 1944), they spent a great deal of time with the President, the Churchills and their staff. 'It was wonderful', said the Princess, 'to meet all the leading men directing the war effort'. They were all 'delightful guests when we were just *en famille*, and we enjoyed many thrilling conversations, off the record, as they say'.[27]

It was during the course of another visit by Churchill, made in the depths of the Canadian winter, that the Prime Minister made one of his characteristically wry remarks. Visitors to Rideau Hall, coming in from the freezing cold outside, often found that the friction of their shoes on the entrance hall carpets would cause an electric spark as they shook hands. And true enough, as Lord Athlone's and Winston Churchill's fingers touched, a spark flew between them.

'This wouldn't be a good house for courting couples,' commented the Prime Minister.[28]

★

'I know that I have many tasks ahead,' wrote Princess
Marina, the Duchess of Kent, to a friend in those desolate
weeks after her husband's death, 'and I pray for strength and
courage to carry on as he would wish me to – for his dear
sake and our children's and the country's. I try not to think
of the lonely future. I know he is always very near me – but
oh, the aching of one's heart and mind . . .'[29]

Within ten weeks of the Duke's death, Princess Marina
was back on duty, inspecting a Wren training centre in
London. And during the following twelve months, as
though dedicating herself to his memory, the Princess took
on almost thirty of her late husband's patronages and
obligations. She even – this least mechanically-minded of
women – replaced the late Duke of Kent in his capacity as an
unofficial factory inspector. Before long, Princess Marina's
official life was busier than it had ever been.

Yet her private life became, as she admitted to a friend,
increasingly lonely. One of the King's new equerries, meeting Princess Marina for the first time, was immediately
struck by her air of melancholy. Her face, he wrote, was of
'an exquisite, almost tragic beauty, with a permanently
wistful expression'.[30] Admittedly, she did have her three
young children as company but she had never been really
close to the other members of her husband's family. The
very British royal family did not share Princess Marina's
Continental sense of dynasty: her view of royalty as a
rarified, supra-national, interrelated caste. She may or may
not have referred to her sisters-in-law, the Queen and the
Duchess of Gloucester, as 'those common little Scottish
girls',[31] but Princess Marina was very conscious of her royal
and imperial descent. Her British relations were never
anything other than kind and supportive but, on the death of
her husband, she felt ever more estranged from them. Their
background and interests were essentially those of the
British aristocracy; hers were more cosmopolitan, more
exclusive.

This difference was brought into sharp focus in the

months after the Duke of Kent's death. During the Second World War, the British royal family had very largely been spared the conflicting loyalties which had proved so harrowing during the First World War: when royal families had not only been cut off from one another but cousins had sometimes faced each other on the battlefield. But with the arrival in Britain – on George VI's instigation – of Princess Marina's sister Olga (Princess Paul of Yugoslavia) to comfort her, the dilemma of divided loyalties again manifested itself.

The trouble had its roots in the period when, as Regent of Yugoslavia, Prince Paul had in March 1941 been forced into signing a pact with the Axis by which Yugoslavia was guaranteed immunity from attack provided German troops were allowed free passage through the country on their way to attack Greece. A subsequent coup resulted in the ousting of Prince Paul and his banishment, under house arrest, to Kenya. (It also resulted in the swift and savage German destruction of Yugoslavia which Prince Paul had been trying to avoid.) The truth was that, like King Leopold III of the Belgians, Prince Paul of Yugoslavia had been deliberately branded a villain and made the scapegoat for the failure of others.

The arrival in Britain of the wife of what the Foreign Office had once referred to as 'this wretched and treacherous creature'[32] gave Captain Alec Cunningham Reid, Tory MP for St Marylebone, a chance to air his fine patriotic prejudices. From the safety of the House of Commons he launched a vigorous and sustained attack on Princess Olga. Prince Paul, thundered Cunningham Reid, was a traitor, a quisling, a war criminal, a collaborator; he could not understand why this man's 'loyal wife', whom he described as a 'sinister woman' and a German sympathizer, was being allowed to move freely about Britain, where she was 'in a position to see, hear and say anything she likes'. In short, implied the incensed Cunningham Reid, Princess Olga was a Nazi spy. 'If you are a quisling and you happen to be royalty,' he declared, 'it appears that you are automatically trusted and forgiven.'[33]

Cunningham Reid's tirade lasted, off and on, for several months. It was not until December 1942, when the Foreign Secretary, Anthony Eden, pointed out that Princess Olga had come to Britain with the government's full 'authority and approval'[34] that the rumpus died down.

These attacks distressed Princess Marina considerably. Not only did they threaten her own position but they would, if repeated to her unsuspecting sister, distress Princess Olga even more. So every morning Princess Marina would scan the newspapers for reports of any Commons debates criticizing Prince and Princess Paul. If any were found, she would either stuff the offending newspaper behind a cushion or destroy it altogether and pretend that it had not arrived that day.

The King was of considerable comfort to the sisters. He visited them twice at Coppins during Princess Olga's stay and she was able to give him a more accurate version of the events which had led to Prince Paul's fall from grace. The King had always been fond of Prince Paul and had never quite believed the Foreign Office's depiction of him as a traitorous stabber-in-the-back. 'Bertie . . .', reported Princess Olga to her husband in Kenya, 'spoke so nicely of you, asked me about our life etc, all of which seemed to touch him . . .'[35] Princess Olga returned to Kenya, after a three-and-a-half-month stay, on New Year's Eve 1942.

Her departure, and the continuing press attacks on Prince Paul and his family, left Princess Marina feeling more isolated than ever. She particularly resented the implication – never anything like as widespread as she imagined – that she had remained a 'foreigner'. 'What must one do to make the English accept you?' she once sighed. 'In any other country in the world I would have become one of them; but however hard I try it seems impossible here.'[36]

Yet she never considered leaving Britain. Princess Marina's consciousness of her royal birth included a full appreciation of the obligations of that birth. She and her three children were members of the British royal family; as such their duty was to that family. Although her closest companions would always be members of her own family and of the cosmopolitan world of her youth, it was as a member of the British royal house that Princess Marina's public life was conducted. 'I could never live anywhere else,' she once said.[37]

And so, wearing her well-cut uniform or one of those defiantly flowered wartime hats, and smiling her lop-sided smile, the widowed Princess Marina continued to carry out her wartime role.

Princess Olga of Yugoslavia was not the royal family's only politically embarrassing relation. The sympathies of the Duke and Duchess of Windsor remained suspect, and one of their ardent supporters – the Duchess of Gloucester's eldest brother, the 8th Duke of Buccleuch – had not only been an outspoken advocate of appeasement but, even after the outbreak of war, had argued in favour of a negotiated peace with Hitler. Germany was full of royal cousins at various removes who were either members of the Nazi party or Nazi sympathizers. But the closest Nazi relation was Princess Alice's brother, Prince Charles Edward, Duke of Saxe-Coburg and Gotha.

Transplanted – for complicated dynastic reasons – from England at the age of 14 to become heir to the Duchy of Coburg, this grandson of Queen Victoria had joined the Nazi party in 1935. As an Englishman-turned-German, the Duke of Coburg's chief obsession was the fostering of a pre-war Anglo-German alliance. At the time of King George V's funeral in 1936, he had been staying with his sister, Princess Alice, at Kensington Palace and had taken the opportunity to have discussions with various prominent personalities such as Anthony Eden, Duff Cooper, Neville Chamberlain and J. J. Astor, the proprietor of *The Times*. As an Old Etonian himself, claimed the Duke of Coburg in a highly coloured and self-congratulatory report to Hitler, he was in a valuable position to sound out the political views of other Old Etonians.

It had been, though, on the new monarch, King Edward VIII, that the Duke of Coburg had placed his highest hopes. In a series of discussions with Edward VIII, the Duke had discovered that the new King was very kindly disposed towards the idea of an Anglo-German understanding. It was '*for him* an urgent necessity and a guiding principle of British foreign policy', reported the gratified Duke. He then went on to make the extravagant claim that Edward VIII had brushed aside the suggestion of a meeting between Hitler and the British Prime Minister of the day, Stanley Baldwin. 'Who is King here?' Edward VIII is supposed to have asked indignantly. 'Baldwin or I? I myself wish to talk to Hitler, and will do so here or in Germany. Tell him that please.'[38]

It is highly unlikely that even Edward VIII would have shown so little appreciation of the constitutional limits of his position. The Duke of Coburg was an unreliable and highly strung personality, ready to go to any lengths to tell the Führer what he thought he wanted to hear.

The Duke reappeared on the diplomatic scene the following year during the Duke and Duchess of Windsor's infamous visit to Nazi Germany. He gave a large dinner in their honour at the Grand Hotel in Dresden. Flouting King George VI's ruling, the Duke of Coburg ensured that the place card set for the Duchess of Windsor bore the German equivalent of 'Her Royal Highness'.

These little diplomatic flurries over, the Duke of Coburg confined himself, during the war, to the less controversial activities of the German Red Cross, of which he was President. None the less, after the war, he was tried for his activities as a 'Nazi camp-follower, category four'.[39] He was accused of having been a member of the Nazi party since 1935, the President of the German Red Cross under the Nazi regime, a *Gruppenführer* in the SA and a Reichstag deputy from 1937 until 1945. He was found guilty and fined.

Crippled by arthritis and suffering, eventually, from cancer, the Duke of Coburg lived out the rest of his life in very straitened circumstances. He died, aged 69, in 1954.

Not unnaturally, Princess Alice was always very reticent about her brother's controversial career. She could only write, in relation to him, that 'Fate sometimes plays a part in our lives and sometimes forces us into situations to which we have to adapt ourselves – often against our inclinations. Several members of my family, including my own brother, found themselves so encompassed by the fatal hands of fortune . . .'[40]

8

Changing Times

'WE NEVER consciously set out to change things; we never said "Let's change this or introduce that." Things just evolved,' claimed the Queen in discussing the modernization and popularization of the monarchy that took place, very largely, during the war years. 'It's just that life was getting more informal.'[1] Up to a point, this was true. The upheavals of the war years certainly accelerated the pace by which the monarchy was automatically adapting itself to a changing world. In less than half a dozen years the rigidity of the court of George V and Queen Mary had all but disappeared. ('My goodness it was stiff,' said one of the new Queen's ladies-in waiting. 'You can have no idea of how stiff it was.')[2] Even George VI's early conviction – that 'a crowned and annointed King must not be too ready to step down from his pedestal'[3] – had been discarded. Due not only to changing circumstances but also to the personalities of the King and Queen, the monarchy was rapidly becoming less hidebound.

But every now and then the royal couple did make a conscious effort to modernize things. One such step was the 'retirement' of the King's Principal Private Secretary, Sir Alexander Hardinge. Hardinge, who had served three kings – George V, Edward VIII and George VI – was very much a product of George V's reign: well-born, serious-minded, discreet, with a highly developed sense of duty and of propriety. The circle surrounding the abdicated Edward VIII ridiculed him as a 'dreary, narrow-minded fogy',[4] and even the more conventional George VI considered Hardinge over-punctilious. The King, and more especially the Queen, regarded him as out of touch, overbearing and obstructive. As Principal Private Secretary, Hardinge was the main channel of communication between the monarch and the outside world; it was very largely on him that the King had to rely as the interpreter of what was happening beyond the Palace walls. The royal couple often felt that Hardinge was preventing them from getting closer to their subjects.

Harold Macmillan, meeting Hardinge in the course of the King's tour of North Africa, professed himself shocked by the secretary's uncooperative attitude. He described him as 'idle, supercilious, without a spark of imagination or vitality' and complained that 'he just doesn't seem to live in the modern world at all. He would have been out of date in the 1900s . . .'[5]

For his part, Hardinge found the King and Queen somewhat difficult to deal with. Things had got off to a bad start with the royal couple's support of, and Hardinge's opposition to, Chamberlain's appeasement policies. A formal man, Hardinge disapproved of the more relaxed atmosphere of the court and was driven to near-distraction by the Queen's notorious lack of punctuality. Accustomed to the independence of action allowed him in the matter of State business by George V and Edward VIII, Hardinge resented George VI's insistence on seeing everything himself; even more, apparently, did he resent the Queen's involvement in these matters. He was very conscious of what he considered to be the couple's inability to take honest criticism or advice. Nor were matters helped by the fact that both George VI and Hardinge were highly strung men, often not in the best of health.

Things came to a head in the summer of 1943, a few days after the King's return from North Africa. Hardinge was faced with the resignation of the King's Assistant Private Secretary, Sir Alan (Tommy) Lascelles. There had never been much harmony between the two men; their views on how the office should be run had always differed sharply. Hardinge maintained that, as the King's Private Secretary, he had a duty to keep certain things from his juniors: Lascelles felt that they should function as a team. After an exchange of letters between the two men, Hardinge, feeling ill, tired, and unable to work with Lascelles any longer, decided that it would be best if *he* resigned. The official reason for his resignation was given as 'ill-health' but there can be little doubt that a stronger reason was that Hardinge felt that he had lost the confidence of the monarch.

Lascelles moved up to take Hardinge's place. Although hardly a shining example of modernity, Lascelles was a more flexible man, less obsessed by the punctiliousness of court life and more ready to delegate responsibility to his subordinates. As a cousin of the 6th Earl of Harewood, the Princess Royal's husband, he could almost be counted as a member of the family. Whereas Hardinge was said to have had a Guards officer mentality, Lascelles was something of a scholar, deeply interested in literature and always ready with an apt literary allusion. As a professional courtier, he knew exactly how to handle the King; there were no more misunderstandings between sovereign and secretary. With the Queen, Lascelles's relationship was less harmonious. It was said to have been 'never more than formal'.[6] Perhaps he considered her role too intrusive; perhaps she found his approach too drily academic.

And although Lascelles's appointment had been planned as a step towards the modernizing of the monarchy, he did not, claims one of the King's wartime equerries, 'adapt himself to the changing times nearly as well as the monarch himself'.[7]

Another member of the family who adapted herself, quite unconsciously, to changing times was Queen Mary. Life at Badminton, claimed her household, was making her 'more democratic than ever before'.[8] The pace of this process

The King on a visit to RAF fighter stations in 1942

18. Monarch and Heir-Apparent: the King and Princess Elizabeth at Windsor

Braving his fear of heights, the King clambers up to a gun turret

20. With General Montgomery sitting beside the driver, the King inspects troops in Nor Africa, 1943

The Princess Royal visits an AA battery in Scotland

. Viscount Lascelles, between companions, on the Italian front

23. Conferring knighthoods at a makeshift ceremony in Italy, 1944

24. The King at a forward observation post at Arezzo, Italy

. Wearing battledress for the first time, the King with General Eisenhower in Belgium

26. With Allied heads of government (*from left to right*): Queen Marie of Yugoslavia, Madame Benes, Queen Wilhelmina of the Netherlands, Madame Raczkiewicz, the King, King Peter of Yugoslavia, King Haakon VII of Norway, the Queen, Monsieur Raczkiewicz, President of Poland, Dr Benes, President of Czechoslovakia

27. Princess Elizabeth's eighteenth birthday. *Front row (from left)*: Queen Mary, the King, Princess Elizabeth, the Queen. *Back row*: the Duke and Duchess of Gloucester, Princess Margaret, the Princess Royal, Princess Marina, the Earl of Harewood

. Followed by Princess Elizabeth in her new uniform, the King and Queen attend the
emorial service to President Roosevelt, 1945

29. Queen Mary entertains Eleanor Roosevelt at Badminton

seems to have been quickened by the entry of America into
the war. Queen Mary was very taken by the American
servicemen who now came crowding into the West Country. She found their frankness, colourful language and lack
of reverence refreshing. Of all the servicemen to whom she
gave lifts in her Daimler, Americans proved the most
diverting. They were never dumbstruck, as British soldiers
tended to be, by her presence. As often as not, they had not
the slightest idea who she was.

'Say, what kind of a set-up is this?' asked one GI as he
clambered into the hearse-like car with its rigidly upright,
elaborately dressed, other-worldly looking occupant.

'It's called a *Daimler*,' answered Queen Mary.[9]

To a couple of bemused American officers who had been
invited to tea at Badminton, she once airily remarked,
'Perhaps we should still be one country, if my great-
grandfather hadn't been so obstinate.'[10] In one sentence, the
Queen had spanned, and reduced to a family matter, the 170
years between the American War of Independence and the
Second World War.

In the furtherance of Anglo-American relations, Queen
Mary once attended a baseball match between two US
Army teams. She listened, with absorbed attention, to the
eager American voices explaining the rules of the game and,
when it was over, agreed to be photographed with the
teams. Among the grinning young men she stood, in her
ostrich-feather-trimmed coat and toque, with a lace parasol
in one hand and, in the other, the ball with which the teams
had just been playing.

Queen Mary's most important American visitor was
Eleanor Roosevelt. In the course of her visit to Britain in
October 1942, Mrs Roosevelt spent a day with the American
forces stationed in the West Country. She was invited by
Queen Mary to stay the night at Badminton. President
Roosevelt had particularly wanted his wife to see Queen
Mary because the old Queen had been 'so nice' to his
mother, the equally redoubtable Sara Roosevelt. Eleanor

Roosevelt was met at the door of the house by Queen Mary herself, who then conducted her to her room. It was 'as vast as a barn' and icy cold but 'very grand with Chinese Chippendale furniture'. The Queen next showed her guest the bathroom and lavatory. They, too, were as cold as ice.

Dinner, as Eleanor Roosevelt put it, was 'not a hilarious meal' in spite of her 'valiant efforts' to keep the conversation going.[11] Nor were the fifteen minutes spent standing stiffly in the drawing-room afterwards any more amusing. Queen Mary then invited her guest, and the Princess Royal who happened to be visiting her mother, into her private sitting-room. Here the three of them spent an hour in conversation. Mrs Roosevelt found it heavy-going: there were so many points of etiquette to be remembered. Queen Mary, however, remained serenely unaware of any awkwardness. 'Mrs R. and I had an agreeable talk both before and after dinner,' she noted in her diary that night. 'She has a wonderful grasp of things in general.'[12] And in a letter to Lord Athlone, the Queen was even more generous in her praise of Mrs Roosevelt. 'I liked her very much,' she wrote, 'she is very intelligent and her grasp of what our women are doing here is splendid, and she hopes to do much in the USA to wake up the women there to emulate our manifold activities. She is on the go from morning till night and I fear will kill her unfortunate secretary Miss Thompson . . .'[13] (When Cecil Beaton complained to Queen Elizabeth about Mrs Roosevelt's 'lack of repose', the Queen's answer was characteristically perceptive. 'Oh! But she has such *animation*,' she protested.)[14]

When the relieved Eleanor Roosevelt left the following morning, Queen Mary presented her with a signed photograph to give to the President. It showed the Queen 'fully dressed in hat, gloves and veil, sawing a dead limb off a tree'. President Roosevelt, apparently, 'loved it'.[15]

Normally so stiff, Queen Mary never ceased to amaze her companions by her unexpected outbursts of informality. One day as she and a guest were strolling through the grounds at Badminton, they met a young woman accompanied by a boy of three or four. Queen Mary suddenly bent down, grasped the child's hands in her own and whirled him round several times. 'Never forget', she exclaimed, 'you've waltzed with an old lady of seventy-five!'[16]

The Queen, noted the guest, was actually 77 by then.

The informality and austerity of wartime were affecting all aspects of her life. Dinner, which was served at precisely 8.30 every night, was confined to the regulation three courses and was, according to one guest, 'by no means plentiful'.[17] In order to save laundering, the table was covered with an oilcloth designed to resemble linen which could be sponged down afterwards, and everyone was obliged to use hitherto despised napkin rings. Queen Mary's was a heavy silver ring, engraved with a crown and her monogram, but the rest of the guests were provided with celluloid rings. Deliberately furling her napkin and tucking it into her ring, Queen Mary once pointed to her deaf old equerry, Sir Richard Molyneux, and said, 'I believe Dick over there disapproves of my doing this, but I've had to do it now for nearly five years!'[18]

Another concession to wartime conditions was the abandoning, by the royal pages, of their scarlet coats in favour of the navy blue battledress with the royal cipher on the breast which the King had introduced at Windsor and Buckingham Palace. Most of the members of Queen Mary's long-serving staff bitterly resented the change. Indeed, one incensed page promptly handed in his notice. Sending for him, the Queen explained that he was guilty of an act of open rebellion against his sovereign's commands.

But nothing – not oilcloth, napkin rings or inadequate food – could lessen the regal atmosphere of Queen Mary's dinner table. The fare might be simple but it was served by no less than four footmen. The Queen always looked superb. 'With her clear skin,' wrote the visiting Osbert Sitwell, 'she could wear white and such colours as usually only girls wear, and still look well in them.' At dinner, she would wear evening dresses of silver lamé or aquamarine sequins, with pearl and diamond chokers, sapphires and 'huge diamond and pearl brooches and pendants'.[19] Churchill's secretary, John Colville, dining with her at Badminton, claimed that 'never have I seen a woman who carries so much jewellery so well'. For her seventy-seven years, he said, 'she is most uncommonly alert, quick and un-bowed'.[20]

Queen Mary insisted on a two-foot space on either side of her at meals and usually drank, during these war years, only water. In peacetime, it was different. Then she drank hock. On the infrequent occasions that she dined out, Queen Mary would be accompanied by her own liveried footman car-rying two half-bottles of hock. One of these he would open and, throughout the meal, keep his mistress's glass – but hers alone – replenished. If she asked for the second bottle to be opened, her hosts knew that their dinner party had been a success.

As dinner-table companions, the Queen preferred men. 'Queen Mary was one of those women', maintained her granddaughter, Princess Margaret, 'who prefer male com-pany. Although my mother [the Queen] always said that she was a wonderful mother-in-law, Queen Mary didn't really like other women. She would put herself out *tremendously* for men, and could be utterly charming. After the war, when some of my men friends were obliged to sit next to Queen Mary at dinner, they would come away enchanted. "She was so interesting," they would say, "and she was so interested in what we had to say."'[21]

This might explain why – at Badminton certainly – Queen Mary never allowed the men to sit on at the table after dinner. She would lead the company into her drawing-room where she would seat herself in her own special chair. This was not an armchair but a high-backed chair, upholstered in red leather, dating from the reign of William IV. This throne-like chair did not, claims Osbert Sitwell, 'suit the room . . . but it did exactly suit Queen Mary'.[22] She had spotted it in a lumber-room and had immediately ordered it to be brought down for her own use.

Once seated, Queen Mary and her lady-in-waiting would whip out their knitting. Not a moment, particularly no moment in wartime, must be wasted. 'Haven't you any work to do?' she would ask of any guest, male or female, who sat with idle hands.[23] Even her host, the Duke of Beaufort, during the times that he was on leave from his regiment, would be compelled to knit scarves by using a wooden framework of pegs.

If she were not knitting, Queen Mary would be employed in some equally profitable fashion: pasting in photographs, sorting papers, identifying pictures. The bombing of 'poor beautiful Bath' in 1942 distressed her considerably. But even this tragic event gave her the opportunity, after having toured the devastated city, of making one of her celebrated, minutely detailed lists, recording the extent of the damage. '*Circus*: 19, 20 & 21 still on fire, large bomb dropped in centre of road. *Assembly Room*: gutted with fire, nothing saved. *Gay Street*: very little damage . . .'[24] Copies of this doleful list were dispatched to various friends.

Their hands usefully occupied, the company would listen to the evening news on the radio. No matter how bad, or good, the news might be, 'never by the flicker of an eyelash would Queen Mary show that she was disturbed, or make any comment', claims Osbert Sitwell. Only once, he says, did he see Her Majesty's expression change during the news. This was at the mention of the word 'Transylvania'. The Queen caught the eye of her niece, the Duchess of Beaufort, smiled 'rather archly' and dreamily repeated the word, 'Transylvania, Transylvania!' 'The joke is', she explained to the rest of the company, 'that some of us come from there.' To those who saw Queen Mary purely as a stiff, uncompromising, somewhat Germanic figure, the claim seemed unlikely but her paternal grandmother had indeed been born in Transylvania. 'Queen Mary's beautiful Magyar or Romanian grandmother', noted the perceptive Osbert Sitwell, 'accounts for many traits in her – her eyebrows, and her eyes, set at an angle; the manner in which she smoked cigarettes; her love of jewels, and the way she wore them; and the particular sort of film-star glamour that in advanced age overtook her appearance, and made her, with the stylisation of her clothes, such an attractive and imposing figure.'[25]

For certainly, in spite of all her concessions and adaptations to a changing wartime world, it was as an *outrée*, decorative, almost unreal relic from another age that Queen Mary was chiefly remarkable. One night at Badminton, as this 'magnificent figure, blazing and sparkling', took leave of the company, Sir Richard Molyneux turned to a guest and said 'in his loud deaf voice, like that of a man shouting from a cave into a strong wind, "I wonder if you realise it, but after that old lady has gone, you'll never see anything like this, or like her, again!"'[26]

One of the decisions taken at the Churchill-Roosevelt conference in Quebec in August 1943 was for the launching of a joint Anglo-American invasion of Western Europe. This offensive across the English Channel was to be known, officially, as Operation Overlord but would come to be known, more generally, as the D-Day landings. It was a venture in which the King was closely involved.

At first, he had not favoured the idea of a landing in Normandy. His attitude had been inspired by the South African Prime Minister, Field Marshal Jan Smuts who, in October 1943, had come to London for a meeting of Commonwealth prime ministers. Smuts, the one-time Boer enemy who had since become an ardent imperialist, was a great favourite with the royal family. Part sage, part simple son of the veld, he had the sort of frank and natural manner which greatly appealed to them. 'He was a wonderful man,' remembered the Queen. 'He knew so much; he was always so interesting.'[27]

The King, who set great store by Smuts's political and

military opinions, was very impressed by his views on the proposed Normandy landings. With the Allies having already achieved a successful invasion of southern Italy, Smuts felt that they should concentrate their efforts on the Mediterranean front. They should consolidate their Italian gains, liberate Greece and Yugoslavia, and move up towards Hungary and Romania. 'If you have a good thing, stick to it,' wrote the King in his diary after his meeting with Smuts. 'Why start another front across the Channel?'[28]

So taken was the King by Smuts's reasoning that he decided to exercise his royal prerogative of advising and warning his Prime Minister. He wrote Churchill a long letter in which he passed on Smuts's views and suggested that the three of them meet to discuss the matter. They met, for dinner at Buckingham Palace, that same night. 'We discussed the whole strategy of the war at length,' recorded the King but, in the end, Churchill was able to convince the other two that – despite his own preference for a strike through the Balkans – neither Roosevelt nor Stalin would agree to a cancellation of Overlord.[29] The Normandy landings would take place, as planned, in June 1944.

In the months before Overlord, the King did whatever he could towards preparations for the great day. He travelled the length and breadth of Britain inspecting and encouraging the troops. He held long discussions with the various commanders, including Eisenhower and Montgomery. He spent several days with the fleet at Scapa Flow. He attended the famous secret conference at St Paul's School at which the final plans for Overlord were presented to a distinguished military audience, including Churchill, Smuts, the Chiefs of Staff and over 150 commanders of the land, sea and air units due to participate in the D-Day landings.

'I could not help reflecting as I looked round the room,' wrote Sir Alan Lascelles, 'that there had probably been no single assembly in the last four years the annihilation of which by a single well-directed bomb would affect more profoundly the issue of the war.'[30]

At the end of the meeting the King, quite unexpectedly, mounted the platform and, without notes, made a speech of 'impressive brevity'.[31] Those who had imagined the King to be little more than a figurehead – an unintelligent, uninformed and inarticulate royal cipher – were very taken by this self-confident speech. 'Absolutely first class,' commented Montgomery.[32]

Something of this same self-confidence characterized the King's handling of another proposed D-Day preparation. George VI was a sincerely religious man, with an uncomplicated, unquestioning belief in God. He was very conscious of his title of Defender of the Faith and few of his wartime speeches did not include a heartfelt and quite unselfconscious call to the Almighty for guidance and comfort. But as a man of simple faith, the King preferred simplicity in matters of worship. This is why he unhesitatingly rejected the idea of staging a grandiose ceremony in St Paul's Cathedral for the hallowing of those servicemen due to take part in Overlord. It had been suggested that on 12 May 1944 – the seventh anniversary of his Coronation – the monarch should attend a service at which the Coronation regalia would be paraded. Not only did the King consider the project distasteful, he also pointed out that the Coronation regalia had already been consecrated to a unique purpose.

The proposal was finally dismissed with another of Sir Alan Lascelles's wry observations. 'This', he wrote, quoting the Younger Pitt, 'is neither a fit time nor a proper subject for the exhibition of a gaudy fancy or the wanton blandishments of theatrical enchantment.'[33]

During the last few days before the launching of Overlord, the King and his Prime Minister were involved in a clash of wills. On 30 May – seven days before D-Day – Churchill, in the course of his usual lunchtime audience with the King, 'glibly' informed the monarch that he intended watching the assault from HMS *Belfast*, one of the 'bombarding ships'. When the King, who had for some time been thinking along the same lines, announced his intention of accompanying Churchill, the Prime Minister was all agreement. And so, on being told about it, was the Queen. 'She was wonderful as always and encouraged me to do it,' noted the King.

Distinctly less encouraging was Lascelles. In fact, he was appalled. That both the sovereign and the Prime Minister should risk their lives in this fashion seemed foolish in the extreme. Who, Lascelles asked the King drily, should the 18-year-old Princess Elizabeth choose as her prime minister in the all-too-likely event of both the King and Churchill being killed?

By the following morning, the King's habitual common sense had reasserted itself. He realized how foolhardy it would be, not only for himself, but also for Churchill to risk his life in this venture. Resigning himself to his disappointment, he wrote to the Prime Minister suggesting that he, too, reconsider the plan. 'I don't think I need emphasise what it would mean to me personally, and to the whole Allied cause, if at this juncture a chance bomb, torpedo, or even a mine, should remove you from the scene.'

But Churchill was not so easily dissuaded. Not even when the King backed up his letter by a visit to 10 Downing Street the following day could Churchill be talked round. When the accompanying Lascelles, who was becoming more alarmed by the minute at the possibility of the King having to find a new prime minister in the middle of the Allied invasion, drew Churchill's attention to the constitutional point that no minister of the crown could go abroad without the sovereign's consent, the Prime Minister had an answer ready. He would not be going abroad: he would be on a British warship and therefore on British territory.

By now the King was equally alarmed at Churchill's continuing obstinacy. 'I am very worried at the P.M.'s seemingly selfish way of looking at the matter,' he confided to his diary. 'He doesn't seem to care about the future, or how much depends on him.'

On the following morning, a mere three days before

D-Day, the King wrote once more to Churchill. In a cogently argued letter, in which he drew attention to his own sacrifice in not accompanying the expedition ('I am a younger man than you, I am a sailor, and as King I am the head of all three Services. There is nothing I would like to do better . . .'), he again begged the Prime Minister to change his mind. 'I ask you most earnestly to consider the whole question again and not let your personal wishes, which I very well understand, lead you to depart from your own high standard of duty to the State.'

Churchill received this second letter just before he was due to set out for Eisenhower's headquarters near Portsmouth. He did not immediately reply to it. The King, by now very worried indeed, decided that there was only one thing left for him to do: he would have to drive to Portsmouth at dawn the following morning to ensure that the Prime Minister did not embark with the invasion force.

In the end, this proved unnecessary. When Lascelles telephoned Churchill, he was assured that the monarch's latest plea had proved successful. In deference to his sovereign's wishes, the Prime Minister had given way.

'He has decided not to go on the expedition,' wrote the relieved King, 'but only because I have asked him not to go.'

Not until six days after the successful D-Day landings did Churchill visit Normandy, and not until four days after that was the King able to follow him. Shepherded by the ebullient General Montgomery, he spent 16 June inspecting the terrain and decorating some officers and men. He was back in Portsmouth at nine that evening.

'A long and interesting day,' he noted in his diary that night. It was most encouraging, he added gamely, 'to know that it was possible for me to land on the beaches only ten days after D-Day'.[34]

On 21 April 1944 Princess Elizabeth celebrated her eighteenth birthday. This milestone was rendered more significant by the fact that, during the previous year, by the

King's express wish, the Regency Act had been amended. Until it was, there had been a curious legal anomaly whereby the Princess would be capable of reigning as Queen once she reached the age of 18 but not as Regent during some incapacitation of her father until she turned 21. A suggestion that she, as the future Queen, be given the title of Princess of Wales was firmly scotched by the King. 'How could I create Lilibet the Princess of Wales', he explained to Queen Mary, 'when it is the recognised title of the wife of the Prince of Wales?' In any case, he added, 'her own name is so nice . . .'[35]

The Princess's birthday was marked by a special Changing of the Guard in the quadrangle at Windsor Castle, at which she was handed the Colonel's Standard, and by a family lunch attended by Queen Mary. That night the royal family went to the Palace Theatre to see *Something in the Air*, starring Jack Hulbert and Cecily Courtneidge.

The Princess's birthday did not, though, bring her much in the way of personal emancipation. In spite of her understandable anxiety to be more profitably employed, she was kept firmly at Windsor. 'Everyone serves', she sighed, '*except me.*'[36]

There had, though, been some progress. The Princess had already been given a lady-in-waiting and, equally important, a sitting-room of her own. Since 1942, Crawfie's somewhat limited educational abilities had been augmented by the appointment of an additional teacher. This was the Belgian-born Madame de Bellaigue, wife of the Vicomte Pierre de Bellaigue, who had escaped to Britain just before the German invasion of her country. A well-educated, highly cultured woman, Madame de Bellaigue taught the princesses history and literature in French. In this way – for 'Toni' de Bellaigue was a more cosmopolitan woman than Crawfie – the princesses' horizons were considerably broadened. Sir Henry Marten, who still had overall control of Princess Elizabeth's education, explained to the new teacher that it did not matter if her pupil forgot dates and events: 'Education broadly speaking was to help a student to learn, to appraise both sides of a question, thus using his judgement.'

From the beginning, claims Mme de Bellaigue, Princess Elizabeth had very good judgement. 'She had an instinct for the right thing. She was her simple self, *très naturelle*. And there was always a strong sense of duty mixed with *joie de vivre* in the pattern of her character.'[37]

When the precocious 14-year-old Princess Margaret asked if she, too, could begin history tutorials with Sir Henry Marten, she was told that for *her*, it was 'not necessary'.[38]

Mme de Bellaigue's mention of Princess Elizabeth's *joie de vivre* is significant. At 18, the Princess was an attractive young woman, with dark brown hair, deep blue eyes and a beautiful skin. Her smile, revealing flawless teeth, was radiant. Although she was reserved with strangers, her manner could become very animated in the company of those whom she knew well. And life at Windsor Castle, particularly during the latter years of the war, was never as gloomy or restrictive as is generally believed. Quite often, the princesses were able to get away. They accompanied their parents to a film studio to watch the shooting of Noël Coward's *In Which We Serve*. They attended the Thanksgiving Service in St Paul's Cathedral for victory in North Africa. (Chips Channon described them 'as dressed alike in blue, which made them seem like little girls'.)[39] They stood beside their parents at reviews outside Buckingham Palace or accompanied them on tours of inspection. They spent short holidays at Balmoral ('absolute heaven', recalled Princess Margaret)[40] and at Sandringham where the lawns had been given over to oats and rye, the golf course to potatoes and the flowerbeds to beetroot and parsnips.

The artist Rex Whistler, serving with the Welsh Guards in Norfolk, was one of a small group of officers invited to dine with the royal family at Sandringham. He was placed on Princess Elizabeth's right. He found her 'gentle and a little demure from shyness but not *too* shy, and a delicious way of gazing – very serious and solemn – into your eyes while talking, but all breaking up into enchanting laughter if we came to anything funny. After dinner I had a most enjoyable talk with the Queen about paintings she had bought – and painters – and books – and poets – and that fantastic *Poetry-reading orgy* [organized by Osbert and Edith Sitwell in the Aeolian Hall on 14 April 1943], and we bellowed with laughter. The K. in very good form, and all as though they hadn't a care in the world!'[41]

On her journeys to or through London, the young Princess Margaret was surprised at how much of the capital had *not* been flattened. 'We heard so much about the bombing', she said, 'that I expected everything to have been destroyed. There was really quite a lot still standing.'[42]

At Windsor the princesses were often visited by their cousins or other young friends. Every day they would chat to the young officers of the Windsor 'Body Guard'. There were usually two more young officers, either on leave or convalescent, who took meals with them, and there were frequent tea parties for visiting American or Commonwealth airmen. The princesses followed the exploits of military heroes as eagerly as did any other young girls. One fighter pilot, on being awarded his DSO by the King, was highly gratified to hear from the monarch that 'Princess Elizabeth will be much excited when I tell her I have seen and decorated you; she follows all your adventures.'[43] The princesses and their companions played charades and parlour games, and, often with Princess Margaret at the piano, enjoyed singsongs. 'The Princesses' lives did not seem secluded to me', maintains Mme de Bellaigue. There was 'plenty of mixed company – all great fun. There were games all over the Castle involving many amusing incidents . . .'

'They never forgot there was a war on and they were much aware of the sadness brought on by casualties,' she continues, 'but there was no feeling of doom and gloom.'[44]

A permanent wartime guest at Windsor Castle was the affable Irish artist Gerald Kelly. Commissioned in 1938 to paint the official portraits of the new King and Queen, Kelly had been obliged, because of the outbreak of war, to move the still unfinished paintings to the safety of Windsor Castle. He had not been long in following them. In order to apply the 'finishing touches' to the portraits, it would be necessary, he explained, for him to be given temporary accommodation in the castle. He stayed for five years. With a bedroom to sleep in, the Grand Reception Room to work in, all meals provided – often in the company of the royal family – Gerald Kelly was in no hurry to finish the portraits. Indeed, it was rumoured that, like Ulysses's wife Penelope, 'he undid each night what he had added during the day'.

To the King's mildly expressed protests about the length of his stay, Kelly remained cheerfully deaf. Nor was he dislodged by the portrayal of himself, in one of the princesses' Christmas pantomimes, as 'Kerald Jelly, the immovable guest'.[45]

Affording Princess Elizabeth the greatest pleasure during these years was her gradually developing relationship with the young Prince Philip of Greece. Five years older than her, Prince Philip had apparently first come to her attention during a royal family visit to the Naval College at Dartmouth just before the war. That she had been taken by the blond, handsome, extrovert 18-year-old cadet there is little doubt. The two of them were distantly related. Prince Philip's father was Prince Andrew of Greece and his mother, Princess Alice of Battenberg, was one of the many great-granddaughters of Queen Victoria. As a Prince of Greece, he was also a first cousin to Princess Marina, the Duchess of Kent; their fathers had been brothers.

Prince Philip's family had been tossed here and there on the turbulent tides of Greek politics, and he was educated mainly in Paris and at the two experimental schools of the celebrated Kurt Hahn: Salem in Bavaria and Gordonstoun in Scotland. From Gordonstoun he had entered the Royal Naval College at Dartmouth. He served throughout the war, chiefly in the Mediterranean and the Far East.

During these war years Prince Philip kept in touch with

Princess Elizabeth. They would write 'cousinly'[46] letters to each other and occasionally he would be invited to stay at Windsor. He was certainly in the audience at one of the famous Christmas pantomimes. According to Crawfie's always sugary account, the fact that Prince Philip, looking 'more like a Viking than ever', was in the front row caused Princess Elizabeth to turn pink and to sparkle in a way 'none of us had ever seen before'.[47] The picture given by one of Prince Philip's biographers – that of a young sailor rolling in the aisle at the dreadful jokes – is probably a more accurate one.

As early as 1941 Chips Channon, who always had an eye for a good-looking young man, was describing Prince Philip as 'extraordinarily handsome' and the future 'Prince Consort'.[48] The burgeoning friendship between the almost penniless Prince and the future Queen was certainly encouraged by the exiled Greek royal family as well as by the young man's dynastically ambitious uncle – his mother's brother – Lord Louis Mountbatten. George VI, though, was not nearly so enthusiastic. When Mountbatten suggested that the Prince renounce his Greek nationality in favour of British citizenship as a first step towards an engagement, the King warned him that he was going too fast. Let the young man change his citizenship but don't let him assume that this would automatically lead to marriage.

'I like Philip,' wrote the King to Queen Mary in March 1944. 'He is intelligent, has a good sense of humour and thinks about things in the right way.' Indeed, the Prince was very much the sort of chaffing, honest, outdoors kind of man that the King liked. But both he and the Queen considered their daughter 'far too young for that now, as she has never met any young men of her own age'.[49]

But Princess Elizabeth, according to the King's official biographer (whose manuscript was read and approved by Queen Elizabeth II before publication), had been in love with Prince Philip 'from their first meeting'.[50] She certainly displayed his photographs, both clean-shaven and bearded, in her sitting-room at Windsor. And Queen Mary had to admit that her granddaughter was the 'kind of girl' who, having fallen in love, would not change her mind. She would always remain 'very steadfast and determined' in her emotions.[51]

9

'Entering as a Conqueror'

GREATLY STIMULATED by his journeys to North Africa and Normandy, the King was anxious to visit the Italian front. That he could consider doing so was due to the dramatically changed situation in that country. Soon after the Allied invasion of Sicily, Mussolini had been deposed; and, on 3 September 1943, the new Italian government had surrendered unconditionally. By mid-1944 the southern half of Italy was in the hands of the Allies while the northern half – including Mussolini's little comic-opera state, called the Republic of Salo – was still controlled by the Germans. Mussolini was now little more than a German puppet.

In discussing his proposed visit with Churchill, the King indicated that he would like to spend a week with the troops and then have a day in recently captured Rome. At this, the Foreign Office took fright. A royal visit to the troops was perfectly acceptable; what was worrying was the proposed visit to Rome. King Victor Emmanuel III had, with what Harold Macmillan called his 'eel-like qualities',[1] recently slithered out of Axis into Allied waters. The Italian King was thus a distinctly controversial figure. Any meeting, in Rome, between King George VI and King Victor Emmanuel would be fraught with difficulties.

Nor should the King meet the Pope. Pius XII's 'very neutral record in this war', warned the Foreign Secretary, Anthony Eden, would make such a visit unpopular in Britain. Churchill's objections were more robustly phrased.

'Obviously if the King enters Italy,' he wrote to Lascelles, 'he does so as a conqueror, and the Lieutenant of the Realm must visit *him*.' It would be much wiser for His Majesty, as the 'representative of the triumphant Monarchy of Britain',[2] to confine his visit to his army and to have no truck with the Italian King, the Pope or the post-Mussolini Italian government.

That settled, the King flew to Italy on 23 July 1944 for an eleven-day stay. His presence was warmly welcomed by General Alexander. 'Alex told me', recorded the King, 'that he was particularly glad I had come out at that moment as the troops rather feared that their campaign had been put in the shade by the Press ever since the landing in Normandy.'[3]

The King enjoyed his tour immensely. Macmillan, who met him on his arrival in Naples and accompanied him for some of the time, described the monarch as being 'in excellent form and most genial'; he was 'in highest spirits till the end'.[4] As the King moved about – sometimes by air, sometimes by road – on his tours of inspection, his accommodation varied considerably. On the Bay of Naples he stayed in the Villa Emma, the house in which Lord Nelson first met Lady Hamilton. From here he visited the former royal palace of Caserta where a luncheon was held in his honour. The great baroque salon in which the meal was served was, claims Macmillan's Private Secretary, 'a finer setting' than either Buckingham Palace or Windsor Castle could have boasted.[5] When the King flew north towards the front, he spent two nights in a couple of caravans at the headquarters of General Sir Oliver Leese overlooking Arezzo. The appointments in these caravans have been described as 'palatial': 'Louis XVI *fauteuils* with flowered satin seats, bowls of pink and white carnations and chintz curtains . . . a large marble bath reposing on a tiled floor . . . the royal lavatory, in a green sentry box, had a walnut seat and a paved and tiled floor'.[6] In the event of any sudden enemy shelling disturbing His Majesty while he was in that marble bath or on that walnut lavatory seat, a special dugout had been constructed behind the caravan.

The caravan provided by General Alexander, on the shores of Lake Bolsena, further south, seems to have been considerably less opulent. The caravan was the General's own and Alexander was amused to discover that the monarch 'was not at all satisfied with my simple comforts, and had fresh lighting installed and a small extra tent attached to the caravan. He also brought a bath made of some sort of rubber stuff – I think it came from a barrage balloon.'[7]

Perched on a pile of folded rugs so as to render him more visible to the troops stationed along the roads, the King was driven in an open car through the wild and hilly country along the front line south of Florence. He would arrive back covered in dust. Sometimes he would stop to chat informally to a group of men; at others he would hold formal inspections, not only of the British and Commonwealth troops but also of units of the American, French and Polish forces which made up Alexander's polyglot army. He toured recent battlefields and watched actual fighting and artillery bombardments.

'I was impressed by his retentive memory and his detailed knowledge of what was going on,' recalled Macmillan. 'When he is talking quietly, his judgement is sound and sensible.'[8]

That the King was in his element there is no doubt. Even the most uxorious husband and devoted father (and George VI's milieu was a particularly feminine one: with the exception of the Duke of Gloucester, his closest relations were all female) sometimes welcomes a period spent in exclusively male company. On these warm Italian nights, as he sat among the military personnel, with a glass of whisky in one hand and a cigarette in the other, the King's pleasure was very apparent. On one occasion he stayed up talking until well after midnight, making the Band of the Grenadier Guards play 'Lili Marlene' three times. On another he joined lustily in the chorus of a Polish folk-song played by a Polish band. When, at an al fresco meal near Monte Cassino, a chair collapsed under the considerable weight of General 'Jumbo' Wilson, the King roared with laughter. Like many shy people, he could become over-excited and voluble in company: 'he is sometimes rather wild in his talk', commented Macmillan.[9]

The King was especially amused by an incident which took place early on the penultimate morning of his stay. He was woken from sleep at the Villa Emma by a commotion on the nearby waters of the Bay of Naples. Sticking his head out of the window, he shouted for silence. Below, in a small fishing boat, sat a couple: a diminutive man and a statuesque woman. She was protesting loudly. The couple were in the process of being arrested by the picket boat which patrolled the waters outside the villa, on the grounds that they 'looked suspicious' and should not have been so close to the King's villa. Finally the incensed woman rummaged about in her fishing gear and shoved a large visiting card under the nose of the naval lieutenant in charge of the patrol. The card identified her as the Queen of Italy.

It appears that King Victor Emmanuel and Queen Elena, having just taken up residence in the neighbouring Villa Rosebery, had set out on an early morning fishing trip. George VI, warned by both Churchill and Macmillan to have nothing to do with the Italian royal family, contented himself with keeping the Queen's outsize visiting card as a souvenir.

'I do hope that you are keeping well through these rather grim days,' the Queen wrote to a friend towards the end of 1944.[10] There were two particular reasons for the grimness of the Queen's days during this period. Her father, the Earl of Strathmore, died in November that year. Although he was 89, his death brought with it the inevitable sense of loss and regret. Contributing to a more general grimness was the launching, in June that year, of Hitler's 'secret weapon': the

V1 flying bomb. These 'pilotless planes filled with explosives' (or 'doodle-bugs' as they were generally known)[11] had a considerable effect on public morale. Not only was this renewed bombing, after a long period of comparative calm, disheartening but the unpredictability of the V1s was unnerving. 'There is something very inhuman about death-dealing missiles being launched in such an indiscriminate manner,' complained the Queen to Queen Mary.[12]

'At Buckingham Palace . . .', wrote one of the equerries, 'I would listen to the V1s as they came roaring in to London. As long as that pulsating noise continued, all was well for those below; but as soon as the ram-jet engine spluttered to a stop it was time to get your head down, thrust your fingers into your ears, open your mouth and wait for the shattering blast.'[13]

Time and again the glass in the windows of Buckingham Palace was blown out and had to be replaced by squares of talc, and a bomb landing on Constitution Hill destroyed seventy-five yards of the Palace's boundary wall. Sixty people were killed when the nearby Guards Chapel at Wellington Barracks was hit. For several weeks after that, the King and Churchill held their weekly lunchtime meetings in the Palace air-raid shelter.

'The King showed remarkable phlegm under fire,' noted one member of the household. Not even when the doodle-bugs were buzzing overhead would he consider curtailing an investiture. Calmly, he would continue to pin on medal after medal. 'Only when one of those sinister missiles was actually visible through the window might he turn and remark "that was a close one".'[14]

It was estimated that during the first fortnight after the launching of the flying bombs, 1,600 people were killed and 10,000 wounded, and over 200,000 houses destroyed, in London alone. Once again, as in the months of the Blitz in 1940, the King and Queen toured the bombed areas. And once again, they were amazed and heartened by the reaction of the public to this renewed threat.

'I do feel so proud of the way our people are going through this terrible ordeal, for it *is* very hard to be bombarded once again,' wrote the Queen. 'It is cruel to lose everything, but the amount of times I have heard people say "Ah well, musn't grumble, must we" and in a philosophical way after escaping with just their lives! It's a great spirit and they deserve many years of real Peace.'[15]

The King, with his practical mind, was very interested in the measures being taken to combat these flying bombs. On several occasions he visited anti-aircraft batteries and fighter squadrons to see for himself what was being achieved. He seems not to have been greatly reassured. Perhaps his presence made everyone nervous, he commented charitably. Making *him* nervous was the 'inarticulate modesty' of many of the young fighter pilots to whom he spoke. Several of them were responsible for shooting down flying bombs but the King found these stiff-upper-lipped men difficult to talk to. In spite of the fact that 'they have all got stories to tell,' he sighed, 'they never say what they have done'.[16]

During one visit by the royal couple to an anti-aircraft battery, six flying bombs suddenly tore over in quick succession. Immediately the anti-aircraft guns opened fire, filling the air with thunderous noise and streaking shells. The King and Queen looked on 'with as much detachment as if it had been a duck shoot', wrote one astonished witness.[17] He could only pray that the guns would miss their targets so as to save Their Majesties from being hit by the debris of a crashing V1.

The V1 was followed by the V2, Hitler's second 'secret weapon'. These ballistic missiles were launched from installations in the Netherlands and the Pas de Calais, and fell with no warning, at great speed and to devastating effect, chiefly in the London area. 'Being supersonic, they hit before they were heard,' wrote one equerry bleakly, 'so the possibility of running for cover did not arise.' One evening, perhaps as 'a gesture of solidarity under the V2 bombardment', the King and Queen invited a young equerry and a lady-in-waiting to dine with them.[18] During the meal, a thunderous explosion rocked the Palace. The King sent the equerry to find out where the bomb had fallen. It had landed on a nearby pub, killing over a hundred people.

Contributing to his increasing self-assurance – and to the prestige of the British crown – was the fact that, of all Europe's monarchs, George VI was the one most firmly seated on his throne. All the other sovereigns were either in exile, in disgrace or virtual prisoners of the Nazi regime. It was to the King of England that most of his brother sovereigns, so woefully down on their luck, were now obliged to appeal for help and protection. And he, very conscious of his royal status, and of his responsibilities as the leading member of the illustrious family of kings, did whatever he could to support them.

London swarmed with exiled crowned heads during the war years. Some, like Queen Wilhelmina of the Netherlands and King Haakon VII of Norway, became symbols of national resistance. King George II of the Hellenes held court, for a while, at Claridges; King Zog and Queen Geraldine of Albania were at the Ritz; Queen Marie of Yugoslavia settled down in the Old Mill House in Grandsden, near Cambridge. Her son, King Peter II, spent some time studying at Cambridge and then won his wings in the Royal Air Force. Ex-Queen Ena of Spain came over for the funeral of her mother, Queen Victoria's youngest daughter, Princess Beatrice. In addition, countless minor members were accommodated in hotels, embassies and the homes of long-suffering friends.

With the British Foreign Office tending to regard the fluctuating fortunes of Continental monarchs as irrelevant to the main struggle, George VI was constantly having to champion their cause. After all, many of them were not only fellow sovereigns but also blood relations. 'If you start looking at Queen Victoria,' explained one exasperated exiled princess to her daughter as the girl sat puzzling over the

Almanach de Gotha, 'you'll find how practically everybody, in all the European Royal Houses, is related.'[19]

The King no more shared the Foreign Office view of King George II of the Hellenes – that he was cowardly, untrustworthy and pro-German – than he had fully believed their propaganda campaigns against King Leopold III of the Belgians and Prince Paul of Yugoslavia. He agonized about the reluctance of the British government to intervene in the affairs of Romania where, early in 1945, young King Michael bravely defied his pro-Axis government, only to become a puppet of the Russians. 'I feel so differently towards [him] than the attitude taken up by the Government,' sighed the King.[20]

But the monarch with whom the King was most closely involved during the war was young King Peter II of Yugoslavia. Born in 1923, King Peter was yet another of Queen Victoria's great-great-grandchildren. His father, King Alexander of Yugoslavia, had been assassinated in Marseilles in 1934; his mother was Queen Marie, one of the daughters of that most theatrical of twentieth-century queens – Queen Victoria's granddaughter, Queen Marie of Romania.

The King and Queen, as Duke and Duchess of York, had attended the infant's christening in Belgrade; in his capacity as godfather, or Koum, the Duke of York had actually held the baby during the ceremony. With Peter being only 11 at the time of his father's assassination in Marseilles, the Regency was entrusted to his father's cousin, Prince Paul. Prince Paul's pact with the Axis in 1941 led to the coup in which he was overthrown and a new government proclaimed in the name of the 17-year-old King Peter II. In just over a week, the infuriated Hitler had crushed the resistance and Peter II had been forced to flee to Britain.

'I am his Koom [*sic*], a sort of permanent god-father . . .', wrote the King in his diary on the night of King Peter's arrival in Britain. 'So I must look after him here. Perhaps it was destiny.'[21]

There was not, in fact, a great deal that the King could do for the small, dark, wilful young King. In any case, the boy's mother, the widowed Queen Marie of Yugoslavia, was by now also living in exile in England. The King saw that the young monarch's coming of age, at 18, was marked by a suitable ceremony in St Paul's Cathedral. He encouraged him to go up to Cambridge: 'The King [George VI] thinks it is much better that he should live the life of an ordinary undergraduate, only going home for the weekends,' wrote the King's Private Secretary to Sir Alexander Cadogan at the Foreign Office. Cadogan was in full agreement. 'We feel', he answered, 'that there is a great opportunity to ensure that the King [Peter] is thoroughly Anglicized during his stay in England. At present, apparently, he appears to admire the United States of America above other countries.'[22]

George VI also encouraged the young King to win his wings in the Royal Air Force. Typically, the one time that he lost his temper with his godson was when King Peter appeared in his presence with his uniform incorrectly worn. George VI, in common with the three British monarchs who preceded him, was obsessed with uniforms, orders and decorations. So the sight of young King Peter with the stiffening taken out of his cap, the top button of his tunic undone and a Cartier gold chain looped gracefully from one breast pocket, through the open buttonhole and into the other pocket, incensed him.

'What have you got all that stuff on for?' he demanded.

When the young man began to stammer out an explanation, the King cut him short. 'It looks damned silly and damned sloppy. Take it off and button up your jacket.'[23]

In the matter of what should have been King Peter's chief concern – the regaining of his throne – George VI was powerless. And so, as it turned out, was King Peter himself. First from Britain and then from Cairo, to which he had moved in order to be nearer his country, the young King could only watch helplessly as his support in Yugoslavia crumbled. Finally, with the Allied recognition of those partisans fighting under Tito as the true Yugoslav opposition to the occupying Nazis, and with Tito wanting nothing to do with the exiled monarchy, King Peter was obliged to return to Britain from Egypt.

Unable to help his godson in the political sphere, the King was able to do so in other ways. Soon after arriving in Britain, King Peter had fallen in love with Princess Alexandra of Greece, daughter of the short-lived King Alexander of the Hellenes and his morganatic wife, Aspasia Manos. The Second World War had deposited mother and daughter in Britain. King Peter's mother, the mannish and dogmatic Queen Marie, was violently opposed to the match. And so was the Yugoslav government-in-exile. Chief among their many objections was that with Yugoslavia so cruelly occupied, the King should be seen as having more serious things than marriage on his mind.

But King Peter, hopelessly in love, was blind to all objections. He and Princess Alexandra became engaged.

George VI proved sympathetic. Several times he received King Peter, alone and with his fiancée, and promised to do whatever he could to help the young couple. Princess Alexandra, meeting George VI and his family at Windsor for the first time, was enchanted by them. '"What a marvellous family," I thought. "How happy and tranquil, and *just right* they are,"' she afterwards wrote. 'This was the sort of home life I wanted, with children and dogs playing at my feet and the simple family jokes between husband and wife. It was nice to be with them; nicer still to share their homeliness for a while; but nicest of all to know, beyond any shadow of doubt now, that they were going to help us to start what I prayed would be the beginning of another such married life as theirs.'[24]

However, it was going to need more than the approval of the British monarch to reconcile King Peter's mother to the proposed marriage. In a violent scene between Queen Marie, King Peter and Princess Alexandra, the young King's mother resolutely refused to sanction the marriage. In the end, the young couple stormed out of her house. Eight days later, on 20 March 1944, they were married at the Yugoslav Embassy in London. George VI, as best man, and Queen Elizabeth headed a galaxy of royal guests, including Queen Wilhelmina of the Netherlands, King Haakon of Norway, King George II of the Hellenes, the Duke of Gloucester and Princess Marina, Duchess of Kent. The presence of the British sovereigns endowed the occasion with an importance which not even the conspicuous absence of the bridegroom's mother could offset. Queen Marie's official excuse for not attending was that she had toothache.

With so many exiled members, both major and minor, of Europe's royal houses crowding wartime London, it was hardly surprising that the general public was often confused about, or even oblivious to, their identity. The majority of them could walk, quite unrecognized, through the streets. Women like Queen Wilhelmina of the Netherlands or Queen Marie of Yugoslavia could easily be mistaken for dowdy middle-class matrons. (In later years Queen Louise of Sweden, rightly assuming that if she were involved in an accident no one would know who she was, always popped a card into her handbag on which was written, in bold capital letters, I AM THE QUEEN OF SWEDEN.)

Of them all, the immensely tall King Haakon of Norway was the one most likely to be noticed and identified. Yet even he could go unrecognized. Long after leaving Buckingham Palace, he regularly strolled over to pick up his mail which was addressed to the Palace so as to keep his actual residence secret. Once, on arriving at the BBC to record a wartime message to the British people, King Haakon announced himself to the receptionist. While she was telephoning through to the person whom he had come to see, the girl turned round to ask, '*Where* was it you said you were the King of?'[25]

★

During his visit to Italy in July and August 1944, George VI had been shown over Monte Cassino, scene of the recent bitter and prolonged battle. His guide was General Alexander. 'This was a great treat,' wrote Macmillan, 'and His Majesty seemed very pleased.'[26] The site would have held an additional interest for the King, for among the British troops engaged there had been his nephew, George Lascelles, eldest son of his sister Mary, the Princess Royal, wife of the 6th Earl of Harewood.

The 21-year-old Viscount Lascelles, serving with the Grenadier Guards, had arrived in Italy during the second phase of the Allied invasion, early in 1944. In what he describes as 'ferociously horrible' weather,[27] he was actively involved in the murderous campaign to capture the reputedly impregnable fortress. 'The mortality rate, or at least the risk of getting wounded,' as he laconically put it, 'was then very high.'[28] Not until 18 May, with the withdrawal of the German forces after relentless bombardment, did Monte Cassino fall to the Allies.

During this campaign, Lascelles was able to spend short periods of leave in nearby Naples. This gave him the opportunity to pursue his burgeoning interest in opera: an interest which was one day to turn him into a knowledgeable musical director. Eventually, he was to become the managing director of the English National Opera. ('It's very odd about George and music,' the perplexed Duke of Windsor once said. 'You know his parents were quite normal – liked horses and dogs and the country.')[29] In the ornate setting of the San Carlo Opera House in Naples, the young Lascelles first saw many of the world's great operas. It was an experience which not even the sometimes makeshift staging and second-rate performances could spoil. 'There must be thousands of wartime operatic converts who will bless the names [of these performers] if they can still remember them,' he later wrote.[30]

With the Germans in retreat, Lascelles's battalion was moved north, bypassing Rome and taking up position in the countryside south of Perugia. On 18 June 1944 they were ordered forward for a day of what Lascelles calls 'attacking and capturing minor German positions . . . a curious day, exhilarating in the speed with which we advanced'.[31] At midnight, in spite of being exhausted, he was sent out on patrol. His job was to discover if the road ahead had been mined. This led, as he wryly put it, to 'a small error of judgement'.[32]

In the darkness, they moved stealthily forward. A sudden shout of *'Halt! Wer da?'* warned them that they had advanced too far. In the resulting confusion Lascelles met with a hail of bullets as he darted across the road. He was hit in several places. 'The main sensation was not of great pain but of a tremendous and disconcerting blow.'[33]

At first light he was helped to a nearby farmhouse. But as he was bleeding so profusely, it was decided that he was too badly wounded to be moved back to base. His blood-soaked battledress was cut away and his wounds bandaged. The delay proved disastrous. Early that afternoon the Germans captured the farmhouse and he, together with four others, was taken prisoner. Except for his boots, beret, watch and bandages, he was naked. In this state Lascelles was briskly marched off, on a stretcher held shoulder-high, by four German soldiers.

In the course of the following month, as the German forces gradually fell back, Lascelles was shunted from one Italian hospital to another. In mid-July, by then almost recovered, he was moved to Germany; first to a prison camp near Munich and then to another near Cassel. In November he was moved yet again. This time he was taken to that most celebrated of German prisoner-of-war camps, Colditz, where the authorities were very interested in the fact that the new arrival was the nephew of the King of England.

For the Duke of Gloucester, Princess Elizabeth's eighteenth birthday – on 21 April 1944 – had a special significance. It marked the end of his term as Regent Designate. From that time on, in the event of any incapacitation of the King, Princess Elizabeth would immediately become Regent. On his death, she would become Queen. But until she turned 18, the Duke of Gloucester would have been obliged to act as Regent. How successfully, one cannot help wondering, would the Queen have adjusted to a situation in which the Duke and Duchess of Gloucester were the country's leading royal couple? She would certainly have been robbed of what were probably her most brilliant years: the six-and-a-half-year period between the end of the war and the death of the King early in 1952.

Although the Duke of Gloucester would hardly have regretted the loss of his position as Regent Designate, it left him feeling more superfluous than ever. 'Ever since September 1942 [when he returned from India]', he admitted to his mother Queen Mary, 'I have felt that I have been doing very little . . .'[34] What his official biographer calls the 'twilight phase'[35] of the Duke's career was given over, very largely, to routine tours of inspection, punctuated by visits to his mother at Badminton and to his brother at Balmoral. Having been obliged to give up his permanent position at the War Office in 1942, he gained most pleasure from the two other passions in his life: shooting and farming. Barnwell Manor, his Northamptonshire country home, remained a haven.

It was not, though, an entirely peaceful haven. The proximity of various air bases brought their own dangers. On at least two occasions, when the infant Prince William was on the lawn, planes narrowly avoided crashing in the grounds; on a third, a German plane jettisoned three bombs not far from the house. As Barnwell was not well guarded, the fear of being kidnapped by a team of enemy parachutists and being whisked off to Germany as royal hostages remained acute. The Duchess had worked out a plan whereby, in the event of such a raid, she would dash across to a nearby farmhouse where she would leave Prince William in the care of the farmer's wife. This woman, claiming that he was her grandson, would look after him until the end of the war. All that was necessary for the conversion of this scheme into a modern fairy-tale was for the farmer's wife to have swopped the royal baby for her own grandson and, many years later, for the handsome young peasant to have been revealed as the true prince.

The noise of the German planes, on their way to bomb Coventry and other Midlands cities, had a very noticeable effect on the animals, claimed the Duchess. 'Neither our ponies nor our bull mastiff paid any attention to the Allied planes passing overhead,' she said, 'but the minute they heard the slightly different sound made by a German engine, the ponies would get restless and the dog would dive under the sofa.'[36]

On 26 August 1944, the Duchess of Gloucester gave birth to a second son. Again Queen Mary was overjoyed. 'I am enchanted,' she wrote. She hoped that they would give the Prince the name of Richard; it sounded so well with Gloucester. The Duke was not so sure. As he, like the King, could not pronounce his 'R's', Richard presented difficulties. But in the end the baby was named Richard, and the Duke had to be content with saying 'William and Witchard'.[37]

By the time of Prince Richard's birth, a new prospect had opened up for the Duke of Gloucester. With Princess Elizabeth having turned 18, the Duke no longer needed to remain close at hand: he was now free to render the crown a different sort of service. It was decided that he should take up the post at one time intended for the late Duke of Kent: the Governor-Generalship of Australia. Perhaps the Gloucesters could prove as successful in Australia as the Athlones were proving in Canada.

Although daunted by this prospect of high office – for the Duke and Duchess remained shy, domestic, country-loving people – they accepted it without question. The couple might lack the strong public image of some other members of the family (Queen Mary was always complaining that their manifold duties were never sufficiently well publicized) but their sense of duty was no less strong. That going to Australia would mean leaving their beloved Barnwell and facing the uncertainties of wartime travel with two small children was simply one of those royal prices to be paid. The Duke hoped, he told his mother, 'to help Bertie' more effectively in Australia than at home.[38] 'Now I feel I have something definite to do makes all the difference,' he wrote gamely.[39]

The Duke and Duchess were seen off, officially, at Euston Station by the King and Queen and Princess Marina. 'I am sure they felt as anxious for our safety as we did ourselves,' wrote the Duchess.[40] As their departure from Liverpool had to be secret, their train was halted at some remote spot between Northampton and Rugby in order to pick up their two little sons and their nurses. They arrived in Liverpool in dense fog. The 3-year-old Prince William, on first seeing the vast bulk of the ship that was to take them to Australia, assumed it to be one of his maternal grandmother's many grandiose homes. Was it 'Granny Buccleuch's house?' he asked.[41]

'I hope they will be a success,' wrote Queen Mary to Lord Athlone after the Gloucesters had sailed away on 16 December 1944, 'it may give Harry a chance of showing what he is made of.'[42]

10

The Soldier Guest

IT WAS WITH the greatest interest that the King watched the advance of the Allied armies towards Germany. By 23 August 1944 Paris had been liberated; on 3 September British troops entered Brussels. By October the Germans had been all but driven out of France, Belgium and the southern part of the Netherlands, and the victorious Montgomery was headquartered with the 21st Army Group in the Dutch town of Eindhoven. 'Ever since you first explained to me your masterly plan for your part in the campaign in western France,' wrote a delighted George VI to General Montgomery, 'I have followed with admiration its day-to-day development. I congratulate you most heartily on its overwhelming success.'[1]

Always ready to bask in a little reflected royal glory, Montgomery invited the King to visit his Group HQ at Eindhoven. The monarch was only too ready to accept the invitation but, as usual, the proposal gave rise to a flurry of official reservations. The Palace was informed that it would be too dangerous for His Majesty to arrive at Eindhoven by air, or even to approach it by road. He was advised to stick to the 'back areas' or, better still, to headquarter himself in safer and considerably more luxurious accommodation in Brussels.

The reactions of the King and Montgomery to these mealy-mouthed suggestions were equally robust. His Majesty, claimed Lascelles, 'would rather put the whole thing off if the only alternative was to go and sit in the outskirts of Brussels'; while Montgomery dismissed the talk of risk as 'complete and utter nonsense'.[2] He would accept full responsibility for the sovereign's safety. That agreed, the King flew into Eindhoven on 11 October 1944 for a six-day stay.

'The visit is being made,' Montgomery had informed Churchill, 'on the very distinct understanding that there are no formal parades or inspections and the visitor is coming to stay at my TAC headquarters as a soldier guest as it were.' The only danger, he added pointedly, 'might be to the visitor's health. I live a caravan and tent life in the country, and it is very cold. I seldom wear less than four woollies and a fur flying jacket.'[3]

The King was accommodated in Montgomery's own caravan ('as an ordinary soldier guest, with no formality at all')[4] with the Royal Presence making no difference to the host's abstemious way of life. Montgomery neither smoked nor drank and went to bed every night at 9.30 sharp. Although the King would have adjusted himself well enough to Montgomery's spartan routine, he would have found some of his host's other traits somewhat trying. Promoted by the King to Field Marshal on 31 August 1944, Montgomery was a complex character. A great commander who liked to present himself as a simple soldier, he was also a fawning courtier. His boasting was legendary and his craving for affection equalled only, it was said, by his 'talent for arousing antagonism'.[5] George VI, always so punctilious about the wearing of uniform, was certainly irritated by Montgomery's insistence on wearing a Tank Corps beret instead of the regulation peaked cap. To the royal suggestion that he discard his beret, Montgomery grandiloquently claimed that it was one of the methods by which he maintained morale; to his men, he said, the sight of it was worth 'at least an Army Corps'.[6]

There is another, apocryphal, story to illustrate Montgomery's reputation for conceit. 'I'm worried about Monty;

I think he's after my job,' Churchill is reported to have said to the King. 'Thank God,' answered George VI, 'I thought he was after mine.'[7]

Yet there is no doubt that the King enjoyed his six-day stay. 'To say that this visit was an unqualified success is to put it mildly . . .', wrote the King's equerry, Sir Piers Legh, to Montgomery afterwards. 'I can recall no occasion when HM was in better form or enjoyed himself more.'[8]

And to Queen Mary's lady-in-waiting, Lady Airlie, the King praised Montgomery warmly. 'I like that man,' he said, when telling her about his Eindhoven visit. 'He has taught me more about the Army than anyone. You can understand what he says. He purposely doesn't confuse you with a lot of military terms.'[9]

During his stay at Eindhoven, the King spent one day visiting the First Canadian Army in its position near Antwerp. At lunch he met Prince Charles, the Regent of Belgium. By now Prince Charles's older brother, King Leopold III, had been deported to Germany, to a fortress-castle near Dresden. This saved George VI the embarrassment of having to decide whether or not he should meet the discredited Belgian monarch.

On another day the King was jolted along 200 miles of bomb-battered roads and over pontoon bridges to visit General Eisenhower in his headquarters near Liège. A few weeks before, Eisenhower had taken over from Montgomery as Commander-in-Chief Allied Ground Forces, an appointment which hardly made for a harmonious relationship between Eisenhower and the resentful Montgomery. Of this resentment, Montgomery would have kept the King only too well aware. But George VI was fond of Eisenhower and the lunch party, with twelve American generals, was a great success. The King was deeply touched by Eisenhower's speech of welcome ('If there is ever another war, pray God we have the British as an ally, and long live King George VI')[10] and Eisenhower, in his memoirs, mentioned the King's popularity with the American forces. Far from being the haughty and unapproachable figure of the average GI's imagination, the King 'liked the simple life of a soldier and was perfectly at home with all of us'.[11]

The King wore battle-dress for the first time during this Eindhoven stay (a style which suited him less well than some of his other uniforms) and he greatly admired the American version. The cloth from which it was made was superior to the stiff, rough-textured variety used by the British Army. He who, in peacetime, gave a great deal of attention to the clothes made for him by his tailors, Benson and Clegg, was very particular about fabrics. Aware of this royal interest, Eisenhower had a length of the American cloth sent to Buckingham Palace as a gift.

As the weather was too tempestuous for the King to fly home at the end of his stay, the royal party returned by sea. This proved equally tempestuous. But the King had been a sailor in his youth and while Lascelles and Legh were prostrate with seasickness, he remained on the bridge from where, dressed in oilskins, he stood staring out at the plunging sea.

While the King was fostering the Anglo-American alliance in Europe, his Canadian representative, the Earl of Athlone, was playing his part in North America. The Athlones kept in touch, both formally and informally, with President Roosevelt, and in March 1945, Lord Athlone and Princess Alice were invited to pay a state visit to Washington.

The couple were given, as Lester Pearson, then Canadian Ambassador to the United States put it, 'the full, red-carpet, head-of-state treatment'. There was an official welcome at the station by the President and Mrs Roosevelt, a roaring cavalcade through the streets of the capital, and a series of formal luncheons, dinners and receptions. The Ambassador experienced one heart-stopping moment when he thought that Lord Athlone, in toasting the President at a White House dinner, was going to refer to the beauty of Washington's famous 'Japanese' cherry blossom; but fully alive to the fact that Japan was the enemy, Lord Athlone deftly substituted 'Oriental' for 'Japanese'.

Lester Pearson was very taken with the Athlones. 'Their natural simplicity and kindliness made them easy and welcome guests. My experience of people has been that the more exalted they are in the social or official hierarchy, the less snobbish and difficult they are with others.' This was certainly true of the Athlones. Pearson considered Lord Athlone to be 'a born tourist, and a very nice, amiable man'. The Princess, though, was an exceptional personality: 'she had surely found the secret of perpetual youth and charm'.[12]

On 12 April 1945, a few weeks after the Athlones had returned to Canada, President Roosevelt suddenly died of a massive cerebral haemorrhage. The King was deeply shocked. He had always looked upon Roosevelt as a father-figure and, in spite of occasional irritation at the President's lapses as a correspondent, remained very fond of him. He had been looking forward to welcoming the Roosevelts to Buckingham Palace that summer. 'We are still under daily bombardment at the moment,' he had written in March, 'but we hope and trust the situation will be better in a few months' time.'[13]

To the King's personal sense of loss was added his appreciation of the national loss. 'He was a very great man and his loss will be felt the World over,' he wrote in his diary. 'He was a staunch friend of this country . . .'[14]

President Roosevelt's funeral brought Lord Athlone back to Washington. This time he came without the Princess and stayed at the Canadian Embassy. Once again, the Pearsons were impressed by his amiability. Heightening the Pearsons' appreciation of their guest was the little service he was able to render them in the matter of their matchless cook, Pearl. She was threatening to leave the Pearsons and return to her native Jamaica. Could His Excellency, begged the Ambassador, appeal to Pearl's staunchly pro-British and pro-Royalist sentiments by suggesting that her continued presence at the

Canadian Embassy was essential for ultimate British victory and as proof of her loyalty to the monarchy?

Lord Athlone complied; and Pearl stayed.

Lester Pearson had one more anecdote. One evening at dinner, Lord Athlone asked James, the stiff-backed British butler, the name of the white wine he was serving. It was a Liebfraumilch, but James, deciding that it would be improper to use a German word to a member of the British royal family in wartime, did a quick literal translation before answering.

'Milk of the Virgin, Your Excellency', came his unblinking reply.[15]

Not until the spring of 1945 did the King give way to Princess Elizabeth's entreaties to be allowed to join one of the women's services. 'Both of his daughters could be immensely persuasive, and had a habit of getting what they wanted in the end. Especially from their father,' wrote their governess. So, after considerable discussion, the Princess was allowed to attend the ATS training centre for drivers at Camberley. A Commandant Wellesley ('very brisk and hearty') arrived at Windsor one morning to whisk the Princess off to the Camberley depot. There she was registered as 'No. 230873, Second Subaltern Elizabeth Alexandra Mary Windsor. Age: 18. Eyes: blue. Hair: brown. Height: 5ft 3ins.' She was issued with the regulation khaki uniform and peaked cap.

From that time on, every morning, Princess Elizabeth was driven over to Camberley to join the squad of other girls going through the ordinary NCO's course. Except for returning to Windsor to sleep, she kept strictly to the routine of the depot, taking her turn as duty officer, doing inspections, maintaining vehicles. She learnt how to strip and service an engine, change wheels, read a map and drive in convoy. She was described as being 'efficient, neat and quick'. As a junior officer, the Princess had to salute her seniors. Crawfie, taking the envious Princess Margaret to tea at the mess, was somewhat disconcerted to see 'how hearty all the lady officers were, drinking sherry and smoking cigarettes'.[16]

There were the usual mishaps, rendered unusual by virtue of the fact that they were being committed by the King's daughter. 'What d'yer think yer doing?' barked one policeman to the girl who had stalled her truck broadside on Windsor Hill. 'I couldn't tell him,' laughed Queen Elizabeth II many years later, 'because I didn't know!'[17]

On the day of the Princess's final test, her parents came down to see her. They watched, fondly and proudly, as with smudged face and greasy hands, 'very grave and determined to get good marks', the Princess carried out her tasks.[18] The final triumph came some time later when she drove her company commander up from Aldershot through the thick of London's traffic to Buckingham Palace. The fact that she found it necessary to drive twice round Piccadilly Circus could have been due, noted one observer, either to high spirits or 'to a less than absolute mastery of the roundabout system . . .'[19]

During the remaining months of the war and, most noticeably, at the memorial service to President Roosevelt at St Paul's Cathedral in April 1945, Princess Elizabeth was frequently seen in public sporting her ATS uniform. The 14-year-old Princess Margaret, still obliged to wear the girlish clothes chosen by her mother, is reported to have been 'madly cross' about this distinction.[20]

For the captured Viscount Lascelles, Colditz Castle proved a particularly forbidding prison. As the nephew of King George VI he immediately became one of the *Prominente*: a small group of prisoners with illustrious connections, highly valued by the Nazis for their possible future use as hostages. Among other *Prominenten* were a nephew of Queen Elizabeth, a son of Field Marshal Haig, a son of the Viceroy of India, Lord Linlithgow, and a couple of members of Winston Churchill's family. Kept together under strict surveillance, the little band could hardly help feeling apprehensive about their future. They could only assume that, as the Allies advanced, so would they be shifted from camp to camp until they reached, somewhere in the mountainous heart of the German Fatherland, what was chillingly referred to as the Final Redoubt. There, as Lascelles put it, 'anything might happen'.[21] If their lives could not be successfully bartered, they would no doubt be executed.

Being a member of the *Prominente* in no way meant preferential treatment. In Colditz young Lascelles had to endure the same hardships and privations as all his fellow prisoners-of-war. His group lived in one room, on the ground floor of the castle. The great stone building was bitterly cold. To keep warm, the prisoners spent most of the day, fully clothed, in bed; at night, if there was any fuel, they would crouch round an inadequate little stove. In later life, Lascelles could not remember washing himself in camp. 'I suppose that we must have had the occasional cold shower but I have no memory of it at all,' he remarked.[22] What he had no difficulty in remembering was the hunger. They were always hungry. Their captors supplied them with a daily bowl of soup and bread; this meagre diet was augmented by Red Cross food parcels. During the first ten weeks at Colditz, Lascelles lost twenty pounds in weight. As a result the prisoners felt permanently lethargic. Occasionally they were taken out for walks but the dreariness of the winter landscape, allied to their own weakened state, made these outings dispiriting occasions.

Although Colditz was famous for its escapes, there were none – attempted or successful – during the five months that Lascelles was held there. This was because the prisoners had been instructed from Britain, by way of the secret camp radio set, that none were to be attempted. It appeared that in the wake of the celebrated plot to kill Hitler in the summer of 1944, a number of escaping RAF prisoners had been caught by the Germans and summarily shot. Any more escapees, found in certain unspecified areas of the country, warned the German authorities, would be similarly executed. This information could hardly have calmed the apprehensions of the *Prominente*.

For the most part, the prisoners spent their days reading and talking. As the *Prominenten* had had the advantage of a good education, their discussions were often on a fairly elevated level: literature, philosophy, religion. Sometimes there were more general, organized activities, involving the whole camp, such as poker schools, history lectures and music appreciation groups. In the end though, sighs Lascelles, 'the cold beat us'.[23] This, combined with the general lack of energy, might also explain why the inevitable flare-ups tended to die down very quickly and why – according to Lascelles – there were so few signs of homosexual activity in the camp.

Information about what was happening in the outside world came chiefly from the secret radio set. Once a day someone would tune in. In this way, the inmates could follow the progress of the war. 'I suspect that the Germans knew that we had a radio,' remembered Lascelles. 'If we were looking especially jaunty at morning inspection, they would know that we had heard good news.'[24] More personal news came by way of occasional letters. The habitual reserve of Lascelles's mother, the Princess Royal, was encouraged by the fact that she knew that her letters would have to pass the military censors. As a result, her letters were simply 'a catalogue of commonplaces: news about the weather, the garden, the names – or nicknames rather – of people who had visited Harewood House'.[25]

If anything, Lascelles's captivity tended to intensify his interest in music. Through the Red Cross he received not only books on music but also records, including all the late Beethoven Quartets, which he was able to play – over and over again – on a wind-up gramophone. His time in Colditz confirmed him in the belief that music must one day be his chief interest in life. 'I really wanted more than anything else to work in an opera house – in *any* capacity; I didn't care.

That was where I felt my contribution in life would be.'[26]

By the beginning of April 1945, with the advancing Allies – the Americans to the south and the Russians to the north – just a few days away, the *Prominente* realized that the hour of decision was at hand. Either they would be left at Colditz, to be liberated with the others, or they would be moved towards the dreaded Final Redoubt. By the night of Friday, 13 April, they knew their fate. They were to be moved on. Together with John Winant, the son of the American Ambassador in London, and half a dozen Polish generals and their staff, the *Prominente* were put aboard a bus.

'In the early hours of the morning we were off,' recalled Lascelles, 'in theory only to another camp, in practice on that journey towards the Final Redoubt . . .'[27]

For Queen Mary, Christmas at Badminton was hardly less of an occasion than it had been at Sandringham during George V's reign. The scale might have been reduced but the ritual remained the same: the house party, the tree, the meals and, above all, the present-giving. The gifts were displayed on an enormous table divided, by forty-year-old ribbons, into labelled sections, beginning with Queen Mary on the left and ending with the least important guest on the right.

Osbert Sitwell, invited to spend the last Christmas of the war at Badminton, was desperately worried about this gift-giving ritual. Where to find, in the depleted wartime shops, and how to pay for, given the high wartime taxes, so many presents? His hostess, the Duchess of Beaufort, had a solution to at least part of his problem. To save exchanging presents with her and the Duke, Sitwell could bring a couple of things he already owned and pretend that they had been given to him by the Beauforts; while they, in turn, could provide him with something of their own to give back to them. Accordingly, Sitwell brought cigarettes and a book as the Beauforts' gifts to him, and the Beauforts provided one of their own books and 'a green-shagreen *étui*, *circa* 1780' as his gifts to them.

Osbert Sitwell had reckoned without Queen Mary's intense curiosity about *objets d'art*. On Christmas Eve she came down to inspect the gifts. Very slowly she moved along the table, leaning forward to examine each item intently. What particularly interested Her Majesty was the *étui* which Mr Sitwell had given the Duchess. *Where*, she asked him, had he possibly found it? One did not often find such things nowadays. Poor Sitwell was obliged to blurt out some sort of reply. He was obviously convincing. 'I think Her Majesty had no inkling of the deceit we practised,' he later wrote.[28]

Osbert Sitwell could not help wondering, as he watched Queen Mary preside over the dinner table on Christmas night, whether she was thinking of 'other Christmasses in the past' when she had sat surrounded by her large family and household.[29] Of all her children, only the Princess Royal was present. The King was with his family, the Duke of Windsor was in the Bahamas, the Duke of Gloucester was on his way to Australia, the Duke of Kent was dead, and her only surviving brother, the Earl of Athlone, was in Canada. Would she rather have been at Sandringham, or even Marlborough House?

Field Marshal Smuts, who had visited Badminton the year before, had also wondered if Queen Mary would not have been happier back in London. This was certainly his impression when he lunched with her that day. 'Queen Mary,' noted Lady Airlie, 'who had a great liking and respect for Jan Smuts, talked animatedly to him at luncheon, but once or twice I saw a rather troubled expression in his eyes as they rested on her.'

In a snatched conversation after the meal, Smuts told Lady Airlie that he thought that 'the isolation of Badminton was depressing' the Queen. 'Queen Mary would be happier in her own home,' said Smuts, 'and there would be more to interest and distract her there than here. She needs to be drawn back into the world. I shall be seeing the King and Queen in a few days and I'll talk to them about it.'

Lady Airlie, although entirely agreeing with Smuts, explained that Queen Mary's chief concern was to cause the King no trouble.

'The King can easily put that right,' answered Smuts.

Together, he and Lady Airlie worked out a 'little plot': he would put the idea to the King and she would put it to Queen Mary.

But when Lady Airlie broached the subject later that evening, she found Queen Mary anything but enthusiastic. 'I don't see how I could possibly go back to Marlborough House with all the windows broken and my furniture all over the place,' she protested. Only later, says Lady Airlie, did she realize that Queen Mary loved the freedom of her life at Badminton; 'and that she had no intention of being pushed back to London'.[30]

If Smuts, on this occasion, was part of a plot concerning Queen Mary, she had once been part of a distinctly more bizarre plot concerning Smuts. There had been a suggestion, in 1940, that if anything should happen to Churchill, he should be replaced, as wartime Prime Minister, by Smuts. This revolutionary idea was eagerly taken up by Churchill's secretary, John Colville. As the King could choose whoever he wished as Prime Minister, argued Colville, why not choose Smuts? He deemed it 'a great Imperial idea': to have a Dominion politician as Prime Minister of England would be a living proof of the solidarity of the Commonwealth.

Colville promptly wrote to his mother, Lady Cynthia Colville, who was one of Queen Mary's ladies-in-waiting, proposing that she put this 'grandiose' scheme to Queen Mary. The old Queen, in turn, could 'filter' it through to the King.[31] Queen Mary was very enthusiastic. She had always admired Smuts; in fact, as she told Lady Cynthia, King George V had favoured the idea of Smuts as Prime Minister. Queen Mary duly passed the suggestion on to the King. His Majesty reacted, she was able to report, 'favourably'.[32]

React favourably George VI might have done (or he may simply have been being polite to his mother) but he could not seriously have considered choosing Smuts, with no mandate from the electorate, to assume the role of British Prime Minister. No more was heard of this 'great Imperial idea'.

Queen Mary's high regard for Smuts was more than matched by his for her.

'You are the *big* potato,' he once said in that homespun fashion which the royal family always found so beguiling. 'Next to you, the others are just *small* potatoes.'[33]

Always encouraged by his visits to the fighting forces, the King had for some time been considering a more ambitious journey: to India and to the troops commanded by the Supreme Allied Commander in South-East Asia, his kinsman, Lord Louis Mountbatten. He had long wanted to visit India and had come to regret the cancellation of his projected Durbar visit in 1937. In those first, uncertain days of his reign, the Durbar had loomed as too overwhelming a prospect; by now the more self-confident monarch was ready to face such challenges. The King was very conscious, too, of the fact that Mountbatten's troops saw themselves as the 'Forgotten Army'. Their planned offensives against the Japanese were constantly having to be cancelled in favour of European operations. Mountbatten, always ready to make the most of his royal connections, had kept the King fully informed on South-East Asian affairs. Writing to him by the 'safe route' – which meant that his letters would go straight to the monarch and not via the Prime Minister or the Chiefs of Staff – Mountbatten would not only send comprehensive surveys of the situation but would also make direct appeals for help.

The King's replies were always models of constitutional propriety. In no position to promise Mountbatten any military assistance, he was anxious to give his troops in South-East Asia some inspirational support. He felt sure that a royal visit to the men of the Fourteenth Army would 'buck them up'.[34] He planned to go in February 1945.

But Churchill was having none of it. The political situation in India was far too delicate. A visit by the King-Emperor might be regarded by the anti-colonialist Americans as some sort of reactionary imperialist gesture, and the Indians might expect a royal pronouncement on their constitutional future. The Prime Minister simply could not allow it.

The King deeply resented Churchill's attitude. He could not agree that a visit to his troops in the field would cause any trouble. But the idea remained in his mind. In early April 1945, when the Burmese front was again active, the monarch's ambitions were fuelled by Mountbatten. 'Once we have got Rangoon do *please* come out,' wrote the Supreme Commander. 'You can easily do a flying visit via Delhi without any previous announcement and go on after a day or two straight to Rangoon.' It would be the King's one chance, wrote the astute Mountbatten, 'of visiting your Indian capital without endless political complications and you have NEVER been there, whereas David [the Duke of Windsor], your father and grandfather all visited Delhi (1922, 1911 and 1876)'.[35]

But by the time Rangoon fell on 3 May 1945, events in Europe had moved on too fast. The last King-Emperor was destined never to set foot in his Indian Empire.

In his various efforts to associate himself more closely with the forces, the King, early in 1944, came up with an imaginative idea. He decided to appoint, as temporary equerries, young men with distinguished fighting records. This meant that they could be chosen from any walk of life and not merely from the customary aristocratic, regimental and interrelated family circles. As the Air Force was the one service not yet represented at court, the monarch approached Air Chief Marshal Sir Charles Portal, Chief of the Air Staff. Could he select a suitable candidate? The appointment would be for three months. Portal chose a much-decorated Battle of Britain pilot by the name of Peter Townsend.

Thirty years old, married and exceptionally handsome, Peter Townsend was a product of the middle classes which had hitherto played almost no part in court life. So adroitly did he adjust himself to his new environment that in very little time Townsend was almost indistinguishable from the other figures surrounding the monarch. His appointment, intended to last for three months, lasted for ten years.

As a newcomer, who came to know the royal family very well, Townsend's impressions of them during these last years of the war are especially interesting. He was first received by George VI, in the green-carpeted Regency Room at Buckingham Palace, in February 1944. 'The King was a man of medium build, lean and athletic,' wrote Townsend. 'His head, rather small, was statuesque, so finely chiselled were his features; his hair and skin had the look and the luminosity of bronze.' His blue eyes had 'a steady regard'.[36] Townsend was immediately struck by the monarch's simplicity. He could sympathize with his hesitancy of speech because Townsend, too, knew 'the agonies of a stammerer'.[37]

There were, in fact, other ways in which the King and his new equerry resembled one another. Both were slender, physically active men, shy, sensitive and most at ease in a small circle. Although Townsend rightly dismissed the claim that he was ever the monarch's confidant or adviser, he was not unlike a son to the King. Townsend was certainly devoted to him and, in time, learned how to cope with the King in his more fractious moments. These, in this trying time of war, were not infrequent. Whenever the King was 'irked or rattled', says Townsend, his blue-eyed gaze would change to an 'alarming glare . . . Then he would start to rant, noisily.'

The Queen conquered Townsend as completely as she conquered anyone whom she met. One never noticed her smallness or her plumpness, he says: 'you were simply swept off your feet by her warm and totally captivating charm. It radiated from her smile . . .' In her beautifully modulated voice she would invariably ask the stranger about *himself*: 'that was the secret of her charm; she gave people the feeling that she was interested, primarily, in them; that she knew them, almost. And when she laughed, her very blue eyes laughed, too.'[38]

She seemed always to be laughing and smiling. The Queen once admitted to Cecil Beaton that she did not know when *not* to smile. Townsend describes her as having 'a delicious and highly imaginative sense of the ridiculous'.[39] She was full of amusing anecdotes and witty asides. Yet it did not take Townsend long to appreciate that the Queen was anything but frivolous; 'beneath her graciousness, her gaiety and her unfailing thoughtfulness for others, she possessed a steely will'.[40] Only rarely, he says, did she show anger, 'and then it was in her eyes, which blazed, bluer than ever'.

The two princesses had inherited their parents' flawless complexions, small stature and blue eyes. Princess Margaret's were of a darker blue, notes Townsend, 'like those of a deep tropical sea'. Princess Elizabeth was 'shy, occasionally to the point of gaucheness, and this tended to hide her charm'. But she was quick and, in an entirely inoffensive way, very conscious of her position. Talking to the new equerry one day about her grandfather, King George V, she remarked that because his manner had been very abrupt, 'people thought he was being rude'.

'I rather like people like that', answered Townsend airily, 'because if they are rude to you, you can be rude back to them.'

'Yes,' answered the future Queen, 'but you can't very well be rude to the King of England.'

Princess Margaret, at 14, was too young to make any strong impression on the newcomer. He describes her as 'unremarkable'; except, he goes on to say, 'when she came out with some shattering wise-crack; then, to her unconcealed delight, all eyes were upon her'.[41] Before many years had passed, Peter Townsend would find Princess Margaret a very remarkable person indeed. Their love affair was to be one of the great royal dramas of the mid-1950s. It is not altogether surprising that this 'dazzling' Princess, who was so devoted to her father, should fall in love – after her father's death – with the man who so much resembled him.

It was after spending his first period *en famille* with the King and Queen – at Appleton House, Sandringham, for Easter 1944 – that Peter Townsend came to appreciate the 'astonishing affection' generated by this little family. 'Perpetual currents of it flowed between them, between father and mother, sister and sister, between the parents and their daughters and back again,' he writes. 'Then it radiated outwards to the ends of the world, touching thousands of millions of hearts who sent, rolling back, a massive wave of loyalty and love to the Royal Family.'[42]

11

Crown of Victory

THE ARRIVAL OF the 44-year-old Duke of Gloucester, as Governor-General of Australia, in January 1945 was greeted with great enthusiasm. The *Sydney Herald* had earlier hailed the prospect of a member of the royal family as Governor-General as 'a magnificent gesture' on the part of the monarchy, and the *Sydney Sun* considered it 'the greatest compliment the throne can pay the Australian people'.[1] The crowds lining the streets of Sydney on that blazing summer day seemed to confirm this view. Their welcome was vociferous. As the Duke and Duchess and their two small sons were driven to Admiralty House, the Duchess heard, for the first time, the characteristically Australian cries of 'Good old Henry!', 'Hullo Dukie!' and 'Coo-ee!' that were to greet them wherever they travelled during their two-year tour of duty.[2]

But the warmth of the Gloucesters' reception was slightly misleading. The Duchess's remark that 'the Australians were feeling a bit fed-up with England at that time because they felt she wasn't doing enough for them'[3] was a simplification of a complex situation. In 1939 Australia, led by its Prime Minister, the young Robert Menzies, had unhesitatingly aligned itself with Britain: the 'Dominion' had automatically come to the aid of 'the Mother Country'. But in 1941 the Labour Party under John Curtin won the election (their success was repeated in 1943) and the Australian govern-

198

ment's enthusiasm for the imperial connection became a little less unequivocal.

The Japanese bombing of Pearl Harbor, followed by the humiliating British defeats in South-East Asia, brought the nightmare of an Asian invasion of Australia very close. Australians felt that Britain, in its preoccupation with the war in Europe, was not paying enough attention to Australia. Already, at the end of 1941, Prime Minister Curtin had issued a significant statement. In it he had indicated that in spite of Australia's traditional attachment to the Empire and to Britain as 'Home', the country would, in future, have to look to America rather than to Britain as an ally. This message, usually regarded as a turning-point in Australia's relationship with Britain, caused a furore in certain quarters. Churchill was particularly incensed. Two days after delivering it, Curtin was obliged to disclaim any intentions of disloyalty to Britain. Australia's loyalty to the King went to the very core of its national life, he claimed.

As the Duke of Gloucester had come to Australia as the representative of the British monarch and not the British government, and as his function was purely ceremonial, he was largely able to distance himself from any such political controversies. In any case, Curtin had hastily assured the Dominions Office in London that 'I do sincerely feel that the appointment of His Majesty's own brother will have excellent results and will show unmistakably to any doubters, how loyal Australians are to the Empire and with what affection they regard the Royal Family.'[4] The Duke was careful to confine himself to the customary viceregal duties: opening Parliament, holding investitures, receiving foreign dignitaries, talking to ministers, attending banquets and receptions, giving garden parties, inspecting troops, taking the salute and applying himself to his desk work.

Making the Duke's job additionally arduous was his shyness. He was always nervous on formal occasions and never conquered his distaste for public speaking. His meetings with the Prime Minister, John Curtin, were especially awkward. 'Being rather shy', as the Duchess put it to Queen Mary, the Duke made 'other people shy'.[5] When faced with someone like Curtin, who was not only shy but also cold and withdrawn, he became more inarticulate still. There they would stand, the Duke grunting, the Prime Minister clearing his throat, as each waited for the other to say something. The King's injunction to his brother that 'your P.M. has got to tell you everything and get all the information from him'[6] was not all that easy to carry out.

Several other factors made the Gloucesters' first months in Australia less than idyllic. Their accommodation was hardly up to viceregal standards. The improvements to Government House in Canberra (then hardly more than a dusty, makeshift town), which had been ordered by the late Duke of Kent in 1939, had never been carried out. Wartime priorities, bureaucratic inefficiency and a lack of interest had left Government House as a sadly inadequate home for a royal Governor-General with a young family and a full diplomatic staff. The rooms were underfurnished, there was not enough bedlinen, the nurseries were lacking in every sort of convenience. The linoleum on the floor of the day nursery, reported the Duchess to Queen Mary, exactly resembled 'pressed beef with a few streaks of orange in it'.[7] The house was buffeted by winds, either searingly hot or glacially cold. It teemed with almost every variety of insect and animal life: silverfish, flies, spiders, mice, rats and snakes. On one occasion, when the Duke of Gloucester was solemnly conferring a knighthood on the kneeling figure of an elderly gentleman, there was a sudden scuffle as a mouse, hotly pursued by a tabby cat, went scampering across the room.

The family all suffered from ill-health. The Duke had trouble with his teeth, a poisoned eye and undiagnosed pains in one of his legs. The 43-year-old Duchess, who had given birth to Prince Richard by Caesarian section only four months before setting out for Australia, had not completely recovered her strength. She often felt tired. Prince Richard succumbed to all the new germs to which he had not yet acquired immunity, and Prince William became very seriously ill with nephritis.

They found the weather, with its sudden changes, very trying. Having usually to be formally dressed, often in uniform (the Duchess was Commandant-in-Chief of several Australian women's services) they suffered badly from the heat. Those long car journeys were especially uncomfortable. The Duchess remembers once looking at her face in the mirror and finding it 'the colour of blackcurrant fool *all over*!!'[8] The frames of her sunglasses would burn her skin and on one journey she had to wipe her husband's sweating back continually with a bathtowel.

Queen Mary once wrote to complain that in none of the press photographs of the Gloucesters had she ever seen her daughter-in-law using the parasols that she had especially given her to take to Australia. The Duchess refrained from explaining that Queen Mary's frail lace and silk parasols, with their jewelled Fabergé handles, were really not much use in a land of blinding dust-storms, boisterous winds and pelting summer rain.

In spite of all these difficulties, the Duke and Duchess of Gloucester uncomplainingly carried out their duties. In the seven months between their arrival and the end of the war, they visited all the states of Australia. By the time they left, after two years, they had travelled some 76,000 miles. Nothing – not gruelling heat, bumpy aeroplane flights, dusty roads, exhausting schedules or inadequate accommodation – ever caused them to shirk their responsibilities. 'It would never have occurred to the Duke', claims one of his secretaries, 'to have refused to do something that he didn't want to do. He would just go ahead and do it.'[9] That he seldom enjoyed what he had to do was apparent only to his intimate circle. 'Do you know what my life has been?' he once said to a confidante in later life. 'Fifty years of bloody boredom.'[10]

In short, the Duke and Duchess of Gloucester epitomized

that devotion to duty which was winning the monarchy so much admiration during the war years. With very little taste or natural aptitude for their calling, they did their job to the best of their abilities. Inevitably there were criticisms. The Duke, with his bluff manner and short temper, might make an undiplomatic remark; the Duchess might be pronounced lacking in the necessary flair for the showier aspects of her task. But if acquaintances found the Duke cantankerous, those who knew him better described him as a conscientious worker, a sympathetic listener and an unpretentious personality. 'He talks our language,' said one Labour Member of Parliament.[11]

And in her old age the Duchess of Gloucester once made a poignant remark. In discussing the Gloucesters' lifelong contribution to the monarchy, she said, 'I don't think that anyone really appreciated how hard we worked. Except in Australia. I think that the Australians appreciated us.'[12]

With the end of the war in sight, the problem of the Duke and Duchess of Windsor, more or less dormant for some years, again became acute. What was the Duke's future position to be?

While, with the best will in the world, the Duke of Windsor's wartime governorship of the Bahamas could hardly be said to have contributed towards the popularization of the monarchy, it was not unsuccessful. Holding the positions of both head of state and head of the executive, the Duke acquitted himself very well. Inheriting a domain notable for bitter political infighting and for an economy dependent on tourism, he did his best to establish a more solvent, stable and – up to a point – equitable society.

The Duchess, too, played her part very well. She ran Government House, Nassau, very efficiently and behaved, in public, with charm and dignity. Often, she revealed a surer touch than the Duke. When, for instance, he once passed for publication an article on the expensive refurbishment of Government House, she made him withdraw his permission. It would never do for the British people, suffering the privations of war, to read about the elegance and comfort in which their ex-King was living.

But such is the way of the world that it was their mistakes rather than their achievements that kept the couple in the public eye. The Duke continued to associate with various politically suspect figures and he formed one of his typically ill-advised friendships with an allegedly pro-Nazi Swede named Axel Wenner-Gren ('Goering's Pal and the Windsors', ran one British newspaper headline).[13] He badly mishandled the investigation into the mysterious murder of the most powerful man in the Bahamas, Sir Harry Oakes, and he is said to have been involved in some illegal currency dealing. The Duchess of Windsor was accused, inevitably and with some justification, of extravagance.

As the Duke of Windsor had no intention of remaining in the Bahamas once the war was over, George VI had to come to some decision about his future. As early as 1942 the King had assured Lord Halifax, the British Ambassador in Washington, that 'the Duke, as a former monarch, could *never* live in England'.[14] To the Duke of Windsor's perennial request – that the Duchess be received at court and be granted the title of Royal Highness – the King replied that it would be impossible: it would 'imply that the abdication had been all a mistake'.[15]

This refusal was backed up by a move on the part of the Queen. She told Sir Alan Lascelles that she and Queen Mary had drawn up and signed a statement to the effect 'that they were *not* prepared to receive the Duchess, now, or at any time, for the same reasons that they would not do so in 1936'.[16] The Queen's icy resolve would no doubt have been icier still had she known the nicknames by which the Duke and Duchess habitually referred to her. One was 'Cookie' because they had decided she looked like a cook; the other, equally inappropriate, one was 'Mrs Temple', with Princess Elizabeth being cast in the role of the cloying child star of the period, Shirley Temple.

As far as the Duke of Windsor was concerned, the Queen's continued refusal to receive the Duchess ruled out any possibility of his living in Britain. If his family were not prepared to treat his wife as one of them, he wanted nothing to do with them. He could not, though, resist a dig at the King and Queen. 'Having been given to understand that they are by now so well and firmly established in the hearts of their people,' he wrote to Lascelles late in 1944, 'I would not have thought that my presence in their midst could any longer be considered so formidable a nuisance to the solidarity of the monarchy.'[17]

With Britain denied to him, the Duke considered the United States as a possible future home. He had always loved America. Halifax had earlier reported that the Duke had his eye on the Washington Embassy for himself. This, warned the Ambassador, would never do: the presence of the Windsors in Washington would encourage the belief, in certain American minds, that the Duke was the rightful King, George VI and Queen Elizabeth merely being 'placeholders'.[18] In the course of several discussions with Churchill and others, various alternative suggestions for the Duke's future role and residence were bandied about. Perhaps he could become a roving ambassador in South America? Or the Governor of Rhodesia? Or of Bermuda? Or of Ceylon? Or of Madras? For one reason or another, all these proposals fell through.

By February 1945, the King had made up his mind. The Duke of Windsor should make his home in the United States, perhaps in a house in the South, where '*in an unofficial capacity*' he could dedicate himself to 'the betterment of Anglo-American relations'.[19] The Windsors might well have settled for this had it not been for the Duke's aversion to paying American income tax – or income tax of any sort. Only in France, it transpired, would the couple be able to live tax-free.

On 3 May 1945, with their future still undecided, the Windsors left the Bahamas. For a while they continued to hope that the Duke might be given some official post and the Duchess some royal recognition but these hopes gradually faded. Eventually the couple settled down in Paris to a life of luxurious, restless and curiously hollow exile.

For Princess Marina, the widowed Duchess of Kent, her husband's death brought an unexpected hardship. She suddenly found herself in financial difficulties. On the Duke's death, his annual income of £25,000 from the Civil List ceased. By an unfortunate oversight, no provision had been made, in the Civil List drawn up at the start of George VI's reign, for the widows of younger sons. No doubt Parliament would have granted the widowed Duchess an allowance but it was considered inadvisable to tackle this always touchy subject in wartime. With so many war widows suffering financial hardship, it would not be seemly for Parliament to vote money for a member of the royal family.

Nor did Princess Marina possess any personal fortune. She had inherited very little from her father, Prince Nicholas of Greece, and the late Duke of Kent had spent a great deal of the money bequeathed to him by George V on his collection of antiques and paintings. He had left his home, Coppins, to his elder son, and the rest of his inherited money was bound up in trusts for his three children, Prince Edward, Princess Alexandra and Prince Michael.

This meant that Princess Marina was forced to meet the considerable expense of educating her three children, running her home and buying her clothes – all to a standard expected of a representative of the monarchy. Both George VI and Queen Mary provided her with undisclosed allowances but charity can never take the place of an independent income. In November 1943 she had to sell some of the furniture bequeathed to her husband by his great-aunt Princess Louise, Duchess of Argyll. This raised almost £20,000. A few years later, yet more of the Duke's possessions had to be auctioned. Not until eleven years after her husband's death, with the passing of Queen Elizabeth II's

Civil List in 1953, did Princess Marina receive an official allowance.

Poverty is, of course, relative, and Princess Marina was never the impecunious widow of popular legend; but not least of the contributions of this publicly active member of the royal family is that for the last three years of the war, and beyond, she carried out her official duties without any income whatsoever from the state.

In the three weeks after being moved from Colditz Castle in mid-April 1945, Viscount Lascelles and the other *Prominenten* were shunted from one prison camp to another. Their chief concern was to avoid being taken to the Final Redoubt. This meant ensuring that they maintained their official prisoner-of-war status. They knew that once incarcerated in a civilian internment camp, they would automatically lose this safeguard. But realizing that not even their POW status would prevent the Nazis from carrying them off as hostages, the little group decided on a delaying tactic. In one of the camps – Tittmonning Castle – they holed up in an excavated wall. Their absence led the authorities to assume that they had joined some others in a recent escape. All the prisoners now had to do was to sit tight in their hiding place in the wall until the castle was liberated. Lascelles spent his time reading, appropriately, Oscar Wilde's *De Profundis*. But after three days their hiding place was discovered. Once more, the group was moved on.

A week later, at dawn on 1 May, the *Prominente* were again bundled into a bus. This time, they felt certain that they were being taken on their final, long-dreaded journey. But, instead, they found themselves being driven south across the old Austrian border to a camp between Salzburg and Innsbruck, named Markt Pongau. Before many hours had passed they realized that they were indeed being held as pawns – but not by the Nazis. They were now in the care of the Wehrmacht who, in their opposition to the Gestapo, were determined not to hand the prisoners over to the head of the Gestapo. This official was after them, claims Lascelles, 'in his own bid for survival'.[20]

The Wehrmacht were successful. The head of the Gestapo was not even able to reach Markt Pongau, let alone get his hands on the *Prominente*. So what was the Wehrmacht planning to do with them? It did not take them long to find out. On the morning after their arrival at the camp there took place what Lascelles calls 'an extraordinary episode'. A fat, dazzlingly bemedalled officer, who introduced himself as Obergruppenführer Gottlob Berger, head of the SS, came to see them. The war, he explained, would be over in a day or two. Although he had received orders to shoot them, he was going to disobey these orders and let them go free. He had made arrangements for them to be handed over to the representative of the Swiss authorities who would escort them through the German lines and deliver them into the hands of the Allies.

The Obergruppenführer was as good as his word. On the afternoon of 4 May 1945 the little group was driven, at snail's pace, in a convoy of vehicles to the German front line. With the Swiss flag on the front of the car they made their eerie journey through no man's land. Eventually, they reached the American front line and were handed over.

Only then did the suppressed apprehension of months manifest itself in a physical form. 'Fear', as Lascelles puts it, 'is a sterile emotion.' The fear which he had experienced during the first few days after his capture had soon subsided. Throughout his captivity he had never, for instance, had any trouble in falling asleep; the mind, he maintains, 'puts up its own defences'.[21] But now, on gaining his freedom, Lascelles suddenly lost his voice. For the rest of the day he simply could not speak.

Within two days of his release he, with his mother the Princess Royal, was dining with the King and Queen at Buckingham Palace. After dinner he smoked an unaccustomed cigar and was violently sick.

★

'Events are moving very fast now,' wrote the King in his diary on 30 April 1945.[22] Every day was bringing the end of the war closer. On 28 April Mussolini had been strung up by the Italian partisans in Mezzegra. Two days later Hitler committed suicide in the Chancellery bunker in Berlin. On 2 May the German armies in Italy surrendered; on that same day the German capital fell to the Russians. On 4 May Montgomery reported to Eisenhower that all enemy forces in Holland, north-west Germany and Denmark had capitulated with effect from eight o'clock the following morning. 'This is wonderful news,' enthused the King.[23] On the morning of 7 May, in a schoolroom at Rheims, a weeping General Jodl signed the instrument of unconditional surrender on behalf of the German High Command. It was agreed that the actual moment for the official cessation of hostilities in Europe would be at one minute after midnight on 8/9 May.

But then there was a muddle. The royal family drove up from Windsor on the evening on Sunday, 6 May, expecting the official announcement of the end of the war, VE Day, to be made the following day – 7 May. Preparations for the celebration of the day had been in hand for months. The Palace balcony had been strengthened and the crimson and gold drapery unearthed for the planned appearance of the family, loudspeakers and floodlights had been erected in the Mall, and the King had had his special victory broadcast recorded and filmed. But then it became known that both Joseph Stalin and the new President of the United States, Harry S. Truman, wanted the announcement to be delayed until 3 p.m. on Tuesday, 8 May.

No sooner had this been agreed to than, quite unexpectedly, the official announcement of the Allied victory was made by Count Schwerin von Krosigk from Hamburg on 7 May. This meant that by the time Churchill made the official announcement at 3 p.m. on Tuesday, 8 May 1945, the news had been known for some time.

None of this, though, could dim the exuberance of the crowds in London on VE Day. And it was to Buckingham

Palace that they surged. A great mass of cheering, flag-waving people packed the area beyond the Palace railings, clamouring for the King and Queen. Finally they appeared – four tiny figures, the King in naval uniform, the Queen in powder blue, Princess Elizabeth in her ATS uniform, Princess Margaret in a simple dress – with the boarded-up windows of the Palace behind them and the badly creased but dashingly fringed and tasselled red drapery adding a splash of colour to the scene. Sometimes accompanied by Churchill, who was in the Palace for his weekly lunch with the King, the royal family appeared again and again before the crowd. 'We went out eight times altogether during the afternoon and evening,' noted the King. 'We were given a great reception.'[24]

At nine that evening the King's victory speech was broadcast, not only to the crowds in the Mall, but throughout the world. Speaking 'from our Empire's oldest capital city, war-battered but never for one moment daunted or discouraged', George VI made a moving speech.[25] It was rendered all the more moving because his deep, resonant voice with its gutteral 'r's was more hesitant than usual. He was clearly tired.

On the last appearance on the balcony that night, the two princesses were not with their parents. In answer to his daughters' entreaties, the King had allowed them to go out and mingle with the crowds. Chaperoned by their uncle, the Queen's youngest brother, David Bowes-Lyon ('It was really his idea; he organized it all,' says Princess Margaret)[26] and accompanied by their governess and a party of young officers, the two princesses slipped out of a side door and joined the surging, roaring, arm-linking revellers. After roaming the streets (the King had forbidden them to go to Piccadilly Circus) they forced their way into the great press of people outside the Palace gates. Here the two princesses stood yelling with the others, 'We want the King! We want the Queen!', and joining lustily in the singing of 'Land of Hope and Glory'.

Years afterwards, Queen Elizabeth II described it as one of the most memorable nights of her life.

In Canada, the King's victory broadcast was heard by the Athlones in Jasper National Park in the Canadian Rockies. Each spring the viceregal couple, who loved the outdoors, would holiday in the Park. Their private railway coach would be shunted into a nearby siding and here, guarded by a handful of Mounties, they would live for five or six days.

The Superintendent of the Park at the time was Major J. A. Wood and, together with his wife, he would take the Athlones on long drives through the immense, thickly forested area. The viceregal couple were very interested in, and knowledgeable about, all forms of wildlife. On their way back to the siding, they would ask to be let out of the car so that they could walk the last two miles. At any spare moment of the day, says Mrs Emily Wood, Princess Alice would get out her knitting. 'She was always knitting army or navy garments for the war effort.'

By that spring of 1945, Lord Athlone's term of office as Governor-General should have ended but he had been asked to stay on. It was generally agreed that until the war, and the inevitable period of post-war confusion, was well and truly over, it would not do to change Governors-General. In any case, as George VI laughingly said to the visiting Mackenzie King, with servants being almost impossible to come by in England, the Athlones would do well to remain at Rideau Hall as long as they could. So Lord Athlone agreed to stay on until the spring of 1946.

This is why VE Day found the couple on their annual holiday in Jasper National Park. They had arranged to go to the Woods' home to listen to the King's victory broadcast. 'When "God Save the King" was played,' remembers Emily Wood, 'the Athlones jumped to attention.' Sheepishly, their hosts also rose to their feet. At that moment, a neighbour happened to pass their window. At the sight of these four figures standing rigid in the middle of the room, the visitor wondered, as well he might, 'whether we had all gone mad'.[27]

From April 1945 Queen Mary began preparing for her return to her London home, Marlborough House. She made a series of visits to the house that spring in order to inspect the damage caused by blast: she found some ceilings down, windows boarded up and doors blown out. Nevertheless, as some parts – including her own first-floor suite of rooms – were quite habitable, she arranged for her furniture and 'treasures' to be brought back from what she called their wartime 'hide-outs'.[28]

'I expect Marlborough House is in a state of eruption, revolt and tumult,' wrote her niece, the Duchess of Beaufort, from Badminton to a friend. 'Vans of boxes and hampers and trunks all marked with the royal cypher continually leave the house.'[29] By the end of May Queen Mary was able to report that her rooms were 'beginning to look quite nice again'. But she arranged to stay on at Badminton House until 11 June 1945.

On VE Day Queen Mary listened to the broadcasts by the King and the Prime Minister. She also heard, with great satisfaction, the roar of the crowds as they cheered the King and Queen at Buckingham Palace. That night she visited the local public house to join in the village celebrations. 'We sang songs,' she noted, 'a friendly affair and amusing.'[30]

'I am much looking forward to going "home",' wrote the old Queen to her daughter-in-law, the Duchess of Gloucester, in Australia, 'though in some ways I shall be sorry to leave this place, especially the "wooding" which I really enjoyed. Do you know we have actually cleared 111 acres in the 5 years and 8 months.'[31]

Before leaving Badminton, Queen Mary gave separate audiences to the nine heads of departments on the estate. To each of them she presented a carefully chosen gift. 'Oh, I *have* been happy here!' she said to one of them. 'Here I've been anybody to everybody, and back in London I shall have to begin being Queen Mary all over again.'[32]

And when she finally left on 11 June, the eyes of this normally impassive-faced and rigidly self-controlled Queen were wet with tears.

'We felt absolutely *whacked*,' admitted the Queen of the three-month period between VE Day and VJ Day.[33] But whacked or not, they had to carry on. The Allies were still at war with Japan and not until victory had been achieved in the Far East could the war be considered over. At home, the King and Queen were plunged into a round of European victory celebrations. On the two days following VE Day they drove through East and South London where, along streets still devastated by the Blitz, they were given a tremendous welcome. Again and again the royal car was brought to a halt by the jostling, flag-waving crowds. At various points they got out to walk among the people.

On 13 May they, together with the two princesses, drove in state to attend a Thanksgiving Service in St Paul's Cathedral. As they passed in an open carriage to and from St Paul's, they were again given a heartfelt ovation. How, the King wanted to know, could the carriage horses – after years spent carting hay and drawing ploughs – be so unaffected by the enthusiastic crowds? It was explained that, during the past few weeks, the horses had been conditioned to strange noises by being made to listen to the Forces Programme on the BBC.

'Their Majesties looked young and smiling,' wrote Chips Channon, who was in the Cathedral that day, 'though the King looked drawn; but he has the Windsor gift of looking half his age.' Behind them, continued Channon, 'walked Queen Mary whom I had not seen since before the war. She looked magnificent – even beautiful, and was gloriously arrayed and bejewelled in a pink-heliotrope confection. She was upright and splendid . . .'[34]

Three days later the King and Queen attended a similar

ceremony in St Giles Cathedral, Edinburgh. By the following day they were back in London where, in the Great Hall
of Westminster, the King received addresses from both
Houses of Parliament. 'They walked down the aisle which
separated the Lords from the Commons; very slowly they
walked, bowing to left and right,' noted Harold Nicolson.
'The Queen has a truly miraculous faculty of making each
individual feel that it is him she has greeted and to him that
was devoted that lovely smile. She has a true genius for her
job.' The King then read a long speech. He has 'a really
beautiful voice', continued Nicolson, 'but his stammer
makes it almost intolerably painful to listen to him'. There
was a poignant faltering when the King spoke of the death of
his brother, the Duke of Kent. At the end of the speech
Churchill called for three cheers. 'All our pent-up energies
responded with three yells such as I would have thought
impossible to emanate from so many elderly throats.'[35] On 7
June the royal couple visited the recently liberated Channel
Islands and then flew to Northern Ireland for a three-day
tour.

'We have been overwhelmed by the kind things people
have said over our part in the War. We have only tried to do
our duty during these five-and-a-half years,' wrote the
King. 'I have found it difficult to rejoice or relax as there is
still so much hard work ahead to deal with.'[36]

Much of this hard work was self-imposed, such as the
King's efforts to meet Stalin and Truman. With the first
post-war meeting of the Big Three due to take place in
Potsdam, George VI was anxious to go to Berlin to see the
Russian leader. For security reasons, the plan had to be
dropped. But Stalin, claims Churchill, 'affirmed that no
country needed a monarchy as much as Great Britain
because the Crown was the unifying force . . .'[37] The King's
efforts to meet Truman were more successful. With the
American President unable to accept the monarch's invitation to Buckingham Palace, George VI suggested that they
meet at sea. Accordingly, they met on board HMS *Renown*

in Plymouth Sound. The shrewd President Truman found the King to be 'a pleasant and surprising person';[38] surprising, not least of all, because of the extent of his knowledge of international affairs.

During lunch, the King was astonished at the openness with which the Americans present discussed the impending dropping of the recently invented atom bomb. He had been told about the bomb in the strictest secrecy; now here it was being discussed in front of the waiters.

Admiral William Leahy, the President's Naval Chief of Staff, dismissed the atom bomb as 'a professor's dream'. 'Would you like to lay a bet on that, Admiral?' countered the King.[39]

It was as well that the Admiral did not. On 6 August an atomic bomb destroyed Hiroshima; three days later another destroyed Nagasaki.

By then Britain had experienced a political upheaval. Throughout the war, the country's affairs had been managed by a coalition National Government made up of Conservative, Labour and Liberal members. The Labour leader, Clement Attlee, had been Deputy Prime Minister. Although Churchill was anxious for this coalition government to continue in office until Japan had been defeated, the opposition parties were not. So, on 23 May 1945, two weeks after VE Day, Churchill tendered his resignation to the monarch. Polling day was set for 5 July. 'The outcome of [the election] is uncertain,' wrote the King to his brother, the Duke of Gloucester, in Australia, 'as no Party may secure a clear working majority . . .'[40]

In fact, the outcome was all too certain. When the election result was announced on 26 July, the Labour Party had a majority of 180 seats. The King was deeply disappointed. Although theoretically above party politics, he was, understandably, a man of conservative views. And so were his entourage. 'There was not a single socialist – at least above stairs – in Buckingham Palace,' claimed Peter Townsend.[41] Rendering the result even more disappointing for the monarch was the fact that it would mean the loss of Winston Churchill. In what he called 'a very sad meeting' with Churchill, the King told the outgoing Prime Minister that he thought that he had been very ungratefully treated. He followed this up with a letter in which he thanked Churchill for 'the great comfort' that he had given him 'in the darkest days of the War'. 'More than perhaps anyone else' did he regret what had happened.[42]

Yet it can be argued that the disappearance of Winston Churchill from centre stage had an enhancing effect on the King's status. Clement Attlee, although in many ways an admirable man and one whom the King came to admire, was completely lacking in Churchill's larger-than-life qualities. With Churchill gone, George VI was able to stand forth as the undisputed national symbol. Churchill's disappearance also emphasized the fact that while prime ministers – no matter how charismatic – come and go, the monarch remains: the personification of stability and continuity.

And there was another factor building up the King's prestige. 'You will find that your position is greatly strengthened,' wrote Lord Mountbatten, 'since you are now the old experienced campaigner on whom the new and partly inexperienced Government will lean for advice and guidance.'[43] Mountbatten might, as usual, have been exaggerating the situation somewhat but there can be no doubt that the King felt more self-assured in his early dealings with Attlee than he had in his early dealings with Churchill.

No such self-regarding thoughts, though, were in the King's mind on 15 August, VJ Day, the day after the Japanese government had accepted the terms of unconditional surrender. 'I wish he [Churchill] could have been given a proper reception by the people,' he wrote in his diary that night.[44]

The King and Queen were certainly given a proper reception. VJ Day happened to coincide with the first peacetime Opening of Parliament which meant that the

King and Queen again drove in state through the clamorous streets. 'H.M. read out his speech, which announced the end of the war . . .', wrote Chips Channon. 'His voice was clear, and he spoke better than usual and was more impressive. But they say that the word Berlin had to be substituted for Potsdam, which he could not have articulated . . .'[45]

Once more the crowds surged towards the Palace, and all through that afternoon – and that night, after they had changed into evening clothes – the King and Queen went out on the balcony in response to the cheers. The writer John Lehmann has left a vivid description of the scene outside the Palace. 'The evening was perfectly clear, warm and still', he says; 'it was impossible to resist going out to see how London was celebrating . . . We made our way past the Athenaeum, where torches were flaming over the portico and all around the Clubs were blazing with lights and hung with flags, down into the Mall, where we were confronted by the same perspective of massed crowds, thickening up to the Victoria Memorial: at the end the great illuminated façade of the Palace, with an enormous, raw half-moon hanging over it. As we came nearer, the noise of singing increased; the crowds were finally jammed beyond movement, and on the Memorial itself people were clustered as thickly as swarming bees. Every few minutes the singing would pause, and the chant would go up: "*We* want the *King* . . . *We* want the *King* . . .". Until at last the french windows on the far, red-draped, fairy-tale balcony were opened, and the King and Queen, diminutive but glittering figures – the Queen's diamonds flashed into the night under the arc-lights – came out to wave and be greeted by cheer after cheer, waving of hands, and the singing of "For he's a jolly good fellow".'[46]

Just over eight years before, on this same balcony, George VI had stood in all his Coronation finery, an insecure, diffident man, stiff as a marionette, while the crowds below had cheered as dutifully as they would have cheered any newly crowned sovereign. Now they were cheering a man who had won their hearts. They were cheering a monarch who had stayed in their midst, who had shared their dangers and privations, and who had worked unremittingly to bring comfort and encouragement. 'This War', as Churchill had told the King, 'has drawn the Throne and the people more closely together than was ever before recorded, and Your Majesties are more beloved by all classes and conditions than any other of the previous princes of the past.'[47]

Supported by a consort of exceptional qualities and backed by what he called 'The Firm' – the extended royal family – King George VI had won tremendous public respect and affection for the monarchy. No less than the country, had the crown emerged triumphant from the long years of war.

George VI had done more than fulfil the symbolic function of a Warrior-King, the focal point of an almost tribal allegiance. He had presided over – indeed, had developed into the embodiment of – a period of unprecedented national unity. Although the wartime fusion of the people and the dissolving of class barriers were never quite as all-embracing as is often nostalgically claimed, there is no doubt that the Second World War saw a dilution of social divisions and a remarkable working together of the entire population. Of this great national synthesis, the crown stood as the unquestioned symbol.

Robert Menzies, the post-war Australian Prime Minister, in paying tribute to the spirit of Britain during the war, spoke of 'an embattled nation, normally not unacquainted with internal divisions and hostilities, in which there was unity, cheerfulness, courage, a common resolution'. It was, concluded Menzies, 'that superb fusing of the common will which defeated the enemy, and did so much to save the world. King George and his Queen Elizabeth were among the great architects of that brotherhood.'[48]

The Queen's summing up was more modest. Sitting in her drawing-room at Clarence House, in the fortieth year of her daughter's reign, the 91-year-old Queen Elizabeth the

Queen Mother – still a straight-backed, charming and vivacious figure – put it very simply.

'Everybody worked together,' she said. 'We just tried to do our best.'[49]

Notes

1. THE UNKNOWN KING

1. Longford, *The Queen*, p. 54.
2. Airlie, *Thatched*, p. 202.
3. Balfour and Mackay, *Paul of Yugoslavia*, p. 135.
4. Princess Alice (Athlone), con. with author.
5. Bradford, *George VI*, p. 242.
6. Wheeler-Bennett, *George VI*, p. 286.
7. Ibid., p. 293.
8. Ibid., p. 297.
9. Bullitt, *For the President,* p. 310.
10. Wheeler-Bennett, *George VI*, p. 380.
11. Roosevelt and Lash, *Letters*, Vol. III, p. 206.
12. Wheeler-Bennett, *George VI*, p. 393.
13. Ibid., p. 380.
14. Bradford, *George VI*, p. 315.
15. Queen Mother, con. with author.
16. Princess Alice (Athlone), con. with author.
17. Bradford, *George VI*, p. 380.
18. Lash, *Eleanor and Franklin*, p. 582.
19. Private information.
20. Nicolson, *Diaries, 1930–39*, p. 405.
21. Lash, *Eleanor and Franklin*, p. 582.
22. Roosevelt, *This I Remember*, p. 153.
23. Wheeler-Bennett, *George VI*, p. 380.
24. Ibid., p. 402.
25. Evans, *Killearn Diaries*, p. 107.
26. Frankland, *Prince Henry*, p. 140.
27. *The Times*, 28 August 1939.
28. Ibid., 2 September 1939.
29. Wheeler-Bennett, *George VI*, p. 407.

30. Ibid., p. 405.
31. Queen Mother, con. with author.
32. Crawford, *Little Princesses*, p. 60.
33. Ibid., p. 62.
34. Ibid., p. 63.
35. Queen Mother, con. with author.
36. Princess Alice (Athlone), con. with author.
37. Wheeler-Bennett, *George VI*, p. 430.
38. Pope-Hennessy, *Queen Mary*, p. 596.
39. Ibid.
40. Colville, *Fringes of Power*, p. 22
41. Princess Alice (Athlone), con. with author.
42. Sitwell, *Queen Mary*, p. 34.
43. Minney, *Private Papers*, p. 238.
44. Vincent, *Crawford Papers*, p. 617.
45. Bruce-Lockhart, *Diaries*, Vol. I, p. 413.
46. Minney, *Hore-Belisha*, p. 238.
47. Ziegler, *Edward VIII*, p. 404.
48. Wheeler-Bennett, *George VI*, p. 417.
49. Ziegler, *Edward VIII*, p. 411.
50. Ibid.
51. Bloch, *Secret File*, p. 151.
52. Nicolson, Balliol, 1 Oct. 1940.
53. Ziegler, *Edward VIII*, p. 392.
54. Bradford, *George VI*, p. 575.

2. A DEFINITE JOB

1. Ziegler, *Mountbatten*, p. 125.
2. Ziegler, *Crown and People*, p. 72.
3. Wheeler-Bennett, *George VI*, p. 428.
4. Roberts, *Holy Fox*, p. 309.
5. Wheeler-Bennett, *George VI*, p. 437.
6. Hardinge, Document, p. 59.
7. Queen Mother, con. with author.
8. Ibid.
9. Hardinge, Document, p. 56.
10. Queen Mother, con. with author.

11. Bradford, *George VI*, p. 411.
12. Nicolson, Balliol, 6 April 1955.
13. Roberts, *Holy Fox*, p. 202.
14. Wilhelmina, *Lonely*, p. 156.
15. Keyes, *Outrageous Fortune*, p. 310.
16. Bradford, *George VI*, p. 422.
17. Wheeler-Bennett, *George VI*, p. 450.
18. Queen Mother, con. with author.
19. Longford, *Queen Mother*, p. 80.
20. Crawford, *Little Princesses*, p. 69.
21. Wheeler-Bennett, *George VI*, p. 464.
22. Olson, *Nicolson Diaries*, p. 188.
23. Channon, *Chips*, p. 259.
24. Princess Margaret, con. with author.
25. Wheeler-Bennett, *George VI*, p. 465.
26. Olson, *Nicolson Diaries*, p. 188.
27. Townsend, *Time and Chance*, p. 164.
28. Princess Alice (Gloucester), con. with author.
29. Alice, *Memoirs*, p. 122.
30. Frankland, *Prince Henry*, p. 185.
31. Ibid.
32. Ibid., p. 141.
33. Ibid., p. 152.
34. Ibid., p. 149.
35. Sitwell, *Queen Mary*, p. 34.
36. RA, Queen Mary's Diary, 28 May 1940.
37. Frankland, *Prince Henry*, p. 155.
38. Ziegler, *Edward VIII*, p. 422.
39. Colville, *Fringes of Power*, pp. 176–7.
40. Ziegler, *Edward VIII*, p. 426.
41. Bradford, *George VI*, p. 577.
42. Ziegler, *Edward VIII*, p. 427.
43. Ibid.
44. Gilbert, *Churchill*, Vol. VI, p. 707.
45. Ziegler, *Edward VIII*, p. 425.
46. Ibid., p. 431.
47. Higham, *Wallis*, p. 211.
48. Ziegler, *Edward VIII*, p. 428.
49. Higham, *Wallis*, p. 239.
50. Bradford, *George VI*, p. 578.

51.   Ziegler, *Edward VIII*, p. 434.
52.   Bradford, *George VI*, p. 580.

3.   'GOD BLESS YOUR MAJESTIES'

1.   Bradford, *George VI*, p. 430.
2.   Wheeler-Bennett, *George VI*, p. 478.
3.   Ibid., p. 479.
4.   Ibid., p. 478.
5.   Milburn, Diary, p. 81.
6.   Lady Hambleden, con. with author.
7.   Anon., *Royal Family*, p. 52.
8.   Dunnett, *Among Friends*, p. 152.
9.   Ziegler, *Crown and People*, p. 72.
10.   Bradford, *George VI*, p. 430.
11.   Ziegler, *Crown and People*, p. 77.
12.   Wheeler-Bennett, *George VI*, p. 470.
13.   Astor Papers, MS 1416/1/4/8.
14.   Queen Mother, con. with author.
15.   Wheeler-Bennett, *George VI*, p. 468.
16.   Crawford, *Little Princesses*, p. 83.
17.   Wheeler-Bennett, *George VI*, p. 469.
18.   Shew, *Queen Elizabeth*, p. 76.
19.   Wheeler-Bennett, *George VI*, p. 469.
20.   Ziegler, *Crown and People*, p. 75.
21.   Townsend, *Time and Chance*, p. 121.
22.   Milburn, Diary, p. 66.
23.   Wheeler-Bennett, *George VI*, p. 472.
24.   Ibid., p. 467.
25.   Queen Mother, con. with author.
26.   Ibid.
27.   Ibid.
28.   Hartnell, *Silver and Gold*, p. 102.
29.   Longford, *Queen Mother*, p. 86.
30.   Wheeler-Bennett, *George VI*, p. 467.
31.   Dunnett, *Among Friends*, p. 152.
32.   Astor Papers, MS 1416/1/4/9.

33. Bradford, *George VI*, p. 437.
34. Ibid., p. 434.
35. Van der Byl, *Shadows*, p. 127.
36. Astor Papers, MS 1416/1/4/5.
37. Lees-Milne, *Ancestral Voices*, p. 160.
38. Bruce-Lockhart, *Diaries*, Vol. I, p. 264.
39. Colville, *Fringes of Power*, p. 351.
40. Bloch, *Secret File*, p. 201.
41. Airlie, *Thatched with Gold*, p. 195.
42. King, *Princess Marina*, p. 132.
43. Warwick, *George and Marina*, p. 121.
44. Ibid., p. 123.
45. Channon, *Chips*, p. 402.
46. Astor Papers, MS 1416/1/4/5.
47. Warwick, *George and Marina*, p. 116.
48. King, *Princess Marina*, p. 166.
49. Ibid., p. 152.
50. Ibid., p. 166.
51. Channon, *Chips*, p. 339.
52. Ibid., p. 402.
53. Frankland, *Prince Henry*, p. 161.
54. King, *Princess Marina*, p. 177.
55. Astor Papers, MS 1416/1/4/5.
56. Donald O. Johnson, *Observer*, 20 Sept. 1985.
57. Pope-Hennessy, *Queen Mary*, p. 578.
58. Sitwell, *Queen Mary*, p. 45.
59. Ibid., p. 51.
60. Pope-Hennessy, *Queen Mary*, p. 605.
61. Sitwell, *Queen Mary*, p. 45.
62. Ibid., p. 29.
63. Wulff, *Queen Mary*, p. 62.
64. Ibid., p. 56.
65. Alice, *Grandchildren*, p. 263.
66. Colville, *Fringes of Power*, p. 211.
67. Bradford, *George VI*, p. 403.
68. Wheeler-Bennett, *George VI*, p. 558.
69. Ibid., p. 447.
70. Ibid., p. 467.
71. *The Times*, 18 May 1943.

4. KING-EMPEROR

1. Wheeler-Bennett, *George VI*, p. 410.
2. Alice, *Grandchildren*, p. 246.
3. Massey, *What's Past*, p. 330.
4. Lord Harewood, con. with author.
5. Pickersgill, *Mackenzie King*, Vol. I, p. 146.
6. Queen Mother, con. with author.
7. Mary Goldie, con. with author.
8. Sir Shuldham Redfern, con. with author.
9. Alice, *Grandchildren*, p. 251.
10. Neville Usher to the author.
11. Sir Shuldham Redfern, con. with author.
12. Ibid.
13. Princess Alice (Athlone), con. with author.
14. Lord Harewood, con. with author.
15. Neville Usher to the author.
16. Harewood, *Tongs and Bones*, p. 75.
17. Sir Shuldham Redfern, con. with author.
18. Lees-Milne, *Ancestral Voices*, p. 45.
19. Hubbard, *Rideau Hall*, p. 202.
20. Alice, *Grandchildren*, p. 250.
21. Sir Shuldham Redfern, con. with author.
22. Wheeler-Bennett, *George VI*, p. 389.
23. Roosevelt, *Rendezvous*, p. 230.
24. Wheeler-Bennett, *George VI*, p. 420.
25. PRO FO 800/326.
26. Wheeler-Bennett, *George VI*, p. 510.
27. Ibid., p. 522.
28. Bradford, *George VI*, p. 441.
29. Wheeler-Bennett, *George VI*, p. 384.
30. Bradford, *George VI*, pp. 441–2.
31. Ibid.
32. Wheeler-Bennett, *George VI*, p. 520.
33. Winant, *Letter*, pp. 28–9.
34. Wheeler-Bennett, *George VI*, pp. 525–6.
35. Ibid., p. 257.
36. Ibid., p. 530.
37. Sinclair, *Queen and Country*, p. 147.
38. Wheeler-Bennett, *George VI*, p. 529.

39. Ibid., pp. 532–3.
40. Alice, *Memoirs*, p. 123.
41. Princess Alice (Gloucester), con. with author.
42. Townsend, *Time and Chance*, p. 164.
43. Princess Alice (Gloucester), con. with author.
44. Ibid.
45. Alice, *Memoirs*, p. 125.
46. Alice, *Memoirs*, p. 125.
47. Frankland, *Prince Henry*, p. 157.
48. Alice, *Memoirs*, p. 126.
49. Frankland, *Prince Henry*, p. 160.
50. Alice, *Memoirs*, p. 127.
51. Frankland, *Prince Henry*, p. 158.
52. Ibid., p. 162.
53. Ibid., p. 167.
54. Ibid., p. 166.
55. Ibid., p. 175.
56. Greacen, *Chink*, p. 196.
57. Channon, *Chips*, p. 334.
58. *New Statesman*, 11 July 1942.
59. Frankland, *Prince Henry*, p. 172.
60. Alice, *Memoirs*, p. 127.

5. FAMILY TRAGEDY

1. Pope-Hennessy, *Queen Mary*, p. 607.
2. Airlie, *Thatched with Gold*, p. 195.
3. Pope-Hennessy, *Queen Mary*, p. 607.
4. Stoeckl, *Not All Vanity*, pp. 239–40.
5. Warwick, *George and Marina*, p. 133.
6. Princess Alice (Gloucester), con. with author.
7. Nesbit, *Aeroplane Monthly*, Jan. 1990.
8. Alice, *Memoirs*, p. 128.
9. Warwick, *George and Marina*, p. 128.
10. King, *Princess Marina*, p. 168.
11. Astor Papers, MS 1416/1/4/10.
12. Colville, *Crowded Life*, p. 131.
13. Pope-Hennessy, *Queen Mary*, p. 608.

14. King, *Princess Marina*, p. 170.
15. Wheeler-Bennett, *George VI*, p. 548.
16. Bloch, *Secret File*, p. 201.
17. Howarth, *George VI*, p. 141.
18. Pope-Hennessy, *Queen Mary*, p. 608.
19. Wheeler-Bennett, *George VI*, p. 549.
20. Ibid., p. 548.
21. Frankland, *Prince Henry*, p. 173.
22. Wheeler-Bennett, *George VI*, pp. 536–7.
23. *Daily Express*, 9 May 1942.
24. Wheeler-Bennett, *George VI*, p. 538.
25. Peter Townsend to the author.
26. Lady Hambleden, con. with author.
27. Ibid.
28. Wood, *A World*, pp. 102–3.
29. *News Chronicle*, 13 Apr. 1953.
30. Milburn, *Diaries*, p. 266.
31. Ziegler, *Crown and People*, p. 70.
32. Bradford, *George VI*, p. 432.
33. Miriam Bloomberg, con. with author.
34. Bradford, *George VI*, p. 433.
35. Anon., *Royal Family*, p. 73.
36. Townsend, *Time and Chance*, p. 138.
37. Lady Hambleden, con. with author.
38. Ibid.
39. Nicolson, Balliol, 4 May 1946.
40. Windsor, *The Heart*, p. 329.
41. Ziegler, *Edward VIII*, p. 457.
42. Ibid., p. 463.
43. Princess Alice (Athlone), con. with author.
44. Ziegler, *Edward VIII*, p. 463.
45. Ibid., p. 468.
46. Princess Alice (Athlone), con. with author.
47. Ziegler, *Edward VIII*, p. 484.
48. Windsor, *The Heart*, p. 329.
49. Howarth, *George VI*, p. 143.
50. Bloch, *Secret File*, p. 200.
51. Bryan and Murphy, *Windsor Story*, p. 355.
52. Harvey, *War Diaries*, p. 275.
53. Rose, *Kings, Queens*, p. 168.

54. Longford, *Queen Mother*, p. 97.
55. Lady Hambleden, con. with author.
56. Roberts, *Holy Fox*, p. 105.
57. Queen Mother, con. with author.
58. Lady Hambleden, con. with author.
59. Soames, *Clementine*, p. 309.
60. Longford, *Queen Mother*, p. 83.
61. Townsend, *Time and Chance*, p. 145.
62. Pertwee, *By Royal Command*, pp. 81–2.
63. Hay, *Theatrical Anecdotes*, p. 305.
64. Pertwee, *By Royal Command*, p. 82.
65. Muggeridge, *Diaries*, p. 360.
66. Welch, *Journals*, p. 75.
67. Lees-Milne, *Ancestral Voices*, p. 45.
68. Blunt, *Slow on the Feather*, p. 133.
69. Lees-Milne, *Ancestral Voices*, p. 151.
70. Alanbrooke, *Diaries*, p. 327.
71. Bradford, *George VI*, p. 610.
72. Wheeler-Bennett, *George VI*, p. 755.

6. FAMILY MATTERS

1. Harewood, *Tongs and Bones*, p. 27.
2. Lord Harewood, con. with author.
3. Harewood, *Tongs and Bones*, p. 27.
4. Ibid.
5. Queen Mother, con. with author.
6. Lord Harewood, con. with author.
7. Harewood, *Tongs and Bones*, p. 27.
8. Lord Harewood, con. with author.
9. Roosevelt, *This I Remember*, p. 264.
10. Wheeler-Bennett, *George VI*, p. 550.
11. Howarth, *George VI*, p. 157.
12. Longford, *Queen Mother*, p. 90.
13. Queen Mother, con. with author.
14. Johnston, *One Policeman's Story*, p. 132.
15. Lady Hambleden, con. with author.
16. Ibid.

17. Jock Webster, con. with author.
18. Hartnell, *Silver and Gold*, p. 102.
19. Queen Mother, con. with author.
20. Alexandra, *For a King's Love*, p. 111.
21. Hartnell, *Silver and Gold*, pp. 104–5.
22. Princess Margaret, con. with author.
23. Queen Mother, con. with author.
24. Crawford, *Little Princesses*, p. 69.
25. Ibid., p. 81.
26. Leslie Congden, *Independent*, 29 Nov. 1990.
27. Sinclair, *Queen and Country*, p. 153.
28. Crawford, *Little Princesses*, p. 84.
29. Warwick, *Princess Margaret*, p. 34.
30. Colville, *Fringes*, pp. 265–6.
31. Longford, *Elizabeth R*, pp. 111–12.
32. Wheeler-Bennett, *George VI*, p. 741.
33. Crawford, *Little Princesses*, p. 80.
34. Alanbrooke, *Diaries*, p. 110.
35. Princess Margaret, con. with author.
36. Van der Byl, *Shadows*, p. 127.
37. Roosevelt, *This I Remember*, p. 209.
38. Alice, *For My Grandchildren*, p. 260.
39. Airlie, *Thatched with Gold*, p. 225.
40. Princess Margaret, con. with author.
41. Airlie, *Thatched with Gold*, p. 220.
42. Wheeler-Bennett, *George VI*, p. 553.
43. Ibid.
44. Butcher, *Three Years*, 12 July 1942.
45. Wheeler-Bennett, *George VI*, p. 554.
46. Gilbert, *Churchill*, Vol. III, p. 249.
47. Ibid., p. 251.

7. 'I KNOW I SHALL BE DOING GOOD'

1. Wheeler-Bennett, *George VI*, p. 611.
2. Ibid., p. 564.

3.   Ibid., p. 567.
4.   Princess Margaret, con. with author.
5.   Wheeler-Bennett, *George VI*, p. 568.
6.   Ibid.
7.   Macmillan, *War Diaries*, p. 123.
8.   Bradford, *George VI*, p. 431.
9.   Laffey, *Beatrice Lillie*, p. 126.
10. Vickers, *Vivien Leigh*, p. 156.
11. Carver, *Out of Step*, p. 166.
12. Wheeler-Bennett, *George VI*, p. 578.
13. Ibid., p. 574.
14. Ibid., p. 577.
15. Ibid., p. 578.
16. Macmillan, *War Diaries*, p. 130.
17. Wheeler-Bennett, *George VI*, p. 578.
18. Hardinge Papers, 12 June 1942.
19. Princess Alice (Gloucester), con. with author.
20. Hardinge Papers, 12 June 1942.
21. Princess Alice (Athlone), con. with author.
22. Beaton, *Self-Portrait*, p. 104.
23. Alice, *For My Grandchildren*, p. 254.
24. Ibid., p. 268.
25. Sir Shuldham Redfern, con. with author.
26. Pickersgill, *Mackenzie King*, Vol. I, p. 528.
27. Alice, *For My Grandchildren*, p. 267.
28. MacDonald, *Titans and Others*, pp. 115–16.
29. Astor Papers, MS 1416/1/4/10.
30. Townsend, *Time and Chance*, p. 164.
31. Warwick, *George and Marina*, p. 136.
32. Bradford, *George VI*, p. 491.
33. *The Times*, 12 Dec. 1942.
34. Ibid., 17 Dec. 1942.
35. Balfour, *Paul of Yugoslavia*, p. 251.
36. King, *Princess Marina*, p. 176.
37. Ibid.
38. Ziegler, *Edward VIII*, p. 267.
39. *The Times*, 5 Aug. 1949.
40. Alice, *For My Grandchildren*, p. 1.

8. CHANGING TIMES

1. Queen Mother, con. with author.
2. Lady Hambleden, con. with author.
3. Morrah, *To be a King*, p. 21.
4. Channon, *Chips*, pp. 45–6.
5. Macmillan, *War Diaries*, p. 120.
6. Rose, *Kings, Queens*, p. 168.
7. Townsend, *Time and Chance*, p. 151.
8. Pope-Hennessy, *Queen Mary*, p. 609.
9. Jock Webster, con. with author.
10. Sitwell, *Queen Mary*, p. 58.
11. Lash, *Eleanor and Franklin*, p. 606.
12. RA, Queen Mary's Diary, 1 Nov. 1942.
13. RA, cc 53/1084.
14. Vickers, *Beaton*, p. 269.
15. Lash, *Eleanor and Franklin*, p. 606.
16. Sitwell, *Queen Mary*, p. 55.
17. Ibid., p. 38.
18. Ibid., p. 39.
19. Ibid., p. 60.
20. Colville, *Fringes of Power*, p. 508.
21. Princess Margaret, con. with author.
22. Sitwell, *Queen Mary*, p. 41.
23. Wulff, *Queen Mary*, p. 62.
24. Sitwell, *Queen Mary*, p. 50.
25. Ibid., p. 40.
26. Ibid., p. 60.
27. Queen Mother, con. with author.
28. Wheeler-Bennett, *George VI*, p. 594.
29. Ibid., p. 596.
30. Ibid., p. 599.
31. Ibid., p. 600.
32. Bradford, *George VI*, p. 474.
33. Wheeler-Bennett, *George VI*, p. 598.
34. Ibid., pp. 601–6.
35. Ibid., p. 592.
36. Longford, *Elizabeth R*, p. 115.
37. Ibid., p. 116.
38. Ibid., p. 119.

39. Channon, *Chips*, p. 438.
40. Princess Margaret, con. with author.
41. Whistler, *Laughter*, p. 261.
42. Princess Margaret, con. with author.
43. Anon., *Royal Family*, p. 116.
44. Longford, *Elizabeth R*, p. 122.
45. Blunt, *Slow on the Feather*, p. 134.
46. Wheeler-Bennett, *George VI*, p. 749.
47. Crawford, *Little Princesses*, p. 86.
48. Channon, *Chips*, pp. 350–1.
49. Wheeler-Bennett, *George VI*, p. 749.
50. Ibid.
51. Airlie, *Thatched with Gold*, p. 228.

9. 'ENTERING AS A CONQUEROR'

1. Bradford, *George VI*, p. 478.
2. PRO FO 954/14.
3. Wheeler-Bennett, *George VI*, p. 612.
4. Macmillan, *War Diaries*, p. 496.
5. Egremont, *Women*, p. 123.
6. Bradford, *George VI*, p. 478.
7. Alexander, *Memoirs*, pp. 129–30.
8. Macmillan, *War Diaries*, p. 496.
9. Ibid.
10. Astor Papers, MS 1416/1/4/8.
11. Wheeler-Bennett, *George VI*, p. 609.
12. Ibid., p. 610.
13. Townsend, *Time and Chance*, p. 151.
14. Ibid., p. 152.
15. Astor Papers, MS 1416/1/4/8.
16. Wheeler-Bennett, *George VI*, p. 611.
17. Townsend, *Time and Chance*, p. 152.
18. Ibid.
19. Alexandra, *For a King's Love*, p. 71.
20. Wheeler-Bennett, *George VI*, p. 618.
21. Ibid., p. 498.
22. PRO FO 371/30265.

23. Alexandra, *For a King's Love*, p. 112.
24. Ibid., p. 106.
25. Michael, *Haakon*, p. 148.
26. Macmillan, *War Diaries*, p. 495.
27. Harewood, *Tongs and Bones*, p. 41.
28. Ibid., p. 43.
29. Ibid., p. 18.
30. Ibid., p. 42.
31. Ibid., p. 45.
32. Lord Harewood, con. with author.
33. Harewood, *Tongs and Bones*, p. 47.
34. Frankland, *Prince Henry*, p. 177.
35. Ibid., p. 175.
36. Princess Alice (Gloucester), con. with author.
37. Frankland, *Prince Henry*, p. 171.
38. Ibid., p. 176.
39. Ibid., p. 177.
40. Alice, *Memoirs*, p. 134.
41. Frankland, *Prince Henry*, p. 179.
42. Ibid.

10. THE SOLDIER GUEST

1. Bradford, *George VI*, p. 480.
2. Hamilton, *Monty*, pp. 115–16.
3. PRO PREM 4/10/4.
4. Hamilton, *Monty*, p. 116.
5. Howarth, *George VI*, p. 169.
6. Ibid.
7. Jock Webster, con. with author.
8. Bradford, *George VI*, p. 481.
9. Airlie, *Thatched with Gold*, p. 224.
10. Howarth, *George VI*, p. 168.
11. Bradford, *George VI*, p. 482.
12. Pearson, *Through Diplomacy*, p. 224.
13. Wheeler-Bennett, *George VI*, p. 619.
14. Ibid., p. 620.
15. Pearson, *Through Diplomacy*, p. 224.

16. Crawford, *Little Princesses*, pp. 87–8.
17. *Majesty Magazine*, June 1986.
18. Crawford, *Little Princesses*, p. 88.
19. Morrah, *Princess Elizabeth*, p. 88.
20. Longford, *Elizabeth R*, p. 120.
21. Harewood, *Tongs and Bones*, p. 56.
22. Lord Harewood, con. with author.
23. Harewood, *Tongs and Bones*, p. 61.
24. Lord Harewood, con. with author.
25. Ibid.
26. Harewood, *Tongs and Bones*, p. 61.
27. Ibid., p. 63.
28. Sitwell, *Queen Mary*, p. 58.
29. Ibid., p. 60.
30. Airlie, *Thatched with Gold*, pp. 220–1.
31. Colville, *Fringes of Power*, p. 271.
32. Ibid., p. 288.
33. Lief Egeland to the author.
34. Wheeler-Bennett, *George VI*, p. 613.
35. Ibid., p. 614.
36. Townsend, *Time and Chance*, p. 144.
37. Ibid., p. 121.
38. Ibid., pp. 144–5.
39. Ibid., p. 123.
40. Ibid., p. 194.
41. Ibid., p. 145.
42. Ibid., p. 146.

11. CROWN OF VICTORY

1. King, *Princess Marina*, p. 151.
2. Alice, *Memoirs*, p. 138.
3. Princess Alice (Gloucester), con. with author.
4. PRO DO/121/52.
5. Frankland, *Prince Henry*, p. 189.
6. Ibid., p. 182.
7. Alice, *Memoirs*, p. 139.
8. Ibid., p. 149.
9. Sir Simon Bland, con. with author.

10. Private information.
11. Frankland, *Prince Henry*, p. 188.
12. Princess Alice (Gloucester), con. with author.
13. *Daily Mirror*, 10 Dec. 1940.
14. Ziegler, *Edward VIII*, p. 469.
15. Ibid., p. 488.
16. Ibid.
17. Ibid., p. 492.
18. Bradford, *George VI*, p. 589.
19. Ibid., p. 590.
20. Harewood, *Tongs and Bones*, p. 67.
21. Lord Harewood, con. with author.
22. Wheeler-Bennett, *George VI*, p. 622.
23. Ibid., p. 623.
24. Ibid., p. 625.
25. Ibid., p. 626.
26. Princess Margaret, con. with author.
27. Mrs E. Wood to the author.
28. Pope-Hennessy, *Queen Mary*, p. 610.
29. Sitwell, *Queen Mary*, p. 61.
30. Pope-Hennessy, *Queen Mary*, p. 609.
31. Alice, *Memoirs*, p. 145.
32. Pope-Hennessy, *Queen Mary*, p. 609.
33. Queen Mother, con. with author.
34. Channon, *Chips*, p. 495.
35. Nicolson, *Diaries*, 17 May 1945.
36. Wheeler-Bennett, *George VI*, p. 627.
37. Churchill, *Second World War*, Vol. V, p. 467.
38. Nicolson, *Diaries*, p. 293.
39. Wheeler-Bennett, *George VI*, p. 645.
40. Ibid., p. 633.
41. Townsend, *Time and Chance*, p. 129.
42. Wheeler-Bennett, *George VI*, p. 637.
43. Ibid., p. 650.
44. Ibid., p. 645.
45. Channon, *Chips*, p. 501.
46. Lehmann, *Brother*, pp. 296–7.
47. Wheeler-Bennett, *George VI*, p. 467.
48. Menzies, *Afternoon Light*, p. 249.
49. Queen Mother, con. with author.

Bibliography

UNPUBLISHED SOURCES

Queen Mary's Letters and Diaries, Royal Archives (RA); Royal Correspondence, Astor Papers, University of Reading; the Private Papers of Lord Hardinge of Penshurst; the Diaries of Harold Nicolson, Balliol College, Oxford; Foreign Office Papers in the Public Records Office, Kew.

PUBLISHED SOURCES

All books were published in London unless otherwise specified.

Airlie, Mabell, Countess of, *Thatched with Gold*, 1962.
Alanbrooke, Viscount, *Diaries: Triumph in the West 1943–1946*, 1959.
Alexander of Tunis, 1st Earl, *Memoirs*, 1962.
Alexandra, Queen of Yugoslavia, *For a King's Love*, 1956.
Alice, Countess of Athlone, Princess, *For My Grandchildren*, 1966.
Alice, Duchess of Gloucester, Princess, *Memoirs*, 1983.
Allen, Peter, *The Crown and the Swastika*, 1983.
Anon., *The Royal Family in Wartime*, 1945.
Balfour, Neil, and Mackay, Sally, *Paul of Yugoslavia*, 1980.
Beaton, Cecil, *Photobiography*, 1951.
—— *Diaries: The Wandering Years*, 1961.
—— *Diaries: The Years Between*, 1965.
—— *Self Portrait with Friends: The Selected Diaries of Cecil Beaton, 1926–1974*, ed. Richard Buckle, 1979.
Bloch, Michael, *The Duke of Windsor's War*, 1982.
—— *Operation Willi*, 1984.
—— *Wallis and Edward, Letters, 1931–1937*, 1986.
—— *The Secret File of the Duke of Windsor*, 1988.
Blunt, Wilfrid, *Slow on the Feather: Further Autobiography*, 1986.
Bradford, Sarah, *George VI*, 1989.

Bruce-Lockhart, Sir Robert, *Diaries 1915–1938*, 1973.
Bryan III, J., and Murphy, J.V., *The Windsor Story*, 1979.
Bullitt, Orville H. (ed.), *For the President: Correspondence between Franklin D. Roosevelt and William C. Bullitt*, 1973.
Butcher, Captain Harry C., *My Three Years with Eisenhower; the Personal Diary, 1942–1945*, 1946.
Carey, M.C., *Princess Mary*, 1922.
Carver, Michael, *Out of Step: Memoirs of a Field Marshal*, 1989.
Channon, Sir Henry, *Chips: The Diaries of Sir Henry Channon*, ed. Robert Rhodes James, 1967.
Churchill, Winston S., *The Second World War*, 6 vols., 1948–54.
Clark, Kenneth, *The Other Half*, 1977.
Colville, Lady Cynthia, *Crowded Life*, 1963.
Colville, Sir John, *The Fringes of Power: Downing Street Diaries, 1939–1955*, 1985.
Corbitt, Frederick, *My Twenty Years in Buckingham Palace*, 1956.
Costello, John, *Ten Days that Shook the West*, 1988.
Crawford, Marion, *The Little Princesses*, 1950.
Donaldson, Frances, *Edward VIII*, 1974.
Dunnett, Alastair, *Among Friends*, 1984.
Egremont, Lord, *Women and Children First*, 1965.
Evans, Trefor (ed.), *The Killearn Diaries*, 1972.
Frankland, Noble, *Prince Henry, Duke of Gloucester*, 1980.
Gilbert, Martin, *Winston S. Churchill*, Vols. V–VIII, 1976–88.
Greacen, Lavinia, *Chink: A Biography*, 1989.
Hamilton, Nigel, *Monty: The Field Marshal 1944–1976*, 1988.
Hartnell, Norman, *Silver and Gold*, 1955.
Harvey, J. (ed.), *The War Diaries of Oliver Harvey*, 1978.
Harewood, Lord, *The Tongs and the Bones*, 1981.
Hay, Peter, *Theatrical Anecdotes*, 1987.
Higham, Charles, *Wallis: Secret Lives of the Duchess of Windsor*, 1988.
Hubbard, R.H., *Rideau Hall*, Montreal, 1977.
Johnston, Sir Eric, *One Policeman's Story*, 1978.
Keyes, Roger, *Outrageous Fortune: The Tragedy of King Leopold III of the Belgians, 1901–1941*, 1984.
King, Stella, *Princess Marina: Her Life and Times*, 1969.
Laffey, Bruce, *Beatrice Lillie*, 1989.
Laird, Dorothy, *Queen Elizabeth the Queen Mother*, 1966.
Lash, Joseph P., *Eleanor and Franklin*, 1972.

Lees-Milne, James, *Ancestral Voices*, 1975.
Lehmann, John, *I Am My Brother*, 1960.
Longford, Elizabeth, *The Queen*, Ch. 4, 1977.
—— *The Queen Mother*, 1981.
—— *Elizabeth R*, 1984.
MacDonald, Rt. Hon. Malcolm, *Titans and Others*, 1972.
Martin, Sir John, *Downing Street: The War Years*, 1991.
Massey, Vincent, *What's Past is Prologue*, 1963.
Menzies, Sir Robert, *Afternoon Light*, 1967.
Michael, Maurice, *Haakon, King of Norway*, 1958.
Milburn, Clara, *Mrs Milburn's Diaries*, 1980.
Minney, R.J. (ed.), *The Private Papers of Hore-Belisha*, 1960.
Morrah, Dermot, *Princess Elizabeth, Duchess of Edinburgh*, 1950.
—— *To Be A King*, 1968.
Muggeridge, Malcolm, *Like It Was: The Diaries of Malcolm
    Muggeridge*, 1981.
Nicolson, Nigel (ed.), *Sir Harold Nicolson: Diaries and Letters,
    1930–1939*, 1966.
Olson, Stanley, *Harold Nicolson: Diaries and Letters, 1930–1964*,
    1980.
Pearson, Lester B., *Through Diplomacy to Politics*, 1973.
Pertwee, Bill, *By Royal Command*, Newton Abbot, 1981.
Pickersgill, J.W., *The Mackenzie King Record*, 4 vols., Toronto,
    1960–70.
Plumb, J.H., *Royal Heritage*, 1981.
Pope-Hennessy, James, *Queen Mary*, 1959.
Rickard, John, *Australia: A Cultural History*, 1988.
Roberts, Andrew, *The Holy Fox: A Biography of Lord Halifax*,
    1991.
Roosevelt, Eleanor, *This I Remember*, New York, 1949.
Roosevelt, Elliott, and Lash, J.P., *The Roosevelt Letters*, New
    York, 1952.
—— and Brough, James, *A Rendezvous with Destiny*, New York,
    1977.
Rose, Kenneth, *Kings, Queens and Courtiers*, 1985.
Shew, Betty Spencer, *Queen Elizabeth, the Queen Mother*, 1955.
Sinclair, David, *Queen and Country*, 1979.
—— *Two Georges: The Making of the Modern Monarchy*, 1988.
Sitwell, Osbert, *Queen Mary and Others*, 1974.
Smith, Godfrey (ed.), *How it Was in the War: An Anthology*, 1989.

Soames, Mary, *Clementine Churchill*, 1979.

Stoeckl, Agnes de, *Not All Vanity*, 1950.

Townsend, Peter, *The Last Emperor*, 1975.

—— *Time and Chance: An Autobiography*, 1978.

Van der Byl, Piet, *The Shadows Lengthen*, Cape Town, 1973.

Vickers, Hugo, *Cecil Beaton*, 1985.

—— *Vivien Leigh*, 1988.

Vincent, John (ed.), *The Crawford Papers*, 1984.

Walker, Alexander, *Vivien: The Life of Vivien Leigh*, 1987.

Warwick, Christopher, *George and Marina: The Duke and Duchess of Kent*, 1988.

—— *Princess Margaret*, 1983.

Welch, Denton, *Journals*, ed. Michael De-la-Noy, 1984.

Wheeler-Bennett, Sir John, *King George VI*, 1958.

Whistler, Laurence, *The Laughter and the Urn*, 1985.

Wilhelmina, HRH Princess, *Lonely But Not Alone*, trans. John Peereboom, 1960.

Williams, Francis (ed.), *A Prime Minister Remembers: The War and the Post-War Memoirs of Earl Attlee*, 1961.

Wilson, Charles, *Australia: The Creation of a Nation*, 1987.

Winant, John G., *A Letter From Grosvenor Square*, Boston, 1947.

Windsor, Duchess of, *The Heart Has Its Reasons*, 1956.

Wood, Robert, *A World in Your Ear*, 1979.

Wulff, Louis, *Her Majesty Queen Mary*, 1949.

Ziegler, Philip, *Crown and People*, 1978.

—— *Mountbatten*, 1985.

—— *Edward VIII*, 1990.

NEWSPAPERS AND MAGAZINES

Aeroplane Monthly, Daily Mirror, Daily Telegraph, Majesty, News Chronicle, New Statesman, Sunday Times, The Times.

Index